THE
ELLACOMBE BOOK

A PORTRAIT OF A TORQUAY PARISH

SYDNEY R. LANGMEAD

DEVON BOOKS

First published in Great Britain in 1998

British Library Cataloguing-in-Publication Data
A CIP record for this title is available from the British Library

ISBN 1 94114 020 1

DEVON BOOKS
OFFICIAL PUBLISHER TO DEVON COUNTY COUNCIL

HALSGROVE
PUBLISHING, MEDIA AND DISTRIBUTION

Halsgrove House
Lower Moor Way
Tiverton, Devon EX16 6SS
Tel: 01884 243242
Fax: 01884 243325

DEDICATION

To my Mother - Violet Oliver (Olive) - who lived almost
all of her 92 years in Ellacombe, and was a well-known
figure in both Church and Parish, and to my Father who
taught me to love, and always respect, the sea.

Printed and bound in Great Britain by Bookcraft Ltd, Midsomer Norton

Contents

Acknowledgements

Before beginning my story of Ellacombe Parish I must acknowledge with gratitude the wealth of information and illustrations I have gathered from books, articles, papers and photographs, from which I have put together a brief amalgam of local history covering Torquay in the early and mid nineteenth century; the objective being to lead the reader into the formation of Ellacombe parish.

Particularly, I would also like to express my grateful thanks to John Pike for his extensive help in my understanding of the mechanics of book writing, and for the use of extracts from his considerable stock of personal literary archives: to Mr Duncan MSc, for his generous offer of access to his comprehensive thesis on social history - again aiding me in summarising a brief religious and educational history of the times - and to Deryk Seymour for extracts from his works and for overseeing my draft script on the foundation of the churches.

I must also thank Mike Thompson, the Deputy Editor of the *Herald Express*, for his support and encouragement, and the use of the newspaper's photograph archives; also the Torquay Natural History Museum, and John Pike, for similar useage. Thanks also to the following people without whose vivid recollections this book would never have been published: Mrs Carrie Pym; Mrs Nora Dowell (Blight); Mrs Amy Stephens (Frost); Mrs Dolly Weymouth (Zaple); Miss Mary Corline; Ken Selley; Ted and Bill Shapley; Mrs Winnie Dyer (Casely); Mr A. A. Bastian; Stanley Crocker; Mr B A Chalker; Lt-Col. Bill Elliott; Archie Skinner; Ted Bragg; Mr and Mrs Les Gibbons; Mr V Fellows; Ken Graham; Ken Lasseter; Percy Dimmock; Mr and Mrs Stan Roberts; Miss Gwen Downey; Henry Hanson; Miss Lilian Brown; Mr and Mrs Gilbert Furneaux; Mrs Stella Margetts (Combe), and Don Roberts.

I would also like to thank Dennis Penny and Don Roberts for their support and encouragement, and the Head of Ellacombe School and the Vicar of Ellacombe for their kindness and co-operation in allowing access to and the use of old records and photographs, both those stored locally, and those held in the Devon Record Office; and Frank Drake who supplied the unique photographs of his family's contracts with the GPO in 1903.

The photographs in this work are individually acknowledged and copyright remains with the owner. If relevant, the origin of a picture is also stated. Where no source is given it may be taken that the photograph is from the author's collection, or that the source is unknown. All royalties arising from publication of this work will be donated to Ellacombe Church and School Funds.

Abbreviations: TNHM - Torquay Natural History Museum; THE - *Torbay Herald Express*; JP - John Pike TFS - Torquay Fire Service

SELECT BIBLIOGRAPHY

ELLIS, Arthur C. *Historical Survey of Torquay*, 1930.
RUSSELL, Percy. *History of Torquay*, 1960.
WHITE. *History of Torquay*, 1878.
HUTCHINGS, Walter J. *Out of the Blue* (Devon Constabulary), 1957.
DUNCAN, G. S. *Thesis on Social History of Early Victorian Torquay*.
JOINT, L. *Torquay United - the First 70 Years*, 1991.
SEYMOUR, Deryk. *Upton Parish Church, Torquay* (St Mary Magdalene): *A Brief History*, also *Upton - the Heart of Torquay*.
PIKE, J. *Torquay, Torbay - A Bibliographical Guide*, also *Torquay - the Place and the People*.
SMITH, Lorna. *The Pilgrim Way*.
CURTIS, S. J. *History of Education in Great Britain*.

Foreword

There are few greater compliments a writer can pay than to produce a history book about the community in which they were born. The hard work that goes into a book of this sort runs into years rather than months of work, and in the case of Sydney Langmead's book, this has been done with no thought of personal reward.

Also, in writing about the places and people he has known from childhood, an author has to take particular care in sorting out fact from fiction, for to get anything wrong results in instant correction from friends and acquaintances met each day in the street. There is no hiding place for the local author! Such a labour of love would only be undertaken by someone who has the deepest affection for his own roots, the people he grew up with, and the community they all share.

The Ellacombe Book is one of a number of books to be published in the Parish History series, and Devon is fortunate in that so many of its parishes retain their centuries-old sense of place. Political and ecclesiastical significance aside, parishes are simply places people feel a strong attachment to, where they are born, raise families, and grow into being part of a community. It is where they *belong*. However, as such boundaries grow less distinct, so much of the commonplace history of the community also fades from view, unless care is taken to conserve it. Sydney Langmead's greatest achievement (though he is too modest to suggest it himself) is in the contribution this book has made to preserving much of Ellacombe's history that would otherwise be lost: the interviews with local people, the photographs of school groups, personal snapshots of fairgrounds, football teams, and church outings, are part of the collective history of a small place which has touched the lives of many people.

It is a great pleasure, and privilege, to have had a small hand in bringing about the publication of this book.

Simon Butler
Joint Managing Director
Halsgrove - Devon Books

ELLACOMBE PARISH
FROM THE 1906 ORDNANCE SURVEY MAP

Scale

0 ————————————————— 1 mile

Introduction

As a genealogist of some fifteen years' experience gained in the research of my family history, I am deeply conscious of the value of written records. Sadly - in many cases involving family lore - much important information has been lost forever through the death of elderly relatives simply because they were not persuaded to 'go on record' prior to their decease.

I was also seized with the idea that although a number of books have been written about the history of Torquay (indeed all of Torbay), no one has written in depth about the Parish of Ellacombe certainly one of the largest in Torquay. Although primarily a working-class area, Ellacombe has sired many an outstanding public figure whose education of began in the local elementary schools of the Parish - particularly Ellacombe School. As evidence will show - this education was sound, thorough and well taught in both the arts and the sciences.

I do not profess a skill in writing professionally, so decided to reach my objective in a somewhat different way. Although a straightforward history of the Parish of Ellacombe would be possible by detailed personal research, and with the help of extracts from works of well-known local historians, in my view, this would lack the human element. So I have introduced my story with, I hope, sufficient material about the Parish's origins, both geographical and historical, and then set out to portray the ambience of my birthplace through the medium of recorded interviews, containing personal memories and recollections of the early 1900s.

I begin these with details of my own family and memories of the area where I was born, and where I spent a large proportion of my early years, and have added to them many more personal reminiscences of old neighbours and friends who have made a substantial contribution to this publication. I must here acknowledge my sister-in-law Margaret (she of the computer memory), and my brother Albert (Bert) - a retired Torquay Postal Superintendent and Justice of the Peace for 26 years - both of whom (in their minds) have never really left the area about which I write. It is with regret that, since this story was initiated, I have to record the sad passing of a number of interviewees.

It should be made clear that all printed recollections are personal, that they may contain errors of fact, and that any inclusions by the author are made in good faith.

Author Henry Mitchell, the American journalist, writing in *Memories*, sums up my intent with this warning: 'Nostalgia is the halfway house by which you love the past and the sweet things in it, without actually committing yourself to the nonsense that life was better then.'

Sydney R. Langmead
Galmpton, Devon
October 1998

Torre Abbey - an engraving by Dennis Penny, taken from an old print.

Chapter 1 - Early History

As stated in the Introduction, it is not the intention of the author to go deeply into the history of Torquay. The purpose of this chapter is to provide only a chronological background to events leading to the emergence of Ellacombe as a Parish, and to highlight the major characters who were influential in the development of the Town in general, and Ellacombe Parish in particular.

Well before 1801, and until the parochial structure of the Town had been extensively modified around 1860, the Parish and Manor of Torre (Mohun) dominated and controlled a division of Manors comprising arable land, meadows and hill pastures which made up the approaches to the little fishing hamlet of Torre Quay. As far back as 1186, the coast between the Teign and the Dart was in the Hundred of Carswell (now Kerswell), and from then (1187) re- named Haitor and later Heytor (not to be confused with the well- known Dartmoor height).

It is of interest to note that the meeting place of the Hundred Court was that area known as Gallows Hill, where the boundaries of the Parishes of Marldon, Cockington and St Marychurch then merged, and that those taking part converged at what is now Nutbush Lane to walk or ride the last mile of country lane to the Court.

St Saviour's Church (Torre Church) was doubtless built on the site of a small Norman church granted to Torre Abbey in 1196. Between 1236-1239 both Torre and Cockington churches were held by the Abbey. From 1539-1881 they were saved by the same incumbent but were then separated and each had its own vicar. The tower dated from the 14th century. TNHM

For many centuries the hamlet occupied by fishermen and sailors at the Strand had either been called 'Flete' (a tidal creek) or 'Tor Key' - later Torre Quay. In the long run, the settlement at the edge of the tidal water became the most important part of the whole area, and the name Torquay was applied to the whole: later still to the Town spreading into the adjoining parishes (Russell). It is a mark of personal sadness to me, as an old Torquinian, that the old Church of Torre (Mohun), the centre of christian life and instigator and arbitrator of local events right up to the mid-19th century when our story begins, should be left to decay to its present state and appearance - bearing in mind it contains the remains and memorials of the Ridgeways and other great families such as Coplestone, Seymour, Denis, Southcote and Cary, who were so much a part of the Town's early history.

The substantial modifications to the Town that began in the early 1800s largely arose from the physical and spiritual needs of an increasing residential and commercial population. In 1811, for example, 29% of the inhabitants of the area were chiefly employed in agriculture, 37% in trade, manufacture and handicrafts, and 34% in other occupations. By 1831, these had changed to 4%, 45% and 50% respectively, and in 1861, the second of these three headings accounted for 79% of the population. In 1801, the Parish of Tormohun served a community of 838 people. By 1861 the parochial structure had been modified in an attempt to adjust to the changes accompanying the growth to a population of 26 641. 'This had consequences for the churches, and the churches consequences for society. They provided services, occupied persons' time, spent money, took stands on issues, provided employment, used up space and transmitted knowledge.' (*Religion in Social Contact* - Demerath & Hammond 1969 Page 191).

Dean Beeke (Dean of Bristol) saw 'three grounds for church extension: to help the course of religion, to provide the moral improvement of the town and to cater for the increase of its inhabitants'. One important consideration was the lamentable failure of the Anglican Churches to cater for the working classes. Churches

Torwood Grange (Manor). Built in 1579 and demolished in 1843, it belonged to the Canons of Torre, and later became the temporary home of Sir Robert Palk. On the left is the old barn in its original form which later became Clifton Grove Cottages. TNHM

participated particularly in the provision of medical and hospital services and in elementary and adult education. Activity was based on the same small circle of decision makers who, although belonging to what might be referred to as the leisured classes, could not have much time to themselves. The clergy, in particular, led the community with a high social status, and were, in the mid-19th century, a highly active group.

Economic factors were of great significance. Several worthwhile projects were never pursued. Even the more 'solid' concerns such as the Dispensary and the National Schools simply existed from year to year as far as financing was concerned. However - apart from the National Society's efforts with elementary education, social improvements were largely local, both in financing and directing; the energy mostly arising from the enthusiasm and vigours of its clergy. Torquay's society was headed by the two main landowners and Lords of the Manor - the Palks and the Carys - the former being Church of England and the latter Catholic. The Palks were relative newcomers to Torquay, Robert Palk having bought the Ridgeway Family's estates in the Town (including Torwood Manor) in 1768.

Robert Palk, born 1717, was the eldest son of Walter Palk of Ashburton, owner of the little farm of Lower Hexborough. Robert attended the old established Grammar School at Ashburton and was sent to Wadham College, Oxford. After being ordained Deacon, he held a small curacy in Cornwall, and later served at sea in that capacity. Later a capable merchant and able diplomat, he was befriended by Stringer Lawrence who appointed him Commissioner and Paymaster in succession to Robert Clive of India. It was later, when General Lawrence died a guest in residence with him at home in England, that Lawrence left the Palk family his fortune of £80 000. A condition of the bequest was that the Palks preserved the name in each generation of the family.

As a result of the Cary family's ownership of Braddons Fields, and their plans for development marring the view, Palk was balked from residing at Torwood Grange, and therefore acquired the great house known as Haldon, on the Exeter side of the lofty Haldon Hill (built in 1735 by Sir Charles Chudleigh). Disputes with the Carys continued - often matters being referred to Counsel. It was at this time the early development of the Town, mainly about the Strand, began.

The Strand, Torquay, 1832, with visitors to the resort promenading under the trees. On the right is Park Place, now Victoria Parade, with an earlier incarnation of the Queen's Hotel. TNHM

Robert Palk, Lord of the Manor, was made a Baronet in 1782 and died in 1798. His son, Sir Lawrence, began an era of providing land and endowments for churches and charitable institutions, and secured authority to improve the harbour. The architect who drew up the plans was John Rennie, afterwards famous as the builder of London Bridge and the Victualling Yard at Devonport. Sir Lawrence (who died in 1813 at the age of 20), together with his son Sir Lawrence Vaughan Palk, were leading spirits in providing suitable accommodation and amenities for visitors to the newly emerging resort. His son (the first Baron Haldon), later sat as Conservative MP for South Devon from 1854-1868, and later, until Peerage in 1880, for East Devon.

In addition to Ellacombe, the Palks gave sites for Upton Church, the Infirmary, the Torquay Market and the Torwood Churches, along with leases to the authorities about the Town.

The splendid new harbour was built at a cost of £70 000. It may well be that Lord Haldon's generosity was perhaps influenced by the cultivation of his Constituency. But by the time Sir Lawrence Vaughan Palk died in 1860, there was increasing evidence that the family finances were on the decline. Neither the son and the grandson of Sir

Robert had the same business acumen as the father.

The man first to persuade Sir Lawrence Palk of the great prospects of the resort was Dr Henry Beeke, Dean of Bristol. He was given this post for his services to the ruling politicians. A Devonshire man, born at Kingsteignton in 1751, he was made a Fellow of Oriel College, Oxford at the age of 24, and Regious Professor of Modern History in 1801. Russell maintained that Dr Beeke was the man really responsible for the formation of the town of Torquay, and would suggest that he motivated Sir Lawrence and his son Lawrence Vaughan in the conduct of affairs from 1803-1813 and onwards. It was Dr Beeke who revealed major discrepancies in the true costs of building the new harbour, because of the failure of the Palks to employ competent agents to oversee the work and accounts.

Referring to earlier times - at the death of William de Brewer in 1232 the Manorial Estate of Torre passed to the powerful Mohun family. The Praemonstratensians built Torre Abbey Barn about 1200 and the rest of the Abbey over the following years. The Mohun gatehouse, however, was 14th. century (possibly between 1310–1330), from a gift of the Mohun family of £200 (Ellis p.47), which paid for the work.

At the dissolution of the monastries in 1539 Torre Abbey was sold as one unit and the Manor as another - the latter being purchased by the Ridgeway family. The son, Thomas, built Torwood Manor in 1579, which survived until 1840 when demolished by the Harvey family. The Abbey, meanwhile, was first purchased from Sir Edward Seymour by the Ridgeways, and then by John Stowell of Bovey Tracey before later assigned to George Cary.

Clearly, the Carys were much longer associated with Torbay, and were not pleased when the Ridgeway/Palk estates 'hemmed-in' the Cary lands. The Carys were the second of the two main landowners and Lords of the Manor which headed Torquay Society. The religious differences between the two also led to some dissention.

The Carys bought the Abbey in 1662, built the present mansion upon the ruins of the former monastery, and survived until the estate was sold to the Torquay Corporation in 1930 for the sum of £40 000. The influence of the Carys was much reduced by financial difficulties towards the mid-1800s. Strangely - it was the Palks who were irretrievably to lose their estates towards the end of the century; the Carys recovered, and there is a Cary Estate Office administering Cary property in Torquay to this day.

When Sir Robert Palk arrived in 1768 the Abbey family were really the leading landowners in the neighbourhood, bearing a name honoured in Devon for many hundreds of years. The lack of harmony between the two was continually the cause of confusion and disarray particularly where their properties bordered each other around Flete Street.

Cockington was a separate manor much earlier than 1316, the de Cockingtons being in residence there in the 13th century. It was not a separate Parish, the Chapel probably being set up by the manorial lords, and served from Torre after 1236. Later, when the Abbey controlled the Parish Church of Torre, Cockington continued to be a chapelry until 1881, when the living was separated. For some 23 years, the manor was held by one of the Black Prince's household, until sold to John Cary. The family held it until 1636.

Next in importance in Torquay's development was the Mallock family, who bought the manor from the Carys. The buyer was a successful merchant of Exeter, Mayor of that City in 1636, who turned over the estate to his second son Rawly Mallock. He was the first of twelve of his family

In July 1836 a conduit was built in Abbey Place to supply the neighbouring houses with water from the Flete Stream. The cost was met by Mr Cary and his tenants in the district. On the left, surrounded by a wall, is Cary Green. TNHM

who made their home at Cockington Court. Church livings dominated the affairs of the Mallocks during the period 1700 to the death of Charles Herbert Mallock in 1873. The estate was finally sold in 1932 - part to a development company and 223 acres to the Corporation of Torquay.

The Revd Roger Mallock, who died in 1846, held the living of Tormohun with Cockington in addition to fifteen others. Roger, as patron, played a key part in the establishment of the Parish of St John's. Two of his sons and three sons-in-law were incumbents of Torre. Another prominent and influential person in the affairs of the new town was William Kitson, second son of Robert Abraham, the first Palk Steward. It was William Kitson and his colleagues who were responsible for the rapid changes which transformed Torquay, having taken over the administration of the affairs of the Manor of Torwood at a critical time. It was his discrimination, foresight and judgement that encouraged improvements and advanced the interests of the Town. He was directly responsible for the planning of the distinctive road system, and allowed the building of the villas comprising the Warberries and Lincombes. He later added banking to his many activities, together with Edward Vivian.

Gradually the responsibilities and initiative of William Kitson reduced the position of Sir Lawrence Vaughan Palk to that of a mere figurehead, and it was at this stage the affairs of the Palk family went gradually into decline. The upkeep of

Cary Parade, named after one of the town's earliest benefactors, the Cary family. THE

Haldon House, one of the largest houses in England, swallowed enormous sums of money, and land and property were sacrificed in an effort to remain solvent, including land at Chapel Hill, sold to the South Devon Railway for £4000.

From 1833 onwards William Kitson was to mastermind the disposal of these leases. He was the brain behind the layout of the new highways, and the new villas, and was the provider of gas and water supplies, as well as the administrator of affairs through a local government council. At the age of 74 he shrewdly withdrew from the Palk Agency in 1874.

On the death of Lord Haldon in 1883, the fortunes of the Palks disintegrated and large auction sales of leaseholds took place in Torquay in 1885. These were followed by disposal of the remaining freeholds and manorial rights. For thirty years thereafter individual owners built with total disregard of their neighbours, before the Town and County Councils were given powers, in the public interest, to intervene.

Belgravia, and other parts of the Cary Estates, escaped this confusion. William Kitson lived, for three years until his death, at Shiphay Manor, which had been in the possession of the Kitson family since acquisition by William Kitson of Painford, near Ashprington, in 1740. After nearly 200 years, the Shiphay Manor Estate was taken over by the Devon County Education Authority as a sixth-form base for the Torquay Grammar School. The Kitson and Vivian Bank, in October 1833 to be known as the Torbay Bank, grew in importance, and by reason of the deposits of residents, was of great service to the Town's development in financing the extensive operations of the master builders. The Bank's premises moved to 1 Vaughan Parade in 1854 and in 1900 was absorbed in the great combine developed from the original Lloyds Bank in Birmingham.

By no means all the important figures in this society were long- standing landowning families. Other well-known Torquay characters of the time were Edward Vivian (1808-1893) - a founder member of the Torquay History Society and a Commander of the Artillery Volunteers in 1859 with the rank of Major, and Henry Cranmer March Phillips (1794-1880), a retiring Officer of the Royal Navy, who made Torquay his home and was closely associated with the building of new churches and other charitable causes. Involved deeply in the religious life of Torquay was Dr J. H. Harris, who accepted the curé of Torre in 1849, was influential in the creation of St John's Chapel and in the fostering of the building of new churches to serve the growing needs of rapidly increasing numbers of people who were, in those days, ardent church goers.

Apart from his quiet and persistent work, and the labours of the Anglican and Catholic Church, and non-conformist clergy, two other personalities figure strongly. The first of these was Henry Phillpotts, Bishop of Exeter from 1831 until his death in 1869. He came to reside in Torquay, where he built the mansion at Bishopstowe (now enlarged as the Palace Hotel). His two outstanding achievements were the advocation of the separation of the County of Cornwall from the diocese of Exeter (1877) and the erection and creation of the new parishes under Peel's New Parish Act of 1843, including the division of the Parish of Torre.

The other prominent and controversial churchman was the Revd Park Smith, made Curate of St John's Chapel in 1837, whose parishioners included March Phillips, Edward Vivian and (as Churchwarden) William Kitson.

In addition to these, of course, were builders and allied tradesmen (of which the Harvey family deserves mention) through election to local government bodies, and also prominent visitors such as the Bishop of Bath and Wells, the Revd Daniel Lyons and Dr Radclyffe Hall, who recommended Torbay for its healing qualities and benefits for resident invalids. Another regular visitor to Torquay was Benjamin Disraeli - a guest of Mrs Willyams, who lived at Mount Braddon. It was thought that a national Conservative organisation called the Primrose League was possibly so named due to Disraeli's admiration of the wild primroses he found in Devon.

View of Abbey Place and Fleet Street c.1870. THE

Chapter 2 - Later Development

As Chapter One has made clear two most eminent citizens, whose foresight and drive, aided by the gifts and leasing of land from the two major Lords of the Manor, made possible the formation of the town of Torquay. The first, Dr Beeke, was more the visionary in the conduct of affairs, whilst the second, William Kitson, actively involved himself in the practical side of development. The Victorian Age can be probably be said to date from about 1833 when the Princess Victoria, together with her mother the Duchess of Kent, landed at Victoria Parade from the yacht *Emerald* and stayed at the Hotel, which later became the Royal.

Whilst the Carys were the leading socialites of that time, it was William Kitson who was responsible for the rapid and structural changes which transformed Torquay. By 1828, some 130 genteel and commodious houses, either occupied by resident gentry or used as lodging houses had been erected. Early Union Street had been constructed, and Jacob Harvey pressed on with his building, including Beacon Terrace. The Parade, with the Lawrence Arch at its landward end leading into the humbler Palk Street, was built on ground reclaimed from the shallow tidal flats on the northern side of the new harbour.

A row of houses on Cary land were erected on the approach to Braddons Hill as well as the new chapel, and four detached villas on the slopes. In 1817 the writer of *Croydon's* (Teignmouth) *Guide* wrote that "both Sir Lawrence Palk and Mr Cary had contributed all in their power to foster up the infant colony". In addition to the extension of Poulton's Hotel, Sir L. V. Palk (now 28 years of age), must be credited, at his own expense in 1821, with the building of a market in Torwood Street under powers granted by a private Act of Parliament. The work was carried out by John Foulston, who was the architect for much fine work at Plymouth and Devonport.

Twenty years later the new market (The Rotunda) languished. Another, supported by both manorial estates, was proposed opposite the present Post Office in Fleet Street, but because of heavy costs in Parliamentary battles over the proposal, the Palk Estates offered the site of the present market.

The Rotunda c. 1822, a drawing by Dennis Penny

The framework of the modern town of Torquay was entirely constructed by the Turnpike Trustees, under their Act of Parliament in 1821. The growth would have been impossible without their activities. Town development was carried through entirely on the Torwood Manor estate, the Abbey estate roads being left out of the scheme. Membership of the Trust was open to any County Magistrate in the district and the capital had to be raised by loans, secured on the tolls. There can be little doubt that this responsibility was accepted by the Palk estate, since the executive office of Clerk to the Trust was first held by the Palk Steward, Robert Abraham, and then by William Kitson. Palk could foresee heavy outlay on the harbour and other works, with very little in return. However, he then embarked on a road scheme to link Torquay with Newton Abbot via Chapel Hill, Lowes Bridge and Kingskerswell, with a notable advance in the construction of a tunnel and 'fly-under' at Kingskerswell. Macadam had brought about a great revolution in road building at about this time. In 1827 the road from Shaldon (toll bridge) was brought into Torquay via Maidencombe, converging with the Newton Road at the north end of Torre Village, thus feeding into the newly constructed Union Street. This remained the approach from Teignmouth until

Victorian Views

Above: *The Winter Garden, proposed in 1880 and erected in 1889, this structure was sold for £1300 in 1903 to Great Yarmouth Council.* THE

Left: *Palk Arch taken a few years before its demolition in 1962. It had stood since 1832 framing the entrance to Palk Street.* THE

Below: *Vane Hill and the Harbour, taken c. 1890.* JP

Left: *Old Torbay Road before the seashore on the left was reclaimed for the promenade.* JP

Centre: *Torquay Harbour and Waldon Hill c. 1880.* TNHM

Below: *Abbey Crescent, 1896.* THE

The Strand in 1906 with the Mallock Memorial clocktower on the right. THE

1898 when the main road debouched into Union Street at Castle Circus (via Lymington Road) and thus became the principal road centre. The Turnpike Trust was responsible for most of the road development in and around Torquay, which included the road from Torwood Valley up to Babbacombe and that which ran from Torre Village up past Warberry Hill to St Marychurch, known as Plain Moor.

Then was cut Upper and Lower Union Street. Upper Union Street was cut through the extensive nursery gardens of the Morgan family. The whole road to Newton was now entirely independent of the Cary owners of the Abbey Estate. The road to Paignton and Brixham was still via Old Mill Road to Livermead, and it was not until the 1840s that the Trustees made their second great advance and built the Torbay Road - but not without overcoming serious opposition from the Carys and the Mallocks. In the meantime much of the construction and development of the Town was being undertaken by such eminent builders as Jacob Harvey (believed to have studied under Nash) and Joseph Beard of Somerset. In the twenty years since 1801, some 165 houses had been erected in the Parish of Torre, of which nearly all were in the harbour neighbourhood - quite a number on Cary land and not the Palk Estate.

The 1866 Ordnance Survey map reveals that Ellacombe was, at that time, largely undeveloped. There was, of course, a main shopping centre stretching from the Strand, through Fleet Street, Lower and Higher Union Streets to Brunswick Square. Commercial works, timber yards and smaller properties lay largely to the south of the main streets, except behind Union Street, and in the Pimlico and Madrepore area. The gasworks was situated behind Temperance Street, and the old Torbay Infirmary and Dispensary was in existence next to the current Court House (which was then Upton School). The National School was in Pimlico. Cumper's Hotel stood adjacent to what is now the Torbay Hotel. There were no Terrace Gardens, and a mud harbour was bounded by the Fish Quay and South Pier.

Torre, within Brunswick Square, Lansdowne Place and St Saviour's (Tormohun) Church, was a thriving village within the town, with the large Torbay Nursery opposite the old hospital. Local Government was centred at the Old Town Hall, at the bottom of Abbey Road, where the building still stands today.

Torwood Street (then Torwood Row) went no further than its junction with Higher Terrace and Meadfoot Road. In the main the rest of the town of Torquay (excluding the Village of St

Torbay Hotel 1875, Standing at the end of Sulyarde Terrace which was named after the mother of Henry George Cary. The houses in the terrace were built between 1853 and 1858, and there were six serious landslides as a result of blasting the rock. TNHM

Marychurch) was composed of large domestic properties, set in their own grounds.

Torre and Torquay Railway Stations were, of course, 'in situ', but the main station was reached from the Harbour by the 'New Road'. Open fields existed between Belgrave Road and the Torquay Station, fronting Torre Abbey, and in Belgrave Road itself, seven large properties lay south of what was later Chestnut Avenue. Lucius Street and Falkland Road were non-existent, with two blocks of terraced villas shown in this area of the Road. About a dozen cottages on the north side ended at Church Street.

Between Upton and Ellacombe, such as it was, no more than a dozen villas, abutting St Marychurch Road, were inhabited. Market Street, as a shopping centre other than the relatively new Market Hall, did not exist at all.

Of prominence, where Ellacombe Road and Princes Road began (at what is now Ellacombe Green), was Ellacombe House (now flats for senior citizens). At the bottom of Princes Road, facing the open space, were Albert Cottages, and on the opposite side (Ellacombe Road) was Ellacombe Terrace, also facing the same open space. These are the same pretty stone cottages that remain inhabited there to this day.

One of the last broad gauge trains leaving Torre Station in May 1892. THE

Contrasting with grand Victorian buildings are these cottages in Belgrave Road c. 1900 (then South Street). Right can be seen Laburnum Row (now Street). The Hotel, left, was once Lacey's, later the Old Mill Inn. THE

Progressing northwards, above the 'Green' was a track (later Victoria Road) - Charles Terrace being a small terraced block where Ellacombe Post Office now stands: to the SW, the beginnings of Alexandra and Princes Roads, with workshops at their rear.

On the west side. a larger block was named Nelson Place. This joined an eastward track, later named Ellacombe Church Road (Hyde Park Terrace). Wellington Terrace (later Wellington Road) and Waterloo Road were terraced blocks, clearly mapped. The area between these groups of small properties and Warberry Copse/Hill (apart from Warberry Mount, now Higher Windsor Road) was totally open/agricultural land. All that broke the open landscape was the Torquay Waterworks Reservoir (in Warberry Copse), a quarry at the bottom of what is now Windsor Road, and another quarry in the dip across the road from Ellacombe Church (built shortly after the OS map was printed).

During the period between 1860 (after Sir L. V. Palk opened up Ellacombe Valley in 1859) and the next published Ordnance Survey Town Map (reprint, dated 1904) a considerable growth in building had taken place. Starting with the Harbour - land had been re-claimed behind the North (Fish) Quay; Cary Green and Princes Gardens set out, and the Royal Terrace Gardens landscaped. Of more significance the Torbay Road had been made up, the Princess and Haldon Piers (1870) built, and with the Pier Pavilion added on (1900), and a more commercialised dock developed at Beacon Quay.

Although the Victoria Parade and Palk Street areas remained relatively unchanged, development had proceeded up Torwood Street (then Row), the Winter Garden was in situ, and the Museum and Weslyan (Methodist) Chapels had

been built. More housing appears above Braddons Street, but the properties abutting Fleet Street and Lower Union Lane remained substantially unchanged - the exception being more housing developement between Warren Road and St Luke's Road North - superseding the Friends Meeting House.

A Doctor Gillow, an enterprising resident, took the lead in a syndicate which bought up a private assembly room in Abbey Road and converted it into a full-scale theatre in 1879 (later to become the Odeon Cinema). A Brewery and an Iron and Brass Foundry had disappeared in Rock Road, and the Drill Hall (seemingly in place of the Foundry) is shown on the map. The number of churches and chapels had increased, including Christ Church, Ellacombe, and the Mission Chapel of St Michael and All Angels at the junction of Pimlico and Market Street.

As mentioned in other publications, the Town Hall and Library at Castle Circus - indeed the whole area behind St Mary Magdalene (Upton) Church and the (old) Torbay Hospital - remained untouched in 1904.

It was in Ellacombe, where the author was later born, that housing and commercial premises multiplied. From the bottom of Market Street to the sparse developement abutting Ellacombe Green and beyond, property grew at quite an astonishing rate - extending to an area enclosed within Windsor Road (then named Lower and Higher Bronshill Road) and ending at All Saints Road to the north, Higher Wellesley Road and Hatfield Road to the west, and Lower Ellacombe Church Road and Princes Road West (no Princes Road East) to the east. Ellacombe Green (one of Sir Laurence Palk's benefactions, given to the town in 1867) had by 1904 been laid out as a small park. By the 1920s, bowls had become a

Castle Circus c. 1906 - a view down Union Street. The empty shops on the left are awaiting demolition for the building of the new public library, the foundation stone for which was laid in Febraury 1906. TNHM

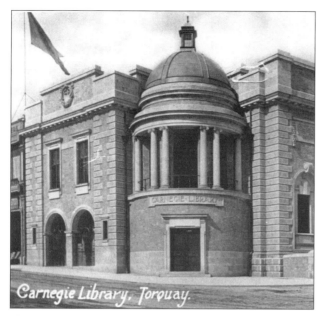

Carnegie Library, Castle Circus, c. 1910. THE

popular activity, with the new and many artisans who lived in the neighbourhood. In May, 1927 the new bowling green opened there for use. Apart from Market Street, at the south end of Ellacombe, the Parish was almost wholly housing development, with a sprinkling of service shops and small industrial units.

Ellacombe now had its Church School, where it still stands today, at the foot of Windsor Road, and later its Parish Church further along Ellacombe Church Road, at its junction with Hoxton Road.

The Old Torbay Hospital started as a public dispensary in 1843, in three rooms at 23 Lower

Torquay Infirmary in Higher Union Street. TNHM

Union Street, and developed into an Infirmary for a few in-patients. Then Sir Lawrence Palk gave a site by Upton Church in 1848, and a Hospital was built on it, fit for occupation in 1853. The Dental Department dates from 1874 and the Eye Infirmary from 1894. In 1878 the 'Provident Dispensary' was set up, whereby the poor, on payment of a few shillings a year, were enabled to secure professional advice and medicine. On 14 April 1898 the site opposite was opened as a hospital recreation ground. Among gifts of shrubs and a shelter was a flagstaff given and erected by H.C.Goss, a Builder of Ellacombe.

Due to the rapid growth of the Town after the War, lack of extension possibilities and ever-increasing traffic in Union Street, it was decided in 1924 to build a new out-of-town hospital, and Major R. P. Kitson of Shiphay Manor offered Hengrave House and its grounds of 15 acres for £8000. Mrs Ella Rowcroft of Pilmuir offered that sum for its purchase. Further donations for the building of the new hospital followed, including a generous one from Sir Mortimer Singer, Major Kitson, Mrs Rowcroft (again) and her sister Miss V. E. Wills. The official opening took place on 17 November 1928.

The Police Force in Torquay grew from very humble beginnings. It seems that at the opening of the 19th century there was but one constable who was to be found at the Watch House, which preceded the old Town Hall. Earliest recollections of the local Police Force for Torquay are recorded in Walter J. Hutchings book *Out of the Blue.*

It was not until 1829 that Sir Robert Peel introduced into Parliament the Metropolitan Police Bill, and in the march of time Devon kept in step and the first Parish Constables were 'sworn in'. In 1855 there were serious bread riots throughout Devon, and in Torquay on 17 May 1847 disturbances broke out in Lower Union Street, where a mob attacked bakers' shops - the contents being carried off by women in their aprons. After hurrying down Fleet Street and the Strand, the mob made its way up to Torre, where they attacked more shops. With the help of 300 special constables, sworn in, the Coastguards and 40 men of the 5th Fusiliers from Exeter, the riots were brought under control.

At one time of crisis the Town Hall - then at the bottom of Abbey Road - was under siege. However, the ringleader and several companions were arrested and lodged in the Watch House. Severe penalties were imposed - two perpetrators were transported for 10 years and nearly a hundred and fifty others imprisoned.

The Old Town Hall at the bottom of Abbey Road, scene of the siege during riots in 1847. THE

A second bread riot took place in the November of 1867 and a further 150 special constables sworn in. Again bread shops in Lower Union Street were attacked and much property destroyed by the mob - the women bringing supplies of heavy stones from Ellacombe to be thrown at the constables. It was not until 5 o'clock in the morning that the disturbances were entirely quelled. At this time the County Police had been established at Torquay for ten years, but no mention is made of any part they played in quelling this riot.

On 30 May 1857 the Torquay Chronical reported that the allotted County Police for the Town of Torquay had been located in the Old Town Hall. Prior to that time a local police force of six constables had operated under a Superintendant Kilby, who resided at 5 Palk Street.

In October 1857 it was ordered that a Station for one cell, a charge-room and quarters be provided within the district. By June 1864, the local force was re-organised as 'F' Division, comprising a Superintendent at Paignton, a First Class Sergeant at Newton Abbot, a Second Class Sergeant at Brixham and Torquay and thirty-two Constables - twelve of whom were in Torquay.

It was not until 1873, however, that Torquay got its new Police Station - then known as the Sessions House. By this time the Police Force must have found its quarters at the old Town Hall most inconvenient, so a separate building was designed which contained both their quarters and the much-needed court accommodation - to say nothing of adequate cells.

The first reference to fire prevention is in 1833 when the 'town' engine, together with those of Newton and Totnes were used to fight a fire at Machetti's Hotel (now The Queens Hotel). The next step was the building of an engine house in 1841 for accommodation of the two fire engines, between the Town Hall and the adjoining premises in the upper yard at the higher side.

The Old Town Hall was not built until 1851 but this was probably the site of the engine house because in 1878 the 'fire engine station' was under the Town Hall in Lower Union Street. There were two separate organisations in mid-Victorian Torquay, the Parish Engine and the West of England Insurance Company Engine. Both existed in 1856, and when Barton Hall was burned down in 1862, difficulty in getting horses delayed the departure of both engines from Torquay and the house was destroyed.

The attendance of Parish & West of England was usual; both were at the scene of a fire at Mr Melhuish's in 1864. (see *Torbay; a Bibliographical Guide* by John Pike).

Chapter 3 - Emergence of the Parish

EARLY HISTORY

Jules-Brown writes: 'Ellacombe, which can hardly be called a valley, is a broad combe or hollow, bounded to the north by Bronshill, on the east by Babbacombe Downs and on the south by Warberry Hill. Even on the west it is shut in by the ridge which ends in Castle Hill, and the only outlet for the rainfall on the slopes of this combe was by the narrow gulley or ravine which is now occupied by Market Street. This is so narrow that from most points of view Ellacombe seems to have no outlet. The rocky sides of Market Street must have been very picturesque in their original condition. The limestone, however, has been so largely quarried on each side of the Street that its natural features are now almost totally destroyed, and changed further since Union Square was built and which obscures the last part of the limestone quarry face.'

There is very little trace of Roman occupation in the Torbay area, other than Kent's Cavern, although Vespasian was rumoured to have landed here in AD49, followed by a battle at Exeter conducted between the Emperor and Arveragus the British King (Arthur C. Ellis - *Historical Survey of Torquay*).

In his *History of Torquay,* White reported traces of a Roman camp between Ansteys Cove and Babbacombe, extending to Warberry Hill, (although this was discounted, later, by R.N. Worth). The earthworks on Warberry Hill were never examined by any competent antiquary. Iron was mined at Torre, between the old hospital and the first house in Higher Union Street, on the side facing Upton, in 1850. Ten years later, some rich samples of iron ore were raised at Sandhill Road, Ellacombe. Prior to 1800 all that existed in the Ellacombe valley was a small estate with a residence and lodge, and there were a dozen modest cottages at Upton.

A brook, whose origin began in Warberry Copse, flowed into and through the old pond at the head of Brewery Park in Lower Ellacombe Church Road, underneath Hoxton and Princes Roads, and so down through Ellacombe Valley, where it reinforced the Flete (meaning 'where the tide comes in') stream and helped to drive the parish mill of Flete - the mill itself standing on the site of the old Union Hotel, with a pond to the eastward covered by Pimlico. The River Flete, rising in Barton, runs through Upton Valley near the bottom of Forest Road, whence it flows under the Lymington Road to Castle Circus, down under

Flete Mill c. 1790, from a watercolour sketch by the Revd John Swete. First recorded in 1618, the mill was in use until 1838. The Flete River, which turned the wheel, rose in Barton and formed a pond at the foot of Market Street. TNHM

Braddon's Hill, otherwise Stentiford's Hill. Notice Higher Terrace which overlooked the harbour. The house with the walled garden was Mount Braddon, the home of Mrs Bridges Willyams, a close friend of Disraeli and his wife who sometimes stayed here. TNHM

Union Street to a spot behind what was once the Union Hotel, and where there was a millpond whose water fed the mill standing on the site of that hotel. Beside the mill, at one time, there were only two other houses in Pimlico. Where the National School once stood, was one occupied by a lime burner named Frank Short, and in the other lived William Stentiford, a gardener, who left his name indelibly upon the western slope of Braddon's Hill, which has ever since been known as Stentiford's Hill.

In 1837 there were 183 voters in Torquay. Under the Reform Act of 1832, two Liberal members - Lord John Russell and John Crocker Bulteel were returned for the South Devon Division (in which Torquay was included), when, prior to this time, South Devon had always returned Conservative members. But in 1835 the two were superseded by Conservatives once again. New Year's Day, 1867, was marked in Torquay by a demonstration among the working classes in favour of reform. A procession of over a thousand men marched to Ellacombe Green, where resolutions were passed calling upon Parliament to extend the franchise. Following the Second Reform Bill of 1867 the County was divided into three Divisions and it was proposed, then, to give a seat to Torquay.

In February 1861, workmen found a large pit in a field on the Warberries. The soil had been carefully removed, planks laid in the cavity, and the top covered with turf. It was presumed that the pit was intended as a cache for the reception of contraband goods. Similar pits had earlier been found on the Torre Abbey grounds.

The lime kiln in the quarry under Braddon Tor was turned into an arbour when one Coulthurst converted the quarry behind South Hill House into gardens. No building of cottage terraces was attempted until the opening up of Market Street and the Ellacombe Valley in 1853, when Mr Lawrence Palk first showed a lively interest in the promotion of schemes for low-rented cottages. On Warberry Hill, a site for an Armada bonfire, is the Quinta, which in the Peninsula, signifies a country house. At Warberry this is recorded as long ago as 1606, at which time it appears that someone 'home from the sea' had set up his place of retirement.

The first large building project for working people was at Ellacombe; this took place in the open lands above Ellacombe House, which ceased to be a residence sometime in the 1850s. It was the first attempt to provide 'houses for the people'. This was on Palk land, and after the second Haldon sale in 1894 more smaller properties were erected. A guidebook of around 1900 states: 'In the neighbourhood of Ellacombe Green, many small and cheap houses will be found, while the general style of the buildings bespeaks owners or tenants in easy circumstances. The price of the better-class houses seems to have declined of late - a fact probably connected with the changes in medical opinion as to the treatment of consumption by climate... Torquay must in future look to the constituency of pleasure-seekers as much as to the invalides, who have been its chief patrons'.

The Ratebook for 1854 lists only a flour mill, water mill and machinery at Ellacombe. Ellacombe House was built sometime before 1823:

Above: *Old Ellacombe Green, 1900. The green was given by Sir Lawrence Palk in 1867. The bowling green was made here in 1927. The premises at right centre were the old 'removals' stables where the Empire Cinema was later erected. The current Ellacombe Post Office lies behind the tree in the centre.* THE

Right: *The Warberries, 1846, pictured from the top of Vane Hill. To the left is Apsley House, and the hedge running up to the Braddon's marks the line of Museum Road. The three houses in the centre are those which stood higher up Babbacombe Road.* TNHM

Above: *The area that was to become Market Street, 1830. In the foreground is the lodge keeper's cottage belonging to Ellacombe House. It stood on the site of St Michael's Church by the entrance to Pimlico. Warren Hill was then a rabbit warren.* TNHM

Top: *Misses Wilson and Warral, residents of 86 Carlton Road, Ellacombe Church road.* Above: *The corner of Ellacombe and Lower Ellacombe Church Road c. 1910.* Dennis Penny/Githa Townsend

Above: *The Torbay Mill shop which stood at the corner of Market Street and the old Albert Road. The author's uncle managed the shop for a time during the 1920s and 30s.* TNHM
Right: *The view down Market Street c. 1960.* THE
Below: *A glimpse of St Michael's and All Angels, standing at the corner of Market Street and Pimlico.* THE

it is shown as 'Allicombe House' in the Tormohun Rate Assessment of 1823, under Sir Laurence Palk's lands, when F Garrett, Esq. paid 2 shillings. (at this time the Rockend Estate was rated at 3 shillings and 11 pence).

A lithograph of about 1830 shows a lodge (Ellis page 325) at the junction of the drive with Union Street (i.e. near Market Corner).

An early issue of the *Torquay Directory* (Jan. 1848) lists as residents 'F. Garrett, Mrs Gardiner and Family'. Mr Garrett made his will in 1853, and refers to him being at Parkhill, Marldon. Possibly he had moved out from Torquay by then

as the earlier Market opened in 1853. By the time the OS map was published in 1860/61, there were houses nearby in Ellacombe Road and Victoria Road as well. Laurence Palk - later Baron Haldon - owned the land, and it was on his initiative he determined that 'low-rented cottages' be built. He proposed that the centre of the vale should be an open space or recreation ground: and around the central spot he proposed that rows of cottages be built, and at the higher elevations streets and villa plots would be provided for. He explained this at a public meeting in September 1859.

He considered that cottages containing a living room, wash-house, pantry, two good bedrooms and closet, with a small garden at the back could be let for £7 and 5 shillings a year. He hoped to reduce it even lower, to £4 per annum, and it would still repay the builder at 7.7% on the capital employed! His good intentions were not realised, and once speculative builders arrived, changes in design and the increased costs of labour and materials raised the rents to between two and three times his original and over-optimistic estimate (White p.69 and Russell p.102).

The centrepiece of ground (Ellacombe Green) was presented to the Town by Sir Lawrence Palk on the occasion of his eldest son obtaining his majority. It was not until 1894 that almost all of

The Methodist Church, Market Street, around 1910. Now demolished the church stood at the corner of Market Street and Ellacombe Green. JP

the Palk Family's estates and properties, which included Ellacombe, were finally sold - the last being in 1914, where the allotments on the Ellacombe Estate were sold to John Short.

When Ellacombe House became derelict is not known, but in 1874 Mr Ginnett was allowed to erect his canvas circus 'on the site of Mr Garrett's House just above the new Police Station'.

The Primitive Methodists were using the old Baptist Chapel in Temperence Street from 1863

(Lorna Smith: *The Pilgrim Way* p.3), and by the 1870s felt strong enough to buy the larger house (Ellacombe House) in Market Street. On 16 July 1877 the memorial stones of Market Street Primitive Methodist Chapel were laid - the building costing £2,500 to build. The Chapel remained a place of worship until 1973, after which the buildings were sold and demolished.

Although the relationship between the Garretts and Gardiners is unknown, there were obviously

Ellacombe Jubilee celebrations c.1881. This takes place on a wet day on Ellacombe Green. Pembroke Villas (below Pembroke Road) can be seen at the top of the picture. The large house on the left later became the headquarters of house removers, C.J. Dimond & Sons, of Victoria Road. TNHM

close ties, because when the Gardiners (one under a married name, Allin) moved to Rawlyn Road in Chelston they took the name Ellacombe House with them. It remained thus until about 1914.

The first Gardiner burial in St Saviour's Churchyard was in 1838, and the last in 1914 - the tombstone can still be seen in Tor Churchyard in excellent condition; being in a hard pink marble (Ashburton or Petitor?).

Mr Ginnett's Canvas Circus existed at the top of Market Street, in the 1870s. This was replaced with a permanent building in 1886 with balconies on three sides. It received the prefix 'Royal' when the Princess of Wales attended a circus performance there. It remained the Royal Public Hall for some time. When Ginnett died in 1892, his will named The Hippodrome, Torquay among his possessions, but it seems never to have been called that publicly.

After a brief spell as the home of a 'People's Mission', and as a theatre, it was purchased by the Salvation Army and used by them for many years until they moved to a purpose-built Citadel next to the Police Station in Market Street.

In 1917 the former theatre was bought by Grey Cars, and became its garage until a larger one was built in Torwood Street. It was then used by the Post Office, also as a garage. After some years as a furniture store, it is now used as a toyshop.

Prior to 1856, water for Torquay was obtained from springs, wells, rainwater tanks or, since1826, from the Palk Water Works, their supply coming from the watershed extending from Barton to the Combe Valley and collected at a reservoir at Ellacombe containing 540 000 gallons. This once existed as Ellacombe Pond, also fed from its own springs. Almost its sole use was to feed the pond and fountain in Cary Green, completed in 1890, but it once fed the Cary parade Conduit and the Palk Brewery - this until the pipe from Ellacombe had been dry for three months and the need for a better supply was discussed and acted upon.

In 1856 the Local Board acquired the plant at Ellacombe, and water was piped from Tottiford. Two reservoirs in Torquay were constructed to contain supplies, one of which was 450 feet high and built on Warberry Hill, holding half a million gallons (Warberry Copse was bought by the Council in April, 1902 for £1000). A second (underground) reservoir was constructed above Rosehill and Grange Roads to hold two million gallons, and opened on 2 October 1872.

In addition to a new reservoir at Great Hill, Barton, a new trunk main from Tottiford to the Warberry Reservoir, to hold and discharge 1.5

Old reservoir, Warberry Copse. The larger, underground, reservoir lies at the edge of Cedar's Road.

million gallons, was approved in March 1912.

Ellacombe Brewery was built, possibly by Henry Swayne of Swayne Brothers, in 1895 and 1900. Brewing seems to have ended about 1930. After being disused for some years, just before the War in 1939, the War Office was negotiating for its purchase and conversion as a Territorial Drill Hall. Presumably because of the war the idea was abandoned, and it remained little changed externally, being used for various commercial purposes including a plan to convert it into a bakery, until recently, when it became a sports club.

When the Market was built, prior to its opening in 1853, the quarry rockface came down to its north wall. By 1900, it had been levelled back for some distance, and Albert Road built as a cul-de-sac from Union Street. Part subsequently became the base for Webber & Steadham's building materials centre. Next door became the Co-operative dairy and stables (established in July 1890), which was built on the quarry floor.

The trams, which were to pass through Ellacombe as part of the 'circular route', beginning and ending on the Strand, were to be a transport lifeline to the working people of Ellacombe, extended as they were to Torre and Torquay Stations, and later to Paignton where they terminated. After four years of discussion and various proposals, the Torquay Tramway Company was authorised to build it in 1905, and then began two years of disruption and chaos, with the closing down of whole streets during its construction.

At first overhead trolleys were not installed, but a 'Dolter' surface contact system used instead - power flowing from self-operating studs between the rails. This system was to cause electrical transmission problems, and many hazards to pedestrians and animals, and was soon discarded in favour of overhead trolleys. As John Pike remarks in *Torquay – the Place and the People*, by 1928, after 21 years of operation, over 109 million passengers had been carried and 11 840 000 miles covered - quite a proportion of which were undoubtedly Ellacombeites. For a time, trolley-buses were in vogue, but by May 1933 trams were superseded by Devon General Buses. The last trams ran in 1934, and the closure of the Westhill Tram Depot was soon to follow.

It was in 1871 that agitation for a new Police Station at Torquay resulted in the provision of a site on the south-east side of Market Street - probably the site of the old Fire Station. On 17 October of that year, the Police Committee reported that work had commenced, but had been abandoned because of falling rock. Another site was purchased and the new station built by Mr A.W. Goss to plans by E. Harbottle. The building was completed and occupied at the top of Market Street early in 1876.

By 1875 the local police had been organised as the Torquay District Police Force, and covered the town, including St Marychurch. It was composed of an inspector, 3 sergeants and 33 constables, and pressure was on for the introduction of women police constables. Of these, in 1878, the constables at Market Street had increased to 23, but later, in 1894, one sergeant was replaced by an additional inspector.

In 1908 a serious disturbance arose in Newton Abbot, due to the visit of the celebrated suffragette Mrs Pankhurst and two followers. A Superintendent Roberts and a squad of policemen from Torquay arrived to assist in restoring order. But it was only when the Chief Constable of Devon arrived on horseback with a small body of mounted policemen and about a hundred on foot that order was finally restored, but not before the body of Sergeant Major Reynell was recovered from the Town Mill Leat.

The Force was seriously depleted during the 1914-1918 War, and it was some time, and much training, before it was brought back to strength. In the 1920s and 30s mechanical vehicles increasingly took over from horse transport and bicycles. In 1921 strength was again depleted when on a temporary transfer to South Wales in connection with the coal strike, and again in 1932 when a

The old Police Station in Market Street, built in the 1870s.

coach-load of policemen from Torquay and Paignton got together and were sent to assist (but too late) in quelling a serious Princetown Prison mutiny.

Little appears to be recorded in the archives of the domestic organisation of, and day-to-day life at, the old Police Station in Market Street. It is known, however, that between 1930 and 1940 it was the headquarters of 'F' Division of the Devon County Police Force, covering Torquay, Paignton, Churston with Galmpton and Brixham, and also Kingskerswell - at that time the largest Division in the Devon Constabulary. It was headed by a Superintendent, A.E. Martin, who lived in a police house in Castle Road. On his promotion to Exeter as an Assistant Chief Constable, he was superseded by a Superintendent Drew, who resided in Higher Warberry Road. Later Superintendent Milford took over.

Next in line in the hierarchy was a Chief Inspector and then an Inspector, who lived on the station premises. Details of the full complement of sergeants and constables is unknown, but a sergeant named Taylor was in charge of the Paignton sub-station. The Police Station entrance was in Market Street with a side door adjacent to Barrows the chemists. Stone stairs led to Supt. Martin's office, with the Magistrates' Court leading off. Here, maintenance payments to deserted

Top: *Devon Constabulary 'F' Division, c. 1920, taken inside the police station yard.* photo Mike Dadly.
Bottom: *Devon Constabulary 'F' Division, 1938. The photograph was taken at Ellacombe Green. Station Sergeant Mair is shown sixth from the right - front row.* photo Mrs M. Langmead

wives were paid weekly, and other business conducted. At the bottom of the stairs, one passed through a small door to the Station Sergeant's office, where Sergeant Mairs and Constable Clements dealt with 'F' Division's administation. Off this room was the Charge Room, which was operated on a 24-hour basis by 3 constables in 8-hour shifts. A passageway led to the cells, where arrested suspects were imprisoned prior to appearing before the Court. The main entrance (an archway) with double doors led into a cobbled courtyard and contained a 'stable' door leading to the Charge Room on the right. The double doors were closed when prisoners were exercised.

The Inspector and his family resided in accommodation to the left of the archway, with a separate access from Castle Lane. Also resident on the

premises was a mess caterer (usually a constable) and his wife. The latter, carrying the title of Matron, was the mess cook, looked after the young recruits (who lived in a 'barrack room' at the rear of the station facing St. Michael's Terrace), and also acted as search officer for any female prisoners. Constable and Mrs Mortimore and Constable and Mrs Hubbard performed these duties - the men also patrolled the sea-front area. Food was taken in the 'mess' kitchen.

Married quarters for police staff were provided in rented properties in parts of Ellacombe: nos. 60, 88, 90 and 117 Ellacombe Church Road, owned by a Mr Tozer (?); 11,13, 21, 23 and 50 Egerton Road; No.1, Congella Road and No.18, Florida Road. There were further rented police houses in Lower Ellacombe Church Road, Cavern

Road and St Michael's Terrace. Residents at that time included Sergeants Gale and Mairs and PC's., Tom Prior, Woolcock, Clements and Gooding. The station had only one patrol car and the officers rode bicycles or walked - and sported the old helmets and traditional wide capes in inclement weather, fastened at the neck by chains. Monthly pay parades were held in the nearby Ellacombe Green.

Enough has been written about Torquay's most famous crime - the murder of Miss Keyse, the subsequent arrest and trial of John Lee, and of the three attempts to hang him at Exeter without success. When released from prison on 18 December 1907, he lived at Abbotskerswell, later married and left the area for Durham.

Another attempted murder took place in 1908. The case was reported in the *Torquay Times* of 16 June 1944 when it was revealed that Sir Edward Carson was briefed to appear for a fee of £1000. Many Ellacombe residents, past and present, will remember that Bruce Reynolds, one of the Great Train Robbers, lived for a time under an assumed name in the Warberries, and was arrested there and charged in the local 'dock'.

The police station in Market Street moved to its current premises in South Street in 1944, and the magistrates' court with it, until transferred into what was the old Upton School - re-built and made into a purpose-built county and magistrates' court in 1960.

As John Pike reports - it was in the 1880s that a new Fire Station was built in Market Street by the Local Board, shortly before the Borough came into existence. At the time the Brigade had 3 foremen, 14 firemen and a driver, ten of whom lived in the Local Board accommodation in Market Street (Corporation Buildings). There were, of course, sub-stations in other parts of the town. Horses were used to haul the fire apparatus until the first motor engine 'Firefly' was introduced in May 1920. In the early days the horses were requisitioned from local livery stables, but by 1910-1911 the Brigade had its own animals, housed in stables behind the Buildings. The most notable fire attended by the Brigade before the First World War was a major one, in 1912, at Slades on the Strand, with all sub-units assisting. The Chief Officer, at the time, was a Mr F.G. Rowland. Earlier a Mr Evans was Superintendent and a Mr

Members of the fire service in Torquay in the late 1800s. Author/Dave Crawford/TFS

Horsepower

Horse-drawn vehicles were vital to commerce in the growing town. The Drake family held the contract with the Post Office for 'the conveyance of mail' between Torquay Post Office and the railway station. Top and top right: Royal Mail coaches c. 1915. Top left: The Drake family house and offices at Bowmanville Terrace, Upper Princes Road. Above: Parade of horses for sale, 1904. Right: Poster of horse sale, 1906. With kind permission of the Drake family

ELLACOMBE, TORQUAY.

To Contractors, Hauliers, Timber Merchants and Others.

Cessation for the time being of Contract to the Torquay Corporation Tramways.

RENDELL & SYMONS

Have been instructed by Mr. F. Drake (who has decided to dispose of his Horses, Carts, &c., owing to the reasons stated above), to

SELL BY AUCTION,

In a Field just beyond Bowmanville Terrace, Ellacombe,

On MONDAY, September 3rd, 1906,

At 2 p.m., the following grand lot of

CART HORSES

COBS, CARTS, TIMBER WAGONS, &c.

HORSES.

1—"BLOSSOM,' grey cart mare, 7 years old, 16·3 h.h., a grand mare, and admirably adapted for timber hauling or other heavy work.
2—"MADAM," roan cart mare, 7 years old, 16·3 h.h., would make an excellent match for No. 1.
3—"DARLING," black cart mare, 7 years old, 16·2 h.h.
4—"PRINCE," bay cart gelding, 8 years old, 16·1 h.h.
5—"CHARLIE," do. do.
6—"MADAM," bay cart mare, do. 16·2 h.h.
7—"VIOLET," brown cart mare, 7 years old, 17 h.h.
8—"LION," bay cart gelding, 8 years old, 16·2 h.h.
9—"BLACK PRINCE," black cart gelding, aged, 16·2 h.h.
10—"BOXER," dark brown cart gelding,aged, 16·3 h.h.
11—"BOB," brown cart gelding, aged,15·2 h.h.
12—"FARMER," bay do. do. 17 h.h.
13—"PRINCE," bay gelding, 6 years old, 16 h.h., fit for 'bus, coaching, or Van work.
14—"POLLY," dun mare, 7 years old, 15 h.h., fit for Cab, 'Bus, or Van work.
15—"DOLLY," bay mare, 10 years old,16 h.h., fit for Cab, 'Bus, or Van work.
16—"BOB," a bay cob gelding, 8 years old, 14·2 h.h., a rare cob to go, and quiet to ride or drive.
17—"BILLY," a brown cob gelding,7 years old, 13·2 h.h., a good worker, and quiet to ride or drive.
18—"LADY BIRD," a grey cob mare, aged, 15 h.h., wonderfully good little Mare, and a rare mover.

CARTS, HARNESS, &c., &c.

Undercarriage Timber Wagon, Top carriage do. to carry 10 tons, to Carts with sideboards, 2 Carts without do., Flat-bottom Wagon by *Jury* with Lades, 2 Spring Wagons to carry 15 cwt. and 13 cwt. respectively, **nearly new Light Varnished Ralli Cart with Lamps and Cushions complete**, nearly new Spring Trap with Cushions
12 Complete Sets of Cart Harness, all practically new ; 2 Sets of Fore Harness ; **nearly new Set of Brown-plated Cob-size Trap Harness;** 4 full-size Sets of Black Trap Harness ; 12 Nosebags.
Lot of Blocks and Chains, Lot of Timber Chains (Roller and Sling), Set of Shear Legs

Torquay Fire Service members in 1910. With kind permission of Dave Crawford, TFS

W. Ferrett his deputy. At this time the Station was at the rear of premises in Laburnum Row.

Mr K.T. Bremridge (Sam), a retired fireman, born 18 June 1926, moved with his family from Plymouth to the Ellacombe area in 1928. This view of life in the old Fire Station in Market Street during the early part of the Second World War, and after the cessation of hostilities is based on his recollections.

Sam joined the Fire Service first as a young motorcycle despatch rider (DR) in 1941. In the absence of modern means of communication, DR's accompanied fire engines, salvage tenders and pumps, etc., on all call outs, apart from daily routine mail services between sub-stations and HQ. He vividly recalls the Divisional HQ of the Torquay Division of what was (pre-war) the Torquay Fire Brigade (TFB), later to become the Auxillary Fire Service, and then the National Fire Service, until renamed the Devon Fire Brigade in 1945. His first Divisional Officer (or Commander) was called Mr Blower, then a Mr Philpotts and after that Mr Kirby took over. The Assistant DO was a Mr Roberts and the Company Officer a Mr Watlin. There were two 'watches' of full-time firemen (now termed firefighters), usually of a maximum strength of 15 each, including a Sub Officer and two Leading Firemen per watch. The figures varied considerably, as there were no staffing reserves employed for sickness, leave, training, etc. Fire attendance numbers were related to the size and type of the conflagration or emergency. The Divisional area of responsibility was considerable - extending through Kingsbridge to Salcombe westwards, Buckfast and Bovey Tracey northwards and through Teignmouth and Shaldon to Dawlish in the East. During the war, of course, there were fire sub-stations all over Torbay and the outlying towns, manned by volunteers. Included, in those days, were the duties of cliff rescue until this was taken over by the Coastguard Service. Also, in the early days, the firemen provided the ambulance services, and the vehicles were garaged within the Market Street depot.

Torquay Council provided ambulance men only during the hours of 9am to 9pm, and firemen were given 'crash courses' in first-aid to provide emergency services outside of these hours. During these early days, before the Newton Road premises were purpose-built and occupied, the Fire Station Control Room was on the ground floor of the Corporation Buildings, on the right of the archway entrance leading in from Market Street. The DO's Office and those of the Station Officers and Sub-Officers were opposite. Behind the Control Room was the watch dormitory (where the betting shop now stands).

The old stables were earlier positioned at the bottom of the yard adjacent to the premises of Messrs Hardings, Ironmongers. Earlier, stores and the motorcycles were kept in the old stalls. Sam remembers that the names of the horses were

Torquay Fire Service members take part in a carnival procession c.1910. With kind permission of Dave Crawford, TFS and TNHM

recorded over each stall. The stables were replaced later by a large dining-room/mess, and service kitchen, and a Mrs Chamberlain was employed during the day as cook. There was also a washroom and large communal bath for men returning from fire duty. A recreation room with billiards and table tennis, etc. was provided in the yard.

At the back, underneath the cliff face, the fire appliances were all garaged and maintained. Within the yard was a training tower, equipment and hose stores, and a boiler room for maintaining constant hot water. On the cliff top Sam recalls a site of a wartime machine-gun post. All fire, cliff and ambulance emergency calls were received by telephone - not on 999 but 2222. Watches were very long at first - 24 hours on and 24 off, with a 96 and then 84-hour week. This was gradually reduced, first to 60 then 48 hours, 2 days on and 4 off. Sam's pay then was £3.19.6d. a week - better than the average pay for manual workers, but hard and dangerous work when fire-fighting or scaling cliffs, often at night and in pouring rain, with only the aid of colleagues and flashlights.

Fitness training consisted of being made to run up the steps adjacent to the Corporation Buildings to Warberry Road West and back in full kit! It was on one night of duty that a large cliff subsidence took place, showering the sheds, boiler room, etc. with stone and rubble, making fur-

ther tenancy of the premises for staff impossible. At this stage - the old Police Station being partly vacant during the early 50s - the Divisional HQ was transferred there, before the new Fire Station was built on old orchard grounds on the Newton Road, where it now stands. Sam had returned to duty as a fireman in 1947 after serving hostility-only duties with the Royal Navy. He recalls the old Courtroom was used as a dormitory, while a kitchen was fitted into the cell block (the firemen using the old Police Mess), and others made into storerooms - the old Police HQ and Charge Room being converted into the Control Room and Divisional offices. Some policemen remained billeted in the Station. While one small appliance was garaged in the police yard, the fire engines, etc. remained in the Corporation Yard, and it was a common sight to see, at that time, the fire crews crossing the traffic in Market Street, hurriedly pulling on uniforms and equipment, and running down to man the vehicles from the Police Station.

The second Divisional Officer, Mr Philpotts, was a clever innovator - designing a purpose-made fire boat, which was built locally and moored in Torquay Harbour. This was propelled by a water jet from water sucked in by means of a petrol engine and expelled from the stern. He was also responsible for inventing an aluminium extending ladder, operated by pulleys, which superseded the old pump escape on large wheels, and is still used in modified form to this day.

Torquay Fire Service members at Market Street Station c.1910. With kind permission of Dave Crawford, TFS

One of Sam's happiest memories concerns the discovery of a box of fourteen old brass helmets in the Market Street Station. These were subsequently used in a charity fun procession with the help of the old steam fire cart drawn by borrowed horses from the Co-op Dairy stables, then situated in the old Albert Road adjacent to Messrs Webber & Stedham's builders yard. Mr Bremridge, now long retired, is the proud possessor of the Queen's Fire Service Medal.

Devon County Fire Brigade with a Metz turntable ladder specially constructed for the Torquay brigade. It could turn out of Market Street without hitting shop blinds etc. On the engine are Archie McElleron (driver), Leading Fireman Whiting, and Firemen Paddon, Ward and Doble. With kind permission of Dave Crawford, TFS.

Cinematic entertainment in Ellacombe was offered in two places - first at the new building (Torquay Market) in Market Street, when a part was leased to a Mr W. Mellor on a three-year lease for cinematograph entertainments in 1909. Earlier there had been unsuccessful attempts to have Italian Band concerts on the site, but roller skating became a popular offering for some years.

It soon became known as the 'Picturedrome'. Performances were screened on Mondays at 8 o'clock, Saturdays at 3 o'clock and at 8 o'clock'. There was also a short exhibition of special pictures on Tuesdays, Wednesdays and Fridays at 11am. to 10pm. Improvements were made in 1913, when red plush tip-up seats 'affording a sense of refinement and comfort' were installed!

The Empire, facing the top of Ellacombe Green, dates from about 1912. On Christmas night during its construction, the main wall (then partly built) blew down! Owing to falling patronage and competition from television, it closed in 1959. It re-opened again in 1962 as a cinema showing continental films, but this did not last long, and soon Mr Lionel Digby was launching his Empire Ballroom there. In the mid-1960s it became Torquay's first 'disco'.

A story of Ellacombe's early days would be incomplete without a mention of the Torquay United Football Club, and its home at Plainmoor. Whilst it is true that the club under this name was introduced in 1921, it was known before under another title from as early as 1899. In 1910 a club known as Torquay Town was formed as an amalgam of Ellacombe and Babbacombe Football Clubs, and took up residence at the Plainmoor ground, when it went professional. Before this time, the game was played at Teignmouth Road, the Torquay Recreation Ground and Barton Road. Much of the early enthusiasm stemmed from the efforts of Charles Dear, who became its first Honorary Secretary. The club first joined the Western League, then the Southern League a year later. It was not until 1927/8 that they were elevated to the Football League, Division Three (South), and their fortunes have fluctuated ever since. The 1925 Great Storm was to blow away the grandstand roof!

Among the outstanding pre-war players for Torquay United was Ralph Birkett, the first TU player to play for England. Another England International was Don Welsh. Other well-remembered players were Babba-combe-born Sid Cann, Phil Joslin and Bert Head. Early post-war the greatest player ever to play for United was Don Mills. Supporters will also remember the outstanding header of the ball, centre forward Jack Conley.

Torquay team members at the first post-war South Devon Wednesday Football League match, held at Plainmoor against an Exeter SDFL team, c.1949. Back row l-r: G. Eden; S. Campbell; R. Mills; R. Bailey; J. Fowler; (?); J. Cordingley; Mr Tickner (Head Postmaster). Front row: J. Catchpole; D. Cox; W. Southcombe; J. Walker; (?).

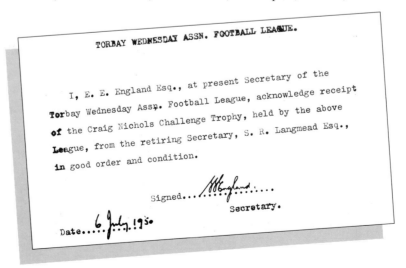

TORBAY WEDNESDAY ASSN. FOOTBALL LEAGUE.

I, E. E. England Esq., at present Secretary of the Torbay Wednesday Assn. Football League, acknowledge receipt of the Craig Nichols Challenge Trophy, held by the above League, from the retiring Secretary, S. R. Langmead Esq., in good order and condition.

Signed...England.....
Secretary.

Date....6 July 1950

Chapter 4 - Elementary Education

Since its founding in 1698, the Society for Promoting Christian Knowledge had, amongst its many aims, the foundation of schools to give a sound education, religious and secular, to the children of the poor (*History of Education in Great Britain*, 1967 S. J. Curtis). The means by which such education was provided were the Charity Schools, financed by subscriptions and the preaching of special 'charity' sermons in local churches at which collections were made for the purpose. Not all charity schools were specifically church schools - private individuals continued to endow schools in the 18th century - many of which had no connection with the philanthropic societies!

Dissenters had their own charity schools. In none of the lists of such schools extant at the time did one for the Parish of Tormohun appear. It must be remembered, however, the close relationship in education between that provided by charity schools, schools of industry and by the sunday schools who opened on weekdays as well.

The 1821 returns show that the parish of Tormohun/Cockington was one of 103 in the Diocese reporting a sunday school. There was a temporary phase when the Sunday School Movement attempted to take over the Charity Schools, but it was soon apparent that the problem was too big for them to handle. This was resolved by provision of the National System of Day Schools. In the early 19th century this was implemented by means of two Societies - the nonconformist dominated British & Foreign Schools Society (formed in 1808) and the National Society for the Education of the Poor in the Principles of the Established Church, formed in 1811. However - Torquay had no non-conformist voluntary schools until as late as 1853 - probably because of the lack of sufficient numbers of nonconformists of means in the Town.

Torquay's first voluntary school appears to have been established in 1826 - referred to as the School at Tormohun cum Cockington, united to the National Society. Blewitt records, six years later, that there were 228 children at the School - 108 boys and 120 girls. This school became known as the Torquay National School or the Pimlico School. The National Society (NS) records

refer later to the Trinity Chapel School (1834) and the Tor School (also known as the Younge School -1836), also an additional part of the NS, independently funded by the St John's Chapel of Ease. Naturally there were many difficulties in the early funding of these schools - much of it by public subscription - at a time when funding was sought for a new church, an infirmary and dispensary. Difficulties included the provision of sites, buildings and teachers. Even the first schoolmaster, Mr Dart, contributed from his only source of income (his wages), and a female servant of the Revd J. Blackmore came to him with an offer of 10/- annually from her princely wages of £10 a year! The estimated annual charge for the Master and Mistress, books, etc. was about £80. At the time Mallock pointed out that in the early days of schooling some 140 scholars were accommodated from an increasing population of the Parish which at the last Census was 3500 and now estimated at 6000.

The completion of Tor School was held to mark the end of a phase in the history of the provision in Torquay. The year 1848 marks the division of the old Parish and the appointment of two new incumbents - one, the Revd J. H. Harris to Tormohun and the other, the Revd R. Wolfe of Leeds (to the newly formed district of Upton, in whose new parish the National School at Pimlico was sited). The Torquay Directory (TD) (of 22.5.1850) reported in some detail the results of a Government inspection of this school in May 1850, conducted by the Revd E. D. Tinling. The following subjects were reported as taught 'reading, spelling, writing, mental and notational arithmetic, knowledge of the Holy Scriptures, the Catechism, english, history, english grammar and composition, mapping, geography and local music'.

The new pupil-teacher system was well under way, and such teachers were required to write papers on the above subjects as a form of examination of their teaching ability! The schools were also subject to Diocesan Inspection.

Concern was expressed by the Master of the Tor National School, in a letter to the TD on 15 November 1851, about the lack of interest of too many parents in the education of their children.

Right: *A photograph c.1880 of the Torquay British School in Abbey Road, opened in 1853. Thomas Viccars was the Superintendant here, and at the Girls ' School in Upton Vale. The British Schools were founded in 1814 as an alternative to Church Schools.* THE

Left: Class 1 outside the First National School, Pimlico c.1920. This was later renamed Madrepore Road C of E school and was closed when the school at Warberry opened in 1972. THE

The Revd R. Wolfe also commented on the fact that his experience of the National Schools also showed how 'regardless parents generally were of the welfare of their children - the average period during which they remained at school not exceeding 1 year' (*Torquay Directory* 19 April 1854).

Typical of working-class education at this time was irregular attendance and the fact that only a small proportion stayed long enough to reach higher classes. Most left early to engage in manual labour. A report in the TD of 1 January 1851 revealed that although the original intention was for Tor School to have a boys section, when it opened in 1845 it provided only for infants and girls. It was not until five years or so later that boys were admitted. Further reports in the TD give a very interesting insight into the conditions of educational establishments obtaining at this time in Torquay.

It was the massive increase in the population of Torquay which occurred during the decades of the 1840s and 50s, and which brought into question the monopoly of provision of day schools by the National Society Schools. The age structure of the population was such as to call for more schools and the population was sufficiently diverse to justify an increasingly significant non-anglican observance. An important meeting took place on 23 December 1852 at the Mechanics Institute 'to elect a provisional committee for the purposes of determining the system of education to be adopted, appointing the teachers and organising and superintending the arrangement of the schools for a period not exceeding 12 months'.

Most of the names of the provisional committee were those of prominent local non-conformists, with the exception of the anglican Edward Vivian - a local example of those who, in an age of strong sectarian feeling, paid little heed to denominational boundaries. As a direct result of this intervention new schools were formed as the Abbey Road Public Schools - the 'Public' signifying their non-sectarian basis. They were set up as rivals to the National Schools in a number of ways - principally in the manner in which they were taught (non-catechatical system). Despite the growing strength of non-conformity in Torquay, however, the Abbey Road Public Schools were not so successful as their rivals, neither in terms of financial support or in numbers of pupils on the books. Indeed the Master later resigned from the conviction that the Schools were not prospering as they might.

For various financial and other organisational reasons the Schools were later designated as the Torquay British Schools, to let the public understand it was a branch of the British and Foreign Schools Society. The contribution of the British Schools during this period was obviously very limited, although 1861 ended with an optimistic note: 350 were on the books and the finances in a somewhat more prosperous condition. The British Schools, in fact, survived until early 1894.

In the meantime the church schools in Torquay consolidated and expanded the adoption of the pupil-teacher system, employing during the 1846 period some six pupil-teachers (three boys and three girls) who were apprenticed to the Master and Mistress for periods of five years, after which they successfully passed their examinations. At this stage the subjects taught were 'Holy Scriptures, Catechism and Liturgy, writing, mental and slate arithmetic, mensuration, geography and mapping, grammar, composition and etymology, history, geometry, books and other useful knowledge'. The girls were also taught sewing and knitting.

Two pupil-teachers were successful in the exams for Queen's Scholarships, entitling them to two year's training and maintenance at Exeter Training College - Exeter being one of the Diocesan Boards to establish a Training College by 1840. It was shortly after this time that a schism within the National Society in 1852 led to the founding of The Church of England Educational Society (CEES) by Mr Colquhoun, as it was felt that the National Society had become too much under the control of Tractarians.

The versatile Mr Vivian took the 'Chair' at this inaugural meeting - commenting at length about the unsatifactory nature and results of the present system, depending so exclusively upon the clergy whereby every change of the incumbent deranged the whole education of a parish. He also referred to the fact that the children of dissenters were excluded from weekly instruction unless they attended the services of the church. After some lengthy debate on the National Society and a proposal of a great debt of gratitude to its educational efforts, the new association was formed with the Revds G. T. Warner and R. Foyle as acting secretaries and E. Vivian as treasurer.

At a meeting of the CEES in 1856 the chairman, Mr Vivian, observed that the Society currently afforded aid by grant for the support of the schools whilst the National Schools Society confined itself principally to the erection of school buildings. Thus they did not compete with each other. He hoped that both Societies would work harmoniously together.

At the end of 1854 the committee of the CEES were elected - comprising H. C. March Phillips, J. Hack, Revd Preb. Ford, F. Spragge, Revd Dr Scoresby, Revds Dr Harris and Wolfe Treasurers. It devoted itself, in the main, to the collection of voluntary contributions. However, the influence of the CEES in Torquay would appear to have been slight, for no further mention of it occurs in the TD after 1859.

The National Society had, in the meantime, continued to expand its activities. A branch infants school to Torre opened in Melville Street - about 70 infants attending there, and another branch of the Torquay National Schools opened at Boston Fields (Plainmoor), an outlying part of Upton Parish. In the following year it was expanded to accommodate 150 children.

It was recorded in the TD of 1854 that there was a population of about 500 poor persons in Boston Fields where a school was much needed 'for the little children who cannot bear the fatigue of walking to Torquay to school'. Sir Lawrence Palk gave the site, and each child was to pay 2d a week. The school was opened in October 1855 - the scholars being later transferred to Ellacombe

School in January 1872. Victoria Park School was built in 1910. Upton Church National School was opened in 1871.

The Parish, through the severence of Ellacombe, had lost two of its three schools - Boston Fields (which was Plainmoor) and Ellacombe. The third school, which was the old National School in Pimlico, had gone to St Luke's when that parish was formed. Upton was thus left high and dry with no school at all, and an increasing population (*Upton – the Heart of Torquay*, Deryck Seymour).

St John's School was, until 20 September 1883, operating in Braddons Street, in a building which served for school and chapel. From that date a new building was opened at the foot of Braddons Street. Concern was felt at this stage about the short time many children spent at school, and the Exeter Diocesan Board of Education took steps to encourage longer stay by means of certificates of merit and prizes. Children above the age of 12 were allowed as candidates.

The year 1861 is marked by the two incumbents of the Parish of Tormohun and Upton each embarking on a new educational venture. A new working mens' area had been growing at Ellacombe and the TD reported that in March 1861 the 'Ellacombe situation had been brought to the attention of the Lord of the Manor by the Revd R Wolfe' who calculated that there were 245 children of school-going age living there. He pointed out that the schools could be used on Sundays for public worship as in the case of Boston Fields. Thus plans were set in motion for both an Ellacombe School and for another to replace the one in Melville Street to be attached to the new church of St Lukes, when completed.

Whilst the early days of education in Torquay, both public and private, have been extensively covered in various publications, perhaps a brief resume of the effects of the Education Act of 1870 and that of 1902 are relevant where both had an impact on the Parish of Ellacombe. Most children in the late 19th century attended either private schools, those run by the Church of England (National Schools) or those run by the independents or nonconformists (the British Schools). Ordinary school-leavers had, until 1918, to leave at the age of 13, but could leave at 12 if they had reached a certain level of education - an incentive welcomed by parents who were anxious to utilise their child's earning capacity in the labour market at an earlier age. The 'Torquay National' in Pimlico was the oldest. There - in the older portion - the upper story was occupied by the girls, and had a separate entrance. The boys were taught on the ground floor, and there was also an infants school there. A new classroom was added in about 1898 and the headmaster had his own house on the site. The School remained in use until 1972, when the children, plus those from the Torwood Junior School in Meadfoot Lane, were (in the main) moved to the newly-built Warberry Church of England School in Cedars Road. Earlier a number of children had moved to both Upton and Ellacombe Schools.

The Education Act of 1902 reorganised the National Schools into Elementary Schools (old names discontinued in 1906). In 1909 the Council bought Homelands Villa and grounds for £5150 and later four additional acres of ground - building Homelands for £7194. The School was officially opened as a school for handicrafts, cookery, laundry work, etc., in 1913. A second handicrafts school was opened at the Old British School in Abbey Road in September 1924.

It was through a Borough initiative that an Open-Air School came into being at Plainmoor, designed for children with health problems. This remained in operation until the Steps Cross Special School opened in Watcombe. Homelands Central School was converted in 1927. The Windmill Hill playing fields were opened for elementary scholars on 8 December 1928.

The School of Arts & Crafts began when the Salem Chapel in Braddons Hill Road West was converted into a School of Science & Arts, and in 1878 it became the Vivian Institute and enlarged. It was organised as a School of Arts & Crafts in 1918, after earlier control became vested in the Governors of the Grammar School in July 1914.

In John Pike's *Torquay – The Place and the People* the author discusses this period in more detail - in particular the subject of selective education and the inauguration of the Torquay Secondary School, the name of which was changed to the Torquay Grammar School in 1928. He also discusses the Torquay Pupil Centre, the Homelands Central School (developed from December 1911, and extended in 1928), and the evolution of the Central Technical School, later to become the South Devon Technical College.

Chapter 5 - Ellacombe School

Before 1861 moves were afoot to construct a school for the children of the 'working classes' in Ellacombe. As has been said before, many artisans and workmen, as well as the servants of the gentry holidaying or settling in the Warberries, Lincombes, and the Bronshill and St Marychurch Road areas of Torquay, were finding acommodation difficult in the (by now) overcrowded areas of Pimlico, the Braddons and Melville Street. Their children likewise found it difficult to find school places. On 23 March 1861 matters were brought to a head as a result of 'a large and influential meeting of gentlemen resident in the town held on Saturday afternoon in the Boardroom at the Town Hall, for the purpose of considering a proposition made by the lord of the manor, Sir L. Palk, to erect schools at Ellacombe'. A full report of that meeting was given in the *Torquay Directory & South Devon Journal* of 27 March 1861, as follows:

Amongst those present were: Sir L Palk, Bart., MP., Revd. Dr Harris, incumbent of Torre; Revd. R.R. Wolfe, incumbent of Upton; Revd. J.R.Hogg, incumbent of St Mark's; H.C.M.Phillips, R Robinson, F H Spragge, A Tower, W Kitson, G H Harris, W H Tinney, N B Edmonstone, W H Kitson, J A Hay, A B Shephard, Smart, J Kitson, and Hartland Esqrs., the Revd. G C Harris, Revd. F Savile, Revd. W B Davis, Revd. Dr. Larden, Revd. W Leeming, Revd. T N Hicks, Colonel Thoresby, Messrs. S Cockings, R C Lemon, Bridgeman, Angel, &c., &c.

Sir L. Palk, who took the Chair, said: Gentlemen, we are met here today in consequence of a paragraph you all saw in the 'Torquay Directory', relating to the erection of schools in Ellacombe: and on that subject I must say that the whole scheme at Ellacombe has been most beneficial to the town. For, had it not been for Ellacombe, which acted as a vent for the increased population of the place, the houses inhabited by the poor would have been most frightfully crowded - to an extent that would have engendered disease and fever in this town. I can tell you it was told me by persons likely to know, that some few years ago there were families amongst the poor, consisting of ten individuals, all

inhabiting one room in Torquay. I am informed that there is still a great want of accommodation for the labouring classes. But as far as the Ellacombe scheme has gone it has been of some service, and I hope to see it still further carried out, and become of greater benefit to the town. In consequence of the scheme succeeding so far, there has been a great accession of children in the district, and at present there is no provision made for their education or their care. As regards their care, we all well know the immense advantage to the wives of labouring, industrial men, to be able to place their children where they can be taken proper care of, while they themselves are attending to their households. As far as the education of the children is concerned , that I believe to be a matter of national importance and, therefore, if we can combine the two objects of taking care of the children and giving them the rudiments of education - we shall be conferring a great benefit upon the mothers themselves, and the country generally. You all know that close by, there is a national school, which I believe is large enough for the wants of the place: there is also another of the same kind at Boston Fields, which, under the care of the Revd. R R Wolfe, has conferred immense benefits upon that locality. I am happy to say that in consequence of the repeal of an Act called the Conventicle Act, in the last session, clergymen may celebrate divine worship in schools properly appointed for that purpose. When Mr Wolfe spoke to me on this subject I at once did what I could. I wished I could have done more. I said I should be happy to give him, as I had at Boston Fields, the site free, and contribute towards the building. With regard to the site, we are really very fortunately situated, for in this instance we have a choice, and I should propose, before this meeting separates, some two or three gentlemen should be appointed as a committee to inspect the ground, and select the best and most judicious for the purpose. Due regard must be paid to those who have houses and villas there; and without putting the school in any improper place, it ought not to be put where it is likely to be a nuisance, or in any way disagreeable to the inmates of the villas. There are various places to be found which might be taken without being a source of annoyance or

Ellacombe School today.

discomfort to any one. It has been mentioned as desirable to build the schools on the centre space between the two rows of houses: I think, however, it would not be judicious to place them there for several reasons. In the first place, it lies very low, and will take the principal drainage of that part of the town: besides that the children will be so over-looked, that it would not be desirable in any respect to build upon that space. In fact, I would rather adhere to my original plan of filling it up, and making pleasure grounds for the working classes residing in that locality. One good site can be obtained on the top of the sand hill, or even in the valley a good site might be found, but that I leave to the better judgement of the gentlemen who may be selected by the meeting. This is all I have to say on this point. I look forward to a very large increase in the population in the vicinity of Ellacombe, and I should be very glad indeed, if in looking forward we could provide some means of securing the performance of divine worship in that locality. I believe it is most important that we should bring the church as near to the poor man's door as we can, and I do hope, that in the course of a very short time, some means might be found for providing a certain amount of remuneration for a clergyman to perform at least one service there on Sundays. This I believe would be a great advantage. I have thrown out this idea that the committee in devising plans for the schools, might so form the building that it may be adapted to the purposes of divine worship.

In the manner of the time the Revd R. R. Wolfe thanked Sir Lawrence and proceeded to provide details of the inhabitants of the area and the type of building that was envisaged.

When he first spoke to Sir Lawrence Palk on the subject, he was not aware of the actual number of the inhabitants at Ellacombe: he had since visited the houses and found that at present there were one hundred and seven houses inhabited - there were several more in course of erection - and in these houses there were 567 persons residing: of these 567, the number of children of a school-going age amounted to 245: again, of this 245, he did not think he should be wrong if he took half, or 120, as being of tender age - from three to six years - unable to go a moderate distance to school, and who came under that class which were to be found in infant schools. As these were physically incapable of walking down to the National School at Pimlico, it was of course necessary that a school should be built at Ellacombe for them...

It was necessary that he should inform the meeting it was only in contemplation to build an infant school, as the larger boys and girls could walk down to the Torquay schools at Pimlico, which was at a reasonable distance. It would also be an advantage if the contemplated building was erected in such a manner as to be suitable for the performance of divine worship on Sunday evenings during the winter months. There would not perhaps be so much necessity for this in the summer, as the people could then easily walk to the neighbouring churches...

In undertaking this work he thought they ought to provide accommodation for two hundred children; they could not calculate for less than that number. A room 50ft. by 20ft. would be sufficient for two hundred children, which would allow five square feet for each child.

The Revd Wolfe described the likely costs of the building based on the costs of the school at Boston Fields. He then outlined the monies already in hand:

Sir L. Palk had given the site and £100; the Revd. Prebendary Ford, who was unable to attend this meeting, had promised £20; Mr. Tower, £10; Mr. Neville £10; Mr. Sheppard, £5; Mr. Spragge, £5; Mr. Dykes, £5; and there were several other smaller donations. Under these circumstances he had not to call upon his friends for any very large donations, but should only require small amounts if they were so disposed to help him. He believed he could provide a school mistress capable of managing the children for about £25 a-year, and if they charged, as he thought they ought to do, a penny or two-pence a head for each of the children, there would be very little to be raised by private contribution. If a certified mistress was obtained, the cost would of course be very much greater; but he believed the person he had spoken of would do very well - at all events, he should have no difficulty in providing a suitable mistress

for that school. It was desirable that a scale of charges should be drawn up, for he believed that there were many persons that could afford to pay more than the penny, and would be very glad to do so...

Mr.H.C.M.Phillips said he had been requested to move the following resolution: "That, in the opinion of this meeting, it is of the utmost importance that public schools should be everywhere established for the instruction of the people in religion and sound knowledge. The meeting therefore has learnt with great pleasure that a free site has been granted, and a liberal donation given in money by Sir L. Palk for the erection of a National School in the populous neighbourhood of Ellacombe; considering that such an undertaking is in every way deserving of general encouragement and support."

The Chairman then put the resolution to the meeting, which was unanimously adopted.

On April 1, 1861 following, the Rev J. H. Harris wrote to the Journal as follows:

Sir, In your reporter's notice, last week, of the few remarks I made at the meeting for promoting the creation of a School Church, at Ellacombe, he only alludes to my having said that I am engaged in the serious undertaking of building a CHURCH; but he omits my statement that I, too, have for some time past been endeavouring to raise funds for building a SCHOOLROOM, which is also to be used provisionally for divine service on Sundays. In the neighbourhood of Melville Street, where

Upton School c. 1890. This was then a National School, becoming Upton Senior School after the 1903 Act, until Audley Park School opened in the 1930s. The building in the photograph was demolished and replaced by Court House incorporating some of the stonework. THE

there is a large poor population for whose children the school is needed, and who are themselves too far off to attend the Parish Church, even if there were any room for them in it; which there is not. I hope we may receive sufficient assistance to enable us to complete, without delay, the new church, whose foundations are already prepared, and so, before long, to meet our great want of church accommodation. But for this we still require £2000 more than as yet subscribed. A much smaller amount (from £300 to £500) will be required for the school I have alluded to; and is much wanted for the two-fold purpose mentioned. About 150 infants have been, for some time, taught in a most inconvenient, and insufficient hired room, and is altogether unsuited for the purpose of holding divine service. Our difficulties with respect both to the church, and school, in this instance, are much enhanced from the fact that we HAVE TO PAY FOR THE SITES, as well as for the buildings to be erected on them. Assistance towards both the above objects, rendered pressingly necessary by the great increase in the population in the parish, will be most thankfully received..."

On Wednesday the 7 August 1861 another report appeared in the T.D. (one of several) indicating that funds were gradually increasing towards meeting the objective of building a church school in Ellacombe, and on 12 October 1861, by conveyance, Sir Laurence Palk granted freely to the minister and churchwardens of Upton/Tormohun a parcel of land of 33 poles, to hold on trust, and all buildings built thereon, for the education of children and adults, or children only of the manufacturing and labouring classes, and other poorer classes.

Authority was vested in the officiating minister for securing the education of the children and for the building's use as a Sunday School. He, his curate and his churchwardens, together with a lay committee were also empowered to appoint schoolmasters and schoolmistresses. On the first lay committee were appointed Alfred Baldry, Robert Dawson Crawford and William Angel. Other members of the lay committee could be co-opted on a 20 shilling contribution to each of the funds of the school, then elected to fill places on receipt of a further 10 shillings. They must each be declared as communicants of the Church of England.

The school was registered with the Charity Commissions on 1 November 1861. No masters or schoolmistresses could be appointed that were not members of the Church of England. A secretary was to be elected to keep minutes. The Lord President of the Privy Council (PC) or the Bishop of the Diocese was to appoint school inspectors and arbitrators. Every January ten ladies, members of the C of E, were to be elected to assist in visiting and assisting in the management of the girls and infants schools. The school first appeared on the grant list in 1862, and was used for church services until Ellacombe Church was built in 1868.

The school stood on the east side of Higher Victoria Road (later Ellacombe Church Road). Under the Deed of 1861 it would appear the school was for infants only, being referred to as such in the manager's minute book. Up to 1871 the boys and girls were taught at Boston Fields School, just over half a mile away. On 10 November 1871, by conveyance, Sir Laurence Palk and Laurence H Palk Esq, granted freely to the minister and churchwardens of Ellacombe a grant of extra land of 1900 square yards, as, by this time, Ellacombe had been created a new ecclesiastical district. The land was to again be held on trust for the enlargement of the school to contain both boys and girls, in addition to the infants. Included in the reorganisation was the Boston Fields School which came under the same management in 1872, but as a school for infants only.

First entries in the minute book of the school, which opened on 12 January 1863, show inscribed inside the front cover the Revd Richard Wolfe (the incumbent of Upton) as the chairman, churchwardens, A. Baldry, E.D. Crawford and William Angel along with an extensive list of committee members.

The work of the teachers and pupil-teachers was vital to the success of the school and the minute book records:

In consideration of additional labour incurred by Miss Vining in preparing her children for the Second Standard in the School, a grant of £5 be made to her'. That with a view to encourage the Pupil Teachers (PTs) to take a greater interest in the prosperity of the School (S), their salaries be raised by £2 each pa., from 1 June 1870, on condition that their salary be divided into 5 equal parts - 4 quarterly and the remainder subject to the PTs passing their next examination. Each candidate will receive £4 in quarterly payments on passing her examination.

Pupil teachers were initially indentured as apprentices and Head Teachers were given an additional bonus when any of their pupils passed their

Top: *Ellacombe School - class of 1904. The photograph was provided by Lily Norrish and a handwritten note reads 'The Good Umbrella - Jan 1904. '* Bottom: *Ellacombe Boys School 1911.* Mrs G. Downey

examinations. This would occur on conclusion of their apprenticeships and was a form of acknowledgement for the training of their pupils.

A scheme for establishing a kitchen was implemented wherein a selection from the girls of the National School might be trained to cook and in general kitchen work. Later it was reported that the six girls who had been selected to cook were giving satisfaction and that others would be added to their number.

In 1877 a new bell was procured for the school, the old one being useless. Mr Goss, having sent the bell to be recast, and the bell turret having been reported by him as being unsafe, the secretary was instructed to see it was repaired before replacement of the bell.

Schooldays

Top: *Ellacombe Boys School Choir, winners of the junior choral class, Southern Counties Eisteddfod, 1924.* Don Roberts. Middle: *Ellacombe Boys School Football Team, 1923-4.* Bottom: *Ellacombe Junior School 1919.* Photos from the school archives by kind permission of Headteacher and Mrs Freer.

Above: *Ellacombe Boys School Choir, Torquay Schools ' Competitive Festival shield winners, 1925.* School Archives

Above: *Ellacombe Girls School Netball Team, 1935-4. Back row l-r: Kathleen Hoskins; Ethel Blackmore; Molly (?). Front row l-r: Kathleen Luxton; (?) Windsor; Nola Lane.* School Archives

Above: *Ellacombe Junior School 1928, heamistress Miss Davies. The picture includes Stan Crocker, Clarice Cornell; Ron Bowden; Gladys Hinder, Ron Waldron; Frank Fellows; Henry Wakeham; Henry Robins; Henry Weymouth; George Martin, and Coombes, Middleton, Smerdon and Tozer.* photo by kind permission of the late Stan Crocker

Left: *Ellacombe School 1927. Teachers include: Hoare, Parr, Cowley, Foulkes and Weaver. Pupils: Abbs, Bentafield, Pook, Mortimer, Wiess, Cross, Watson, Cheeseworth, Gitsham, Phillips and Obroshki.* School Archives

With a view to the more efficient administration of discipline, it was resolved that regulations for the guidance of the teachers should be drawn up and exhibited in the school.

In the early years of the 1870s children were expected to bring their pennies to help pay for their schooling. A caretaker was appointed at a salary of 3 shillings a week, and also a sergeant to drill the boys once a week for 1 shilling and 6 pence. It seems that teachers in those days were not held in high esteem by the school authorities, and in 1875 they were told that they could not be given an advance of salaries as such a practice was 'pernicious, and should not be allowed!'

The logbook of Ellacombe Girls' School for the 1920s reveals a fascinating insight into school life in the early part of the present century. Conditions were still somewhat primitive, and lighting poor. Indeed, on 7 November 1921, a stong complaint was made about the latter. There were only three incandescent gas burners, two of which were 'any good', and it was reported that 'many could not see'. By 27 November 1922, apparently very little had been done to improve matters, as the lighting was still reported as 'very poor', and there was a further complaint that the high windows were also 'very dirty'. The caretaker was taken to task for the latter. There were regular inspection visits by a school inspector appointed by the Department of Education and by the parish incumbent of the time, the Revd A. C. Stratton, together with other members of the education committee. There were other regular visitors: 'Harry' Terry, the Headmaster who served from 1879 until he retired in 1920, visited as a 'corresponding manager' and also a school manager by the name of W Kerswell, who would 'call the register'.

The attendance officers, Mr Jaggs and Mr Rooke, also called frequently to assess the number of absentees, and then went forth to harrass the parents of the recalcitrants! It seems it was common, at this time, for many children to be absent at any one time - not necessarily because of sickness - but because they were kept at home to run errands and to mind baby sisters and brothers for their parents.

In December 1920 a heavy fall of snow was reported. This, when added to sickness and other causes, meant only 55 per cent of the total pupil numbers were in attendance.

A swimming class was introduced under the control of a Miss L. Perryman and organised games took place at the Homelands playing fields.

Empire Days were regularly celebrated with the singing of patriotic songs, followed by half-day holidays. On 23 June 1921, an extra holiday was given 'in deference to HRH the Prince of Wales'. On 21 December of the same year, one of the foundation managers - a Mr Lord - was recorded as having 'passed away'.

The total pupil numbers seemed to have varied between about 230 and 240 in the 1920s. There were frequent changes in staff and recording of the names of pupil-teachers in training, and a regular ritual of paying staff monthly salaries. The following samples are taken from the school logbook of the time from the 20s and 30s:

Miss Bradbury and Miss Lowmass left in October. Mr Leicester, visiting the school, commented on its dirty state. Visit by doctor & nurse December - Miss Packe commenced duty. 1923. Report by Miss B F Cooke, HMI - Excellent work, considering four large classes taught in undivided room of inconvenient shape and size. Furniture very antiquated and unsuitable. Some adjustment needed for overcrowding. Reading material nearly exhausted. Homework encouraged. Several pupils of senior class given use of 'free library'. April - Very bad attendance. 48 out of 224 absent. Many girls kept away twice a week. S holiday - celebration of wedding of Duke of York. August - new domestic classes started at Abbey Road and at Homelands. November - two girls behaving badly and were punished. Bad leaks reported in roof. Water on desks and books spoilt. Bucket needed in centre of room. Nothing done. Two doors and many windows let in cold air. Heating only from one stove at one end. Children too near, too hot. Those away, too cold. Artificial lighting very poor. Caretakers rarely clean properly. High windows very dirty. Latter say - not their work! December - Headmistress resigns. Presentation on leaving given by Revd. Stratton and his wife, Mr Kerswell (manager), Dr.Strangeways, Miss Dawes and Mr Collett. 'Auld Lang Syne' sung. 1924 - January - Miss B.G.Phillips commenced duty as new Headmistress. May - 5 scholarships awarded to Iris Anderton, Eileen Marles, Irene Lamble, Dorothy Greenslade and Nora Williams. S closed in June for Torquay Historical Pageant at Rock End. In September, 29 scholars attended performance of 'Julius Caesar' at Royal Theatre - part of term's English Scheme. Miss Simpson's services terminated in December. Wedding present presented as token of affection and esteem. Mrs Laskey commenced duty in place of Mrs Ellis. Miss Fairbairn, CT, commenced. Miss Davies presented on her retirement from IS. Miss Saunders (UA) terminated her engagement after 38 years loyal and faithful service. A presentation was made by Revd. Stratton. 1925 - Mrs Lowmass left. In April Miss D Terry joined as CA. In June - older girls paid visit to Buckfast Abbey.

In November there was a report on S by Miss Cooke, HMI. Older girls transferred to buildings formerly used by Is. Structural alterations made and improvements following removal of a gallery, making new classroom. Electric light installed. Girls to be trained in neatness. More advanced schemes in Upper School. Formation of small reference library for older girls. Needlework requires reconsideration. 1926 - Structural alterations made in Xmas holidays. On Empire Day - the National Anthem and patriotic songs were sung and recitations given. Girls were addressed by Mr A.Constantine on part of women in making a great empire.

In November 1928 - skylights blown from over cloakroom and many slates from roof during heavy gale. Musical Festival in December. First & second places won out of 61 competitors. Third place in Junior Section and two in Open Section. 1929 - Miss B.Cooke, HMI, visited and inspected S. Playground and lavatories in very shocking condition. Report of school inspector. 50% of

whole school, including 3 senior classes, taught in same room. Excellent report on work of Headmistress and staff. More specialisation in subjects. Offices and playground to receive attention. S closed at 4pm on 20 December. Winning team presented at 2.30.pm. with Elementary Schools' Swimming Gala silver brooches.

1930 - Two new 'Tortoise' stoves installed during holidays. Lavatory basins installed and seats renovated. S closed in May. Girls assembled at Torbay Hospital to greet visit of HRH the Prince of Wales to the Hospital. S closed from September until 20.10.1930 for drainage to be put in order. Temporary accommodation to be found at Homelands Central, Westhill and Babbacombe Junior Schools. Very poor attendance in November - 167 out of 248. Exceptional storms. HMI and LEA visit proposed site for new schools at Ellacombe and Hele.

1931 - 343 on register. In February - Miss D Terry absent through illness. Mrs Wood, CT, deputising as ST. Miss Terry presented with token of affection by Headmistress on behalf of elder girls and staff on termination of her services a AM in April. Moving to Kingston-on-Thames. Specialisation in geography, history, literature and needlework to cease. Each teacher to teach all class subjects.

Ellacombe Girls School choir, 1934-5. The picture includes l-r: Dorothy Mardon; Gladys Helmore; Nancy Gilpin; Gwen Phillips; Josephine Watson; Peggy Hawkins; Iris Wakeham; Mary Venables; Olive Smythe; Daphne Salmon; Connie Smith; Edna German; Lilian White; Gwen Mudge; Betty White; Muriel Hookway; Mr C. Parr, Kathleen Hoskin, Joyce Hookway; Audrey Phare; Margaret Watson; Grace (?); Ethel Blackmore; (?) Lander; Gwen Connellaus, Joyce Hatton; Marjorie Elliott; Muriel Windsor; Dorothy Crossing; Betty Sherwood; Ruby Sparkes. THE

Ellacombe Boys School, 1937. THE

1932 - S re-opened. 11 children admitted, 4 from IS, 6 from other schools in Borough and 1 from outside. H. Terry, corresponding manager, issued a memorandum recording that, as from 1 January 1932, E Church of England Ss ceased to exist as such, and were transferred to the LEA for a period of 99 years at a nominal rent. This step had been rendered necessary through the financial demands of the B of E with which the Ss managers were quite unable to comply. The S dentist inspected the girls' teeth. S closed in July for the Torquay Schools Senior Sports at Windmill Hill. The Schools Girls' Schools Cup was won by E girls. The Junior Torquay Schools' Sports were held at Windmill Hill. The Junior Schools' Cup was won by ES. S dis-organised and closed due to the preparation for removal to temporary premises whilst S re-modelled.

1936 - No new admissions due to lack of accommodation. S closed on 10 January afternoon whilst elementary schools attended a party given by the Torquay Rowing Club, and again on the 28th. for the funeral of King George V. Lengthy report given in June on S by the 2 HMIs. "Overcrowding of IS due to continued presence of seniors. This limits the use of playground and deprives juniors of a hall. Staff strong. Headmistress and assistants spare themselves no trouble in educating the children.

1937 - Attendance low owing to sickness - 233 out of 320. Miss Collihole absent in London in February to receive an investment of 'The Order of a Serving Sister of the St. John's Ambulance' - the

only lady in Devon to receive the 'Honour' on this occasion. April - 44 children and 3 teachers departed on educational visit to London Zoo and to see the Coronation decorations.

November - 1 case of diptheria reported - Henry Wyatt removed to the Isolation Hospital. Ronald Bowden (aged 8) cut the top of his head on a peg in the cloakroom. Taken to Dr. Ward for 3 stitches to be inserted. Lessons suspended whilst Xmas concert, arranged by pupils, was given to children assembled in hall. 1938 - Many children absent due to chicken-pox and measles.

1939 - Miss Bolding did not attend on Friday afternoon, 28th. Inadvertently locked in S by caretaker and not freed until 1.30pm. May - 55 absentees - list sent to LEA ES. Early attention to be given to poor attendance. Further report followed showing only 80% and Infants 64%. June - attendance officer reported that there were too many absentees for him to visit.

Chairman, vice chmn., Councillor Phillips, Revd. Every and ES met Headmaster to discuss preparations in event of air-raid. Owing to outbreak of war with Germany on Sept. 3, attendance was less than 40%. Number on roll 336, attendance 94% after 1st. week. Members of EC visited in connection with playground improvements. S still awaiting advice on air-raid precautions. Mr C.A. Tomlins commenced work as teacher. October - Councillor Cruse (v.chmn. of EC) visited S and inspected air-raid drill. ES called to discuss coal rationing for SS.18.12.1939.

The war years between 1939 and 1945 saw the school caught up in many of the exigencies felt by those fighting on the home front. Though Exeter and Plymouth caught the main force of Hitler's raids in the westcountry, Torquay also suffered a number of hit and run air raids. The school records give some flavour of these times:

The winter of 1940 was severe, with frozen pipes. 120 parents expressed the wish for children to be sent home after an air-raid warning. There was no protection provided for the 250 children remaining. In June, 15 children evacuated from London commenced at S followed by 36 more shortly after. In July it was decided that, owing to prevailing conditions, the S would remain open during the whole of the summer holiday period - teachers to take holidays in rotation.

There was a re-organisation of teaching staff: Form IVA - Mr Parr; Form IVB - Mrs Carroll (evac. LCC teacher); Form IIIA - Miss Crocker; Form IIIB - Mr Cowling; Form IIA - Miss Packe; Form IIB - Mrs Sayer (evac. LCC teacher); Form IA Miss - Mudge; Form IB - Mrs Tomlins (ST); Infants - Class I - Miss Bolding; Class II - Miss Collins; Class III - Miss Kirkham. There was visit on 9 Sept. regarding provision of air-raid shelters.

In October 77 more evacuees arrived plus 61 private ones. The shelters were erected on 28 October. By 16 December evacuated teachers from LCC were now Miss Joyce; Miss Blake; Mrs Carroll; Mr Rees; Miss Parker, and Mr Moss-Yarham. In 1941 the winter was again extreme. Because of frozen pipes, the children were sent home. Shortage of coal aggravated the situation. There was much changing of staff due to sickness and other reasons. On 24 February Mr H.C. Cowling retired after 37 years at the S. There was much collecting of funds for War Weapons Week and Warships Week. On March 20 1942 Mr F.C. Collett, the Headmaster, retired, and Mr Moss-Yarham from the LCC took a temporary post in his place.

Mr Parr was made temporary Headmaster. On 20 October an abnormal rainstorm burst the window of the babies room and flooded the classroom, but the children suffered no harm. On 6 June 1944, during the Whitsun holiday period the S was damaged by the blast of a bomb which fell in the vicinity. However - the S opened with modifications to the timetables whilst repairs were made.

School certificate for Torquay Music Festival, 1934.

On 8 May 1945 the S was closed for VE Day celebrations. On 29 May the children were invited to the Regal Cinema, by invitation of the Mayor, to take part in further celebrations.

In a 'sum-up' of the contemporary educational scene in the Parish in early 1900, it would be to report that schooling standards were at a high level, considering the fact that Ellacombe School was in the centre of a working class area.

Reference to school journals shows clear evidence of good quality grammar, punctuation, spelling and essay writing and there is no reason to doubt that the mathematical side was equally sound. Further evidence confirms that the teachers were dedicated, and held a personal interest in their pupils well into their later lives and careers.

Examination of the 'Punishment Book' reveals that although caning by the Headmaster and Headmistress (girls too!) was common at that time, it was rare that children transgressed more than once again - indicating that the method was clearly effective. Offences were often of disobedience, incorrigible laziness, disorderly behaviour, rudeness to staff, persistent talking, avoidable lateness after repeated warnings and misbehaviour of other types. One notable exception stands out (who shall be nameless), and who's name appears on several successive pages of the 'Book'. It would appear that no amount of corporal punishment had any effect upon *his* continued misbehaviour!

In the early 1900s the school-leaving age was set at 14, when the majority of Ellacombe children left to take up employment in the Town or surrounding areas. There was only one fee-paying grammar school in the Torbay area. Scholarships were available - and were at a premium. In general - working class families could ill afford to pay for necessary books and clothing, even if their children were bright enough to pass the entrance examination.

Research has shown that pupils at Ellacombe rarely received more than a small number of opportunities a year to gain places at the Torquay Grammar School. 'Near misses' were awarded places at the Central School at Plainmoor (with commercial leanings) or to the distinct Commercial College, then in Upper Union Street. Nevertheless - many children who received a very good elementary educational grounding at the

School are known to have made fine careers in commerce, industry and the civil and public services.

The TD of 1897 records an enlargement of the S in 1895 which may well have been associated with the closure of the British Schools in Torquay. Following the Education Act of 1902 the school continued under the Torquay Borough Council as the LEA and was maintained as a Voluntary Church School until the managers could no longer meet the cost of necessary improvements.

On 31st. December 1931 the school was transferred from the Church (Revd. J.L.Cobham) to the Borough of Torquay under an agreement that recommended no charges were to be made for heating, lighting and cleaning, and that the premises were to be made available to the church authorities for parochial purposes and for use as a Sunday School.

In the reorganisation of 1932 Ellacombe became one of the Torquay schools with a senior department, until the more comprehensive reorganisation of 1938, and following the opening of the new Senior School at Audley Park. From this point onwards Ellacombe School has been a Junior, later termed Primary School.

Sports teams from the 1920s and 30s. School archives

Bits and pieces from the Ellacombe School Journal

THE ELLACOMBE JOURNAL
1924 - Midsummer

Editor	E Tanner
S/Editor	A Clarke
Manager	C Windsor
Committee	H Bengafield, R Fields
	and W Coombe

Prizes for Seniors & Juniors
For "Best Home-made Toy",
Materials n/e 6d. in value

Articles

Visit to Wembley; Southern Counties Eisteddfod at Town Hall, Torquay;

Report on New Partition Screens and 'Table Desks ' (Contributors to funds - Messdames Wedden, McIver, Moore, Paterson, Hunt, Richards, Martin, Cowling, Parr, Turner, Lowmass; the Misses Collihole, Tremlett, Blackler, Cowling, Scholes, Prowse; and Messrs. Dennis, Collett, Preston, Johns, Dear and Bradford

A Seaside Adventure; Sport, and Head-master's Letter. Written by: George Eden, E Powesland, W Phillips, H Benjafield, Ernest Elford, H Stentiford (Hon. Sec., Old Boys Association), E Turner and Major F G Collett.

School Leavers (1924)

H Harding, F Warring, A Steer, R Pierce, J Hicks, S Wotton, F. Abbs, M Leaman, W Mann, F Andrews, R Abraham, E Hingston, J Ridsdale, K Cross and H Yelland.

House Captains

DRAKE	M Millman
GILBERT	C Windsor
RALEIGH	R Fileds
GRENVILLE	J Gitsham

Sport

1st. Eleven Football Team had an unbeaten season in the Schools League. Goal Scorers - Gitsham (20) Leaman (11) Knapman (7) Tozer (2) and Bradford & Pook (1 each).

Cricket
Progress slow. R Fields elected Captain

A Rhyme by H Langmead (1927)

You should see our old dad with his wireless,
His efforts are practically tireless;
If all's not quite right
He'll sit up all night,
Till he finds there's a valve that is fireless.

✦

ELOCUTION (1925)

Six girls were chosen from our school to enter the yearly Open Elocution Contest. As we met outside the Baptist Church on a hot June afternoon, ready to compete, most of us felt very "nervy." The adjudicator, Miss Irene Sadler, was seated at a large oaken desk, a few yards from the platform, while the competitors were given seats on chairs and benches around the room. The first girl was called - she recited and was applauded heartily. One by one the members of Ellacombe School went up. It needed great self-possession to face the sea of up-turned faces. Soon we had finished and were listening to the adjudicator who told us our faults and demonstrated how the poems should have been recited. IRIS WAKEHAM

ADVERTISERS IN THIS EDITION (1924)

A G Priston 47 Market Street Tobacconist Stationer Fancy & Leather Goods

T L Burgoyne Opposite the School The Ellacombe Pharmacy

R H Tozer 29 Princes Road Butcher

J F French 22 Hoxton Road Butcher

J J Richards All kinds of Saddlery, Harness, etc

Jacksons Ltd Hat & Boot Specialist

H Corline & Sons 20 Victoria Road Wholesale & Retail Potato Merchants

H Alford 20 Princes Road Lummaton Farm Dairy

H Mitchelmore 5 or 10 Woodville Road Boot & Shoe Repairs

M L White 30 Princes Road Hairdressing & Shaving

W Farleigh 30 Ellacombe Church Road General Grocery Stores

A J Boon Ellacombe Road & Market Street Boot Repairs

R W Hodder Opposite the School Seedsman, Florist & Fruiterer

T H Easterbrook of Market Street for Jewellery

Hepworths 71 Union Street Clothier

A J Dyke 33 Victoria Road Groceries,Sweets, Cigarettes, Tobacco & Farm Produce

P W Rendle 48 Victoria Road Practical Umbrella Maker

C Wedden 57 Victoria Road Newsagent, Tobacconist & Confectioner

Wills ' Cakes 53 Woodville Road Cake Shop

L P Gambrell 17 Market Street Poulterer, Fruiterer & Greengrocer

The Dairy 32 Victoria Road Fresh Butter, Eggs & Vegetables - Cream by Post

SCHOOL LEAVERS 1928

W Potter - Apprenticed as Plasterer with T Guest

G Andrews - Errand Boy at Bethel Cafe

G Bovey - Devon General Parcel Delivery

H Pearce - Butcher Boy at R H Tozers

C Wannell - Errand Boy

W Stevens - Errand Boy at Slades

K Saunders - Apprenticed at Newton's Bakery

L Middleton - Butcher Boy at Torquay Coop

E Algar - Paper Boy at W H Smith

G Emmett - Apprenticed at G Davey's Upholsters

G Tucker - Errand Boy

Representing Torquay Schools at Football:
A Emmett, T Endacott, F Greenaway and F. Coles.

Rowing Regatta - Bronze Shield
Team - H Langmead, F Avenall and V Best.

THE ELLACOMBE (SCHOOL) JOURNAL
MIDSUMMER 1935

EDITORIAL STAFF

Editor	
Art Editor	B Hookway
Manager	E Adams
Committee	S Langmead
	A Phare, A Splatt,
	A West

EDITORIAL

Dear Readers

Once again "Magazine Time" is here. This is the second birthday of the "Ellacombe Journal" and I think we could best celebrate it by purchasing a copy for ourselves, and, by doing our utmost to get our friends to do the same.

We wish to thank our many contributors for their articles, and although we are unable to publish them all we hope that every member of the school will try to send a contribution to the next issue. We will enlarge the staff, if necessary, to cope with the result of this reminder.

A very happy summer holiday to you all.

THE EDITOR

THE JUBILEE (1935)

The King is keeping his Jubilee
And so we all from work are free
On the sixth of May, his Jubilee day,
When all our nation will kneel and pray.

Gifts still come from home and abroad,
From Italy, France, Norwegian fiord,
The Colonies, too, loyally send
Wishes and gifts to their King and friend.

Long live the King! Long may he reign!
Our feet march to this joyous refrain,
Thro ' sunshine and shadow we know he will set
An example to follow, we 'll never forget.

A SPLATT

THE SILVER JUBILEE - IN CITY, TOWN AND VILLAGE

On Monday, 6th May 1935, the whole of England and the Dominions celebrated the Silver Jubilee of King George V and Queen Mary. In the City of London, the royal procession drove from Buckingham Palace through wildly cheering crowds to St Paul's Cathedral, where a thanksgiving service was held. In the evening, there was a special display of fireworks at the Crystal Palace. In Torquay the streets were decorated with flags and bunting. In the morning a thanksgiving service was held, and a dinner, at which the Mayor was present, was given to the old folk of the Town. In the afternoon a display of dancing was given by the schoolchildren of the Town. Afterwards the children went to Torre Abbey, where they were given tea and a Jubilee mug. In the evening there was a Confetti Dance for the older people and fires were also lit on the seven hills of Torquay. The village of Lydford consistes of twenty or thirty cottages in the country. Here there was a competition for the best decorated cottage and I helped to decorate the one in which I was staying. We plaited paper strips of red, white and blue and hung up three balloons with the portrait of the King and Queen painted on them. We used the plaits to decorate the porch and windows. In the afternoon there was a small procession consisting of three lorries. One carried a Jubilee Queen, another a May Queen and her attendants, and in the third was a band. These lorries went around the Memorial and then on to the sports ground. The celebrations were concluded with a bonfire and a firework display.

JOAN LANG
CONNIE SMITH
PAT DANIEL

FOOTBALL

Following a season of team building and moderate success, we have for the first time been successful in winning the Torbay Schools Association Shield. In the Knockout Competition we succumbed to Westhill in the 2nd. Round. Although the team contained no player of brilliance, yet through playing hard to the end of each game, were successful many times by the narrowest of margins. We are hoping for further successes next season.

RESULTS

v Barton	W 9 - 0	W 5 - 0
v Chudleigh	W 4 - 0	D 2 - 2
v Upton	W 1 - 0	W 2 - 1
v Westhill	W 2 - 1	D 0 - 0
v Paignton	W 4 - 3	W 3 - 2
v Highweek	W 1 - 0	D 1 - 1
v Brixham	W 3 - 1	L 1 - 2

TEAM

V Tuck (Goal); R Nicholls, F Reed (Backs); H Beer, W Bunch, A Bowden (Halves); R Annear, C Wilbourne, L Honeywill, W Bowden, A Pym (Forwards).

HOUSE CHAMPIONSHIP

Final   Athens 4   Troy 1

SCHOOL NOTES

On Wednesday 12th December, the school choir gave a recital of carols to the parents. We began with "O little town of Bethlehem" and throughout the evening a group of two or more carols was followed by a group of poems recited by the girls. One poem called "Night Wind" just before the interval caused much amusement. After the interval the carols were even more interesting because several boys sang solos. At the end, our Headmaster thanked the parents for coming and then everybody in the room joined in the singing of "The First Nowell", which concluded an enjoyable evening.

B CREWS

EMPIRE DAY

We celebrated Empire Day on May 24th. The scholars sang patriotic songs interspersed with readings of poems. Councillor Rowland Ward, who was accompanied by his wife, gave a stirring address to the school on the significance of Empire Day, which was greatly appreciated by the children. Short addresses were also given by Alderman R. A. Johns, Councillor R. J. Bullied and Revd R. Ford. The whole school adjourned to the playground for national and folk dances by the scholars and, at the conclusion, the whole school marched past and saluted the flag.

FORM NOTES

Form 1A
1935 has been a busy and important year and work has gone forward as usual. Two school visits have been made, one to Kent's Cavern and one to the Natural History Museum. The boys made a shelf for our Reference Library at the woodwork centre. Last term, newspaper groups were formed, each group taking charge of the newspaper for a week, cutting out important items for the notice board and giving a summary to the class at the end of the week.

GLADYS HELMORE

Form 1B
The girls visited the Co-operative Bakery Department in the Easter Term with our Mistress, and the boys went to Longpark Pottery. On Empire Day L.Roberts of our form had the honour of carrying the Flag. At the Musical Festival, M.Davy won a Merit Certificate for Elocution.

SHEILA WILLIAMS

Form IIA
The past year has been one of steady work. We paid visits to Kent's Cavern and the Museum in the Easter term. A "thermometer" on the blackboard, with "mercury" gradually going up one degree for each contribution, proved an incentive to those with short memories. In March, every member of the class contributed to the Hospital Box.

MARY VENABLES

Form IIB
At the beginning of the year our class moved to Chard's Hall and consequently we now start each lesson with a brisk walk. The girls visited the Co-operative Bakery and the boys visited the "Herald & Express" Printing Works and the Ice Works during the year.

THE SWIMMING GALA

Ellacombe Schools held their first swimming gala at the Torquay Corporation Baths on April 10th. There were no fewer than 33 events in the programme - a record number for a gala in Torquay, and they were run off in the remarkably quick time of two hours. Some keen and exciting racing was witnessed. During the evening and interesting exhibition of trick and fancy swimming was given by Messrs G.H.Clow and F.P.Moon, both old Ellacombe scholars. The prizes were presented by Mrs G.W.P.Laskey.

PRESENTATION OF THE ROWING SHIELD

In December last, Major Ball, accompanied by Messrs Luscombe and Manley, presented the Rowing Shield and medals won by one of the crews of our school, N. Blunt, E. Waldron and R. Brown (cox), at the Torbay Regatta. Two of our crews were successful in getting into the final for the Shield. A fine race resulted, there being only half a length between the three crews.

THE MUSICAL FESTIVAL

Our school was again successful at the Torquay Musical Festival, and the Boys ' Choir won the first place with 165 marks. On the morning we were to sing, the members of our choir came to school attired in their best suits. Soon we set off for the Town Hall. When we arrived, the Junior Schools ' Choirs were singing and we had to wait until they had finished. Our choir was the last to sing in the Senior School choirs. We listened attentively to our rivals singing, wondering how we should fare singing the same songs. At last our turn came and then we sat waiting to hear the adjudicator's remarks. We were all pleased when we learnt that we had won first place and upheld the honour of our school.

E. SHAPLEY.

FOLK DANCING

On Friday, May 31st., our school sent a team of girls to compete in the Folk Dancing Festival at the Town Hall. We arrived there early and had to wait some time before we went on to dance. When we did reach the shining floor, we danced as we 'd never danced before. Each school had to do two dances, "Christchurch Bells" and one of our own choice, which was "If all the world were paper." Our girls looked very neat in their gym-slips and long stockings. The adjudicator was very pleased with our dances, except that we did not smile; we gained eighty marks and were very proud of them. Highweek (Newton Abbot) School was first with eighty five marks. The adjudicator was excellent and showed us herself the mistakes that some schools made. As there were a few minutes before the Infants were to do their dances, she let all the schools dance "Old Mole" together.

BARBARA TOZER

Chapter 6 - The Anglican Church

At the beginning of the 19th century the only place of worship for the parishioners of Tormohun was the old Parish Church of St Saviour as distinct from the Abbey - for whom it was *not* built. It was supposed to have been erected in the early 14th century (White - *History of Torquay*), but others refer to it as possibly dedicated to St Petrox - perhaps dating from the 7th century.

Torre and Cockington were, in fact, a united benefice in the gift of the Abbot of Torre, until 1881. Nevertheless Cockington was in practice treated as a separate Parish at the time of a survey by the Diocese of Exeter in the period 1811-1825 when the population, according to the 1821 Census, was 1925, of which only 180 were adjudged to be practising communicants.

By 1821 the population of Torquay had risen from 828 to 1925 (1821 census). As the old Church of St Saviours, Tormohun, could accommodate no more than 500, something clearly had to be done. Keeping church accommodation in line with population increase was a perpetual problem. Nevertheless, a need was recognised by the Lord of the Manor, Sir Lawrence Palk donating initially land and £300 towards the building of the Torquay Endowed Chapel of St Johns, despite a great deal of acrimony about its financial effect on the living of Torre within the ministration of the Revd Roger Mallock. This was, however, eventually resolved. The only other place of worship available was the Trinity Proprietary Chapel, financed out of pew rents and subscriptions, and only attracting worshippers who could afford to maintain them. Clearly proprietary chapels could hardly be relied upon to meet the needs of a growing population of working classes.

Until well into the 1840s no modification of the parochial structure of the Anglican Church in Torquay occurred after the building of St John's Chapel of Ease and the unexpected and unplanned acquisition of Trinity Chapel. These were considered inconvenient and irritating devices to supply the deficiency of church accommodation. The original large Parish of Tormohun remained intact until the first sub-division occurred in 1848, when the district of Upton was created. Its Parish Church, St Mary Magdalene, was opened for services in 1849. In 1855 the District of Torwood was formed, its Parish Church of St Mark opening in 1857 and the daughter Church of St Matthias in 1858.

St John's Chapel of Ease was made the Parish Church of the new District of St John in 1861. It is clear that many upper and middle class people were involved in the Established Church's new projects: the Palks, William Kitson, H.C. March Phillips and Jacob Harvey.

The immediate motivation behind efforts to establish new churches was undoubtedly population pressure on accommodation, and it was this latter which chiefly prevented the poor from attending church. Thus the main purpose was to provide for the rapid increase of the labouring classes. It is sad to report that the first extension, the Parish of Upton, took over a decade to be brought to completion, although St Marks and St Mathias were completed in a much shorter span of time. One reason may well have been the diminishing enthusiasm of the Mallocks, particularly as the original intention had been to make the New Church (Upton) the new Parish Church of Tormohun.

Some time in May 1845, however, the Bishop of Exeter changed his thinking, motivated an Act of 1843 (Better Provision for the Spiritual Care of Populous Parishes), and the positioning of the Church of St Mary Magdalene in a more central and prominent part of the fast growing Town (Upper Union Street). Although the population of Torquay in the Census of 1861 still showed that St Saviours, Tormohun was dominant (at 16 419 of a whole of 25 641), the new Torwood Parish was formed from the latter and St Marychurch.

The changes were accommodated in A Bill to Facilitate Erection of One or More Churches in the Parishes of Tormohun and St Marychurch, Torquay - The Torquay Churches Act of 1855. The Churches that followed the Ancient Parish of Tormohun were, in chronological order, Upton (1848), St Mark's, Torwood (1855), St Mathias, Wellswood, (1858), St Johns (1861), All Saints, Babbacombe (1867), Christ Church, Ellacombe (1868), St Lukes (1869), The Mission Chapel of St Michael & All Angels (1877), Ilsham (1880), All Saints, Torre (1889) and Holy Trinity (1896).

Ellacombe Church.

Chapter 7 - Ellacombe Church

Until the coming of the railways in the 1840s, Torquay (Tormoham or more correctly Tor Mohun) had (apart from Trinity Chapel) only the little village church of St Saviours, Tormohun, to provide for the religious needs of a rural population. This had increased from 838 in 1801 to nearly 6000 in 1841. This increase had been fuelled mainly by the arrival of large numbers of servants brought into the district by each household of distinguished people, and by craftsmen and tradesmen needed to service this expansion. Religious requirements for this considerable increase in population rose proportionately. Because of the practice of 'sittings ', poor people were unable to afford to worship within the church. However - a local benefactor by the name of Charles Dawson was so incensed by the unchristian nature of this practice that, when he lay dying, he expressed a wish that £2000 from his estate should be given to the founding of a new church where the seats were to be free and unappropriated for ever.

From this bequest, and with other donations from various sources, the sum of £5000 was eventually raised, and in 1844 the first foundation stone was laid for the erection of the Parish Church of St Magdalene, Upton. But it was not until 12 April 1849 that the Parish Church was finally consecrated, and its first Rector, Prebendary R. R. Wolfe MA, took over administration of the Parish. The tower and spire were not added until 1854. All three remain dominating the Town Centre to this day.

By the 1860s the population had increased to such a size that a number of new churches and chapels were erected, and parts of the old parish boundary of Upton 'hived-off ' to form new ones. Christ Church, Ellacombe, was one of these, and Prebendary Wolfe undertook its construction. Although it was the Revd Wolfe's great ambition to complete Upton Church the astonishing growth in Ellacombe caused him to belay his intentions and transfer them to a new modern housing estate of artisans' dwellings there.

In 1848 only one large house existed there (Ellacombe House). Now Wolfe had already raised thousands of pounds to complete Upton Church, and thousands more to build schools. How was the money to be got to build yet another church? Although Bishop Phillpotts agreed to the building of a church he only agreed to a first donation of £50. Wolfe himself describes the manner in which the money in this case was forthcoming. He was discussing the matter of Ellacombe with a Mr Haliburton - a member of his congregation and said 'Oh that I could find a man with a large heart and a long purse to build a church!' In his own words, 'About three days later Mr Haliburton called on me and said, 'What you said the other day about looking for such a man has been ringing in my ears ever since, and I cannot get rid of it. I have been thinking I may be able to help you in providing a church! And that good man did build the church.' Haliburton in fact contributed £5000, and Christ Church, Ellacombe, was opened in 1868 (*Upton - the Heart of Torquay*, Deryck Seymour).

Before this took place, and the Parish of Ellacombe formed, this area was, of course, part of the larger Parish of Upton. This, in 1848, took in almost the whole centre of the Town, down to the Old Town Hall - extending to Warberry Hill and Babbacombe Road. Warberry Hill went to St Marks, Torwood, and the lower part of Abbey Road went to St Lukes: the Shirburn Road district became part of the new Parish of St James (later returned to Upton). The lower part of Market Street was given to St Michaels, and the Daison Estate formed the boundary between the Parish of Upton and that of St Marychurch. In 1868 the *Torquay Directory* suggested that readers were:

already aware that by the united exertions of the Rev R R Wolfe, Mr A F Haliburton, and other gentlemen, a movement was on foot a few years ago to provide church accommodation for the new town which has sprung up at Ellacombe. It is now an accomplished fact, or will be so in another week or so, when the new building of Christ Church is opened and consecrated for divine worship. The London Gazette *of Tuesday, contains an Order in Council by which Ellacombe is erected into an ecclesiatical district, or sub-parish, in the same manner as St Marks and St Johns. The district is thus defined: "All that part of the new Parish of Upton, sometime part of the Parish of*

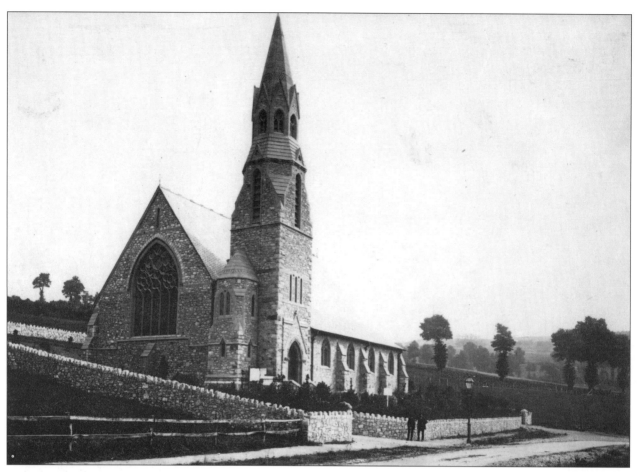

Ellacombe Church viewed from the south-west in 1870 The church was built betweern 1867-8 on a site given by Sir Lawrence Palk. TNHM

Tormohun, in the County of Devon, and in the Diocese of Exeter, wherein the present incumbent of such new parish now possesses the exclusive care of souls, which is comprised within and is bounded by an imaginary line commencing upon the boundary which divides the said new Parish of Upton from the Parish of St Marychurch, in the County and Diocese aforesaid, at a point in the middle of the said St Marychurch Road near the houses called or known as Boston Fields; and extending thence, first south-westward and then southward, for a distance of two and a half furlongs, or thereabouts, along the middle of the said road to its junction with Butterhill Road; and extending thence, south-eastward, along the middle of the last-named road to its junction with Wellesley Road; and extending thence, first southwards, and then south-eastward, along the middle of the last-named road to its junction with Wellington Road, at the north-western end of a certain footpath leading from Wellington Road aforesaid past Ellacombe House to Market Street; and continuing thence, still south-eastward, to and along the middle of the said footpath to its

junction with Market Street aforesaid; and, extending thence, southward, along the middle of the same street as far as the steps leading to Queen Street; and extending thence, south-eastward up the said steps to their junction with Queen Street aforesaid; and extending thence, first northward to and then south-eastward along the rear of the houses situate on the north-eastern side of the

The interior of Ellacombe Church c.1870. An un-usual feature is the iron columns supporting the arches, one of which can be seen on the right. TNHM

Ellacombe and its church viewed from the south, c.1906. THE

same street to a point on the northern side of Hoppaway Hill Road; and extending thence, southward, across the last-named road to and along the wall which divides the houses known as No. 1 Bedford Row, from the premises of the Upton National School to the boundary dividing the said new Parish of Upton from the Consolidated Chapelry of St John, Torquay, in the County and Diocese aforesaid; and extending thence, generally eastward, along the last-described boundary as far as the point where Upper Braddon's Hill Road is joined by Lower Warberry Road, and by a certain cross-road leading to Higher Warberry Road; and extending thence, north-eastward, along the middle of the said cross-road (thereby crossing Middle Warberry Road) to the junction of the same cross-road with Higher Warberry Road aforesaid; and continuing thence, still north-eastward, across the last-named road to a point in the middle of the south- western end of a certain footpath which leads over Warberry Hill, past the reservoir to Babbicombe; and continuing thence, generally north-eastward, along the middle of the last-described footpath to the boundary dividing the said new Parish of Upton from the new Parish of All Saints, Babbicombe, in the County and Diocese aforesaid; and extending thence, generally

westward, along the last-described boundary to its junction with the boundary which divides the new Parish of Upton from the Parish of St Marychurch as aforesaid; and extending thence first south-eastward, and then north-westward, along the last-described boundary to the first-described point in the middle of the St Marychurch Road aforesaid, where the said imaginary line commenced.

The consecration and opening of Christ Church, Ellacombe took place on 15 April 1868 - the event, again according to the *Torquay Directory*:

was the occasion of much sincere rejoicing amongst those who have the welfare of the large population of that district at heart... Twelve years ago there was but one house, at the entrance to the valley, occupied by the Rev. Francis Garrett; now the valley itself with its two outlets, the one stretching towards the Warberry Hill, and the other in the direction of St Marychurch Road, are intersected with roads and streets in all directions, and containing a population that consists exclusively of the poor. How that district has grown is certainly a matter of astonishment to all who have witnessed it. Within but a few years, green pasture meadows, watered by a streamlet from the

Ellacombe Church - a view taken around 1920.

hills, allotment gardens and fields, have all disappeared. The natural features of the place have been altered, and in many cases the old landmarks removed. Literally, hills have been levelled and valleys filled up. The history of Ellacombe is briefly told. Fourteen years ago the dwelling accommodation for not only the poor, but respectable artisans, was extremely limited. Swan Street, Pimlico, Melville Street, and some parts of Torre, were their haunts(!). At length the overcrowding became so great by reason of the demand for labour, that the necessity of providing adequate house-room was forced upon the minds of the people. At this juncture Sir L Palk came forward and relieved the town of a great difficulty by opening the valley of Ellacombe, as building ground for houses of a kind suitable for the working classes; the row of cottages on the south side of the central piece of ground was first built and occupied, then street after street was quickly added, and now at this moment the population of that district alone cannot be less than four thousand. But whilst the sanitary and material welfare of the people was thus secured, it was soon found that there was a

great spiritual destitution. The Rev. R R Wolfe, already burdened with a large and poor district, compared with other parts of the town, courageously endeavoured to meet the difficulty, but the vastness of the numbers he had to cope with almost paralysed his efforts; he had not only Upton, Boston Fields, Pimlico, and the district of Union Street, all thickly populated. as belonging to his own proper parish of Upton to care for, but this new place - a new town, as it were - was added to his already arduous work. Happily, amongst his own congregation he found lay helpers who were willing to assist in any good work that he might undertake. To meet, in some degree, the growing need of church accommodation, he caused the school to be built which, besides being used as a school in the week, has been devoted to chapel purposes on the Sunday. By this means, and also by the aid of Scripture readers, Bible women, Mothers' Meetings and other kindred institutions, the truths of the gospel have, in one way or another, been brought home to the people. At this time an unexpected source of relief came to the Rector of Upton. One of our resident gentlemen offered to *build a church; and Sir L Palk, who had for a long time previously contemplated the necessity of such a work being undertaken, had set aside a piece of ground for the future needs of the place in this respect. It need hardly be said that the offer of Mr Haliburton (for that is the name of the gentleman who had undertaken so munificent a work) was accepted thankfully and prayerfully. And the same grand and noble aim that animated Mr Haliburton spread itself to others: Sir L Palk and his Son willingly gave the ground, and contributed to the endowment of the church; and other ladies and gentlemen residing here have given large donations, fifty and one hundred pounds at a time, towards the same object. So, greatly encouraged thereby, the good enterprise was entered into, and thirteen months ago the foundation stone of Christ Church, Ellacombe was laid. On Thursday the Church was opened, and consecrated by Bishop Chapman, of Colombo, acting on behalf of the Right Rev. the Lord Bishop of Exeter. The building is in the early gothic style of architecture, and has been constructed of the limestone of the neighbourhood, with dressings of Bath stone. It consists of a nave, ending in an octagonal apse, and is ninety-five feet long from east to west, and is fifty-three broad, including a south aisle, which is divided from the nave by Gothic arches supported by light iron columns with enriched capitals. At the south-west angle is a tower, serving as an entrance lobby to the church below, and having an organ gallery above. The tower terminates in an octagonal belfry, and a Bath stone spire. The church internally is very spacious and open, all interruptions of the view having been carefully avoided in the design; the acoustic properties of the church are also very good. Accommodation has been provided for seven hundred worshippers, and provision has been made for the future enlargement of the building. Arrangements have also been made for heating the church with hot water. The roofs of the building are internally of light open Gothic woodwork, and are externally covered with slates relieved by bands of others of a green colour. The font is partly of Devonshire marble, and the pulpit and reading desk are made of oak. The whole of the works have been carried out under the superintendence of Messrs E Harbershon, Brock and Webb, Architects, of 37, Bedford Place, Russell Square, London, and the works have been executed by Messrs Call & Pathick, Builders, of Plymouth. Mr A A G Colpoys has overseen the works for the Architects from the commencement. The doors of the building were opened about half-past ten o'clock, and very soon the seats were all occupied, a considerable portion of the congregation being ladies and gentlemen themselves contributors more or less to the building, and who by their attendance showed their hearty sympathy. The pews are open, with low backs; over the entrance to the chancel is the inscription "God is a Spirit, and they that worship Him must worship Him in spirit and in truth". Within the communion rails the furniture is exceedingly plain and simple. There is no elaborate 'altar piece' over the communion table, but the plainly-lettered words "This do in remembrance of Me". At eleven o'clock, Bishop Chapman met the clergy at the west door, and having accepted the petition of the parishioners, praying that he would be pleased to Consecrate the Church, His Lordship, accompanied by the Bishop's Chaplains, the Rev. Preb. Barnes, the Rev. R R Wolfe, the Rev. Preb. Harris, Rev. T Kitson, Rev. R Fayle, Rev. Baring Gould, Rev. W B Davis, Rev Parkes Smith, Rev. R Elrington, Rev. A Carey, Rev. J FitzTaylor, Rev. - Elliott, Rev. W Villiers, Rev. E Grinstead, and other clergymen from neighbouring parishes, proceeding up towards the east and repeated the 24th Psalm. The usual form of prayer on such occasions was proceeded with, and the instrument of consecration having been read and signed by the Bishop, the Church was declared to be Consecrated. The morning service was then proceeded with, the officiating clergyman being the Rev. Baring Gould; the first lesson was read by the Rev. T Kitson, the second lesson by the Rev. J FitzTaylor. The communion service was read by His Lordship the Bishop, the Rev. R Barnes reading the epistle, and the Rev. R R Wolfe the gospel. An eloquent and effective sermon was then preached by the Ven. the Archdeacon Downall, from the 4th and 5th verses of the 2nd chapter of the 1st Epistle of Peter. A collection was made at the close in aid of the organ fund. The training of the choir had been undertaken by Miss Ainsworth, who had bestowed much pains and trouble in bringing them up to the present most creditable standard. Mr Gregory conducted the singing on the harmonium. Jackson's "Te Deum" was very well sung. After the services, Mr & Mrs Haliburton entertained upwards of a hundred ladies and gentlemen at lunchion, which was provided by Mr Ralph in admirable style at the Mission Rooms (later United Services Club). The Chair was taken by the Rev. R R Wolfe, who was supported on his right by Bishop Chapman, Mrs Haliburton, and others; and on his left by Mrs Fayle, Sir L Palk, Bart., MP., Mrs Wolfe, ChancellorPhillpotts, and others, and most of the clergy who were present at the consecration. Grace before and after meat was said by the Rev. R R Wolfe, and the health of Her Most Gracious Majesty the Queen was drunk with the usual honours. There followed a series of long speeches and further toasts to the distinguished guests present. The Minister who had been appointed to the Church was the Rev. Baring Gould - a Devonshire man related to the Barings of Lewtrenchard, where his Brother was the Squire and another Brother the Rector (the Revd Sabine Baring-Gould - writer of the hymn 'Onward Christian Soldiers'). In replying to a welcome from the Ven. the Archdeacon Downall, the Rev. Baring Gould said he had sought divine guidance in debating whether to come back to his native county. He had felt satisfied that the Providence of God had directed him - to what he described as the most beautiful spot in the most beautiful county in England. The Chairman asked the company present to return hearty thanks to Mr & Mrs Haliburton for what they had done for the Parish. Mr Haliburton had provided everything; not leaving a single thing except the organ. He added the company's grateful thanks to Sir L Palk for donating the site, and for such a large contribution to the endowment fund. Mr Haliburton rose to return thanks, with a speech at some length, and received quite an ovation - as did Sir L Palk. The proceedings were then brought to a close. A dinner was provided for the members of the choir, the pew-openers, and others connected with the Church, at Baker's Country House Inn; and a dinner was also given to those of the workmen engaged in building the Church who remained in the place; the Rev. Baring Gould afterwards delivered to them an interesting and suitable address. The schoolchildren of Ellacombe and Boston Fields (about three-hundred in number) were regaled with cake, and the elder children were each presented with a hymn and prayer-book. This evening (Tuesday) three hundred of the parents of the school-children are to have tea in the Mission Rooms, after which they will be addressed by several friends. On Sunday, the Rev Baring Gould preached in the morning to a large congregation on the text which is inscribed on the Chancel Arch, "God is a Spirit, and they that worship Him must worship Him in Spirit and in Truth". In the evening there was an overflowing congregation, chiefly of the working class, when a most impressive and eloquent sermon was preached from the words "God forbid that I should glory, save in the Cross of our Lord Jesus Christ, by whom the world is crucified unto Me, and I unto the World".*

CHRIST CHURCH, ELLACOMBE
ARCHIVES BENEFICE

In 1873 new trustees of the right of patronage of Ellacombe District and of the nomination of its incumbent were appointed.

In 1906 a conveyance was signed, together with a plan, for transferring part of Bronshill Field, in the parish of Tormoham to form a site for a parsonage house for the sum of £322.

The parties concerned in the transaction were - on the one part, Lucius Falkland Brancaleone, of The Quinta, Babbacombe, a retired colonel, and Arthur Hingston Dymond of Exeter, solicitor, testamentary trustees of Robert Sheddon Sulyarde Cary, late of Torre Abbey, deceased, on the one part and the Governors of the Bounty of Queen Anne and the Revd John Percy Baker, vicar of Christchurch, Ellacombe on the other. Again in 1906 a further conveyance was signed tranferring land adjoining a new road leading to Bronshill Road in the parish of Tormoham for the sum of £90. The parties, in this case, were George Henry Francis, of The Excelsior Works, Plainmoor, Torquay, mineral water manufacturers on the one part, and (again) the Governors of the Bounty of Queen Anne and the Revd Percy Baker, vicar of Christ Church, Ellacombe on the other.

During 1909-1911 the new vicarage was built out of a local building fund and that held by the Governors of the Bounty of Queen Anne, and improvements were made to the building in 1925. In 1934 the vicarage was converted into two flats, and in 1960 more money was raised for extensive alterations and improvements.

CHURCHWARDENS' ACCOUNTS 1903

Additions were made to the parish rooms from a specification, plan and building agreement.

1907-09: Faculty, with plans, for a new chancel and sentence of consecration were considered and executed.
1928: Details of a new chancel door were recorded.
1934: The Borough of Torquay issued a licence for the erection of a scout hut.
Undated: A new oak screen, chapel and childrens 'corner, plus panelling for a baptistry were proposed. Also one for a west porch and a stained-glass window showing Christ on the right panel and St George, St Nicholas and St Cyprian on the left.

Ellacombe Church, c. 1910, looking towards the altar. TNHM

CHURCH CHARITIES 1892-1905

Mrs Louise Neville Haliburton made a bequest of, inter alia, £500 for the relief of the sick and needy of the Parish.

1909: Mrs L. J. Grice made a bequest of £100 for the benefit of the poor of Ellacombe.

1928: Miss Pain left a legacy for the erection of a door to be built on the south side of the church.

EARLIEST MINUTES
VESTRY MINUTE BOOK

The earliest minutes in the Vestry Minute Book of Ellacombe Church are dated 29 March 1869, and record the Revd A Baring-Gould in the Chair as vicar. Other church members present were Mr Haliburton, Mr Pannel, the Revd Sidney Robinson, Capt. Perkins (Vicar's Warden - Resigned), Mr Walker, Mr Halsey (Appt. Vicar's Warden) and Mr Baker. Church Accounts were examined and passed. It was determined that Offerings on the first Sunday Morning in each month would be reserved for the poor of the Parish and that of the third Sunday for Church expenses. In 1874 the Revd Charles Camp expressed dissatisfaction with the state of the local roads, and proposed that a petition be sent to the Local Board for some action to be taken. In 1876 Dr Tombe was appointed Vicar's Warden and Mr G. Drake People's Warden. Miss Ainsworth was given a vote of thanks for services to the Choir - proposed by the Vicar - Revd I A Jamieson.

In 1877 the Stipend of Mr Smerdon - presumably the Verger - was raised from £2 to £4. The following year the current vicar in the chair was minuted as Revd I. Holdernep. Dr Tombe, Mr F. Hoare and G. Drake were listed as being present.

The 1880 Minutes noted that, because of the parlous state of Church Funds, there could be no further increase in Mr Smerdon's income. Nothing of moment was recorded until 1895 when it was minuted that the number of sidesmen would be reduced from 12 to 10. In 1896 Church Funds showed a balance of £151:11:0d and the singing of Kyries was introduced into Morning Service.

The 1897 Minutes gave the following list of personnel present: the vicar, the Revd A P Cox in the chair; followed by the Revd H. Laine, and Messrs. J. M. Curzon, C. Chambers, W. H. Lord, G. Drake, Knight, Hoskin, Davis, Ferris, Brock, Murray, Pedrick, Packe, Lee, A. Smith, Allward, Tretheway, R. Smerdon, Walker, Tucker, Pearce and A. J. Pratt. At this Meeting Mr Curzon was made Vicar's Warden and Mr G. Drake remained People's

Warden. The Church Council, formed on 29 November 1883, was to be resuscitated, and a Jubilee Fund to be created - to be named 'The Mission Chapels & Church Repair Fund'. The Vicar's House, thanks to the generosity of Mr and Mrs Haliburton, was now made a Vicarage. Early noted incumbents included the Revd A. Baring Gould (1869), the Revd J.A. Jamieson (1876), and the Revd A.P. Cox. From 1900 a succession of vicars were appointed, including: 1900 - the Revd C.H. Druitt; 1902 - the Revd Percy Baker; 1914 - the Revd R.A.C. Stratton; 1926 - the Revd W. Higgins; 1931 - the Revd Leslie St Aubrey..

PAROCHIAL CHURCH COUNCIL

The following selected extracts from the PPC minute books, from 1883 until 1895 throw an interesting light on the day to day workings of the church in Ellacombe and highlight the perennial problems concerning finances, and the reliance upon local beneficiaries in ensuring that costs were met. The earliest recorded congregation meeting of Ellacombe Church took place at Ellacombe Vicarage on November 29, 1883 (the new vicarage, off Bronshill Road, was not built until 1909). The vicar, Revd J. A. Jamieson, took the Chair: Dr Lombe and George Drake were the churchwardens present and Messrs J. Austin, D. Love and R. Slowman, sidesmen, together with Col. Martin, A.R. Hunt, Esq., Capt Perkins, Capt W. Fame Tucker and Messrs Pratt, Adams, Blackwood, Baker, Dodd, Daymond, Gibbs, Phillips and Tozer were present. It was resolved that: 1. a Church Council be formed with the object of relieving the vicar of the secular business connected with Ellacombe Church; 2. the Council would consist of the Vicar, the Churchwardens and Sidesmen (ex officio) and other members now to be elected at this Congregational Meeting with power to add to their number; 3. it was proposed and seconded that Mr T. Baker, Mr Gibbs, Mr Tozer and Mr Daymond be unanimously elected as Members of the Council; 4. the first meeting of the Parochial Church Council (PCC) be held at the Ellacombe parochial room on Monday 3 December 1883 at 7pm; 5. proposed by Mr Austin and seconded by Capt. Tucker, in consequence of sufficient money not be forthcoming for Church Expenses and the Parochial Fund, a collection be made every Sunday morning which shall be divided between these two objects, excepting that when other special societies and charities are pleaded for. And if there be any surplus, Church Council shall have the power to transfer such sur-

plus, or any part of it, to any parochial object which may require such assistance. Carried unanimously and signed by J.A. Jamieson Vicar.

The first meeting of the new PCC was held at the Parochial Room on Monday, 3 December 1883 at 7pm. Mr R. Gibbs undertook the Secretaryship and a Mr Thomas Adams was added to the members of the Council. Capt Fame Tucker remained Treasurer of the Ellacombe and Victoria Park Schools and the Sunday School Clothing Clubs. Dr Lombe undertook the Secretaryship of both the Senior and Junior Curates' Funds, Mr Drake the Ellacombe Mission Churches, the Revd E. L. Fawcett the Young Mens' Institute and Mr Gibbs the Secretary and Treasurerships of the following: the Scripture Readers' Fund, the Parochial Relief Fund and the Ellacombe Coal Fund. Mr Drake to remain Secretary of the Churchwardens' Account.

3 April 1884: The Secretary read the minutes of the previous meeting, and gave a summary of the quarterly accounts showing a balance of cash in hand. It was suggested by the Secretary that the insurance on the fabric of the Church was insufficient to cover the cost in case of fire. It was proposed and carried that the insurance be raised from £2000 to £4000. A question having arisen with regard to the gates of the Church enclosure now being used as swings by children, the matter was referred to the Vestry Meeting. A large pile of bricks lying in the Church enclosure were to be laid down. It was suggested a lamp be placed at the Church entrance, after many complaints of poor lighting. The matter was left to stand over until Mrs Haliburton's return, as that lady would no doubt be glad to present the lamp to the Church. There was also comment on the state of the road in front. The Vicar promised to write to the Local Board to take over this piece of ground and roadway.

7 July 1884: Accounts for the last quarter were submitted by the Secretary. He advised that the road in front of the Church was still in the same condition as when the Council last met and the Local Board, not having fulfilled their promise to give notice to the houses abutting on the roadway to put it in repair, the Vicar was again requested to write to the Board upon the subject. Nothing having been done to the Church gates Mr Drake promised to have them repainted at once and padlocks provided. On the recommendation of the Secretary, it was resolved that in future all accounts excepting the regular monthly ones be submitted to the Council before payment and countersigned by the Vicar or either of the Churchwardens. It was proposed and carried that the weekly offertories of all monies accruing to the different funds, either from collections or donations be handed to the Treasurer for him to bank the same.

The Coal Fund being very much in arrears, it was urged that a special appeal be made to the congregation to cover the amount of Mr Manley's account of £19.6.9d., but upon a motion put forward and agreed it was recommended that the appeal would be more successful at this time of the year if made for general purposes. It was resolved accordingly that the third Sunday in July be for this object, the third Sunday in August for the Scripture Fund and the third Sunday in September for the Curates' Fund.

The question of the remuneration of the organ player was then addressed. It was agreed that his salary be increased to £4 per annum - an amendment to make the increase £5 being unsupported was lost.

16 January 1885: The balance sheets were again presented, showing a general deficit of £59.19.4d., afterward supplemented by £8.12.5d. being an amount collected at Xmas for the 'Torquay Charities' not added in error to the Parochial Fund, making together £68.11.9d. A discussion of the work plan upon the different balances, as compared with the previous ones of the Secretary, ensued and the Vicar handed over the School accounts from Capt Fame Tucker. The Choir Fund was remarked upon as showing the most serious deficiency and it was decided to merge the Church expenses and the Choir Fund into one account in the report. The Secretary was also instructed to take over the charge of the Curates' Fund hitherto kept by Dr Lombe and to pay in all monies received on account of the Young Mens' Institute to the Church Fund at the bank. It was further agreed that the Secretary draw a cheque once a quarter covering the allowances to the church attendance bell ringer and other sundry outgoings in connection with church expenses and parochial funds.

10 July 1885: Report of balances of the various Church funds and the Curates' Fund showing a general deficit of £49.4.8d. increased to £79.3.7d. by the outstanding accounts for coal, gas, taxes and printing, a discussion followed as to the best method of immediate clearance of this deficiency. The Vicar proposed, and it was agreed, to issue a circular to the congregation and friends of Ellacombe Church setting forth the particulars of the deficiency and inviting their contributions. The Secretary was requested to draw up the said paper and submit the same to the Vicar prior to its

being handed to the printer. Volunteers offered to distribute them. Mr Drake enquired if it was the intention of the Council to have the internal walls of the Church coloured or simply cleaned this year. In reply to Dr Lombe, Mr Drake roughly estimated the colouring, involving the erection of the necessary scaffolding, at between £30 and £40. The Vicar interposed that as he intended to invite the widow ladies of the congregation to each contribute a memorial to relieve the interior, it would be well to postpone the colouring to another season. Mr Drake was therefore instructed to proceed with the cleaning.

14 January 1886: The Secretary presented to the Council a separate balance sheet for each of the various funds connected with his secretaryship, showing a general deficit on the whole of £206.16.1d. The Vicar stated that the arrears in the School Accounts would bring the total up to over £300, and a discussion thereupon ensued as to the best method of bringing the facts before the congregation, when it was ultimately decided to have the accounts printed forthwith and leave it to the discretion of the Vicar to make a personal appeal to some of the wealthier members prior to the circulation of the report.

1 April 1886: The Secretary presented the various balances showing a surplus of £52, in addition to which the Vicar handed a cheque from Mrs Haliburton for £86, making £138 against which there were accounts still unpaid of £56, leaving a clear balance of £82 to meet current expenses of the ensuing quarter. The Vicar, however, stated that all the subscriptions had not come in and it was therefore decided to leave the apportionment of the deficit fund of £158.8.6d. in hand and the other funds still in arrears until the next meeting in July. The Vicar then stated that the former caretaker of the Parochial Rooms had resigned and left. It was proposed that Mrs Smith should take charge of the Rooms and attend to the cleaning, for which services she asked the sum of 3/6d. a week. The general feeling appeared to be that this sum was fair remuneration for her services and it was unanimously agreed that Mrs Smith be engaged for the work.

15 July 1887: General Fund balance of £183, but by year end a grand deficit of £117:2:1. Moved that entire collections for one month be appropriated exclusively for Parochial relief of Coal Funds, etc. Deficit to remain in year's account.

2 Feb 1888: Revd Hamlyn in Chair. Letter from Mrs Haliburton enclosing £122 cheque entirely clearing adverse balance - from 1 Jan. Mrs

Haliburton thanked on behalf of Council. Report given on 'relief of poor'.

May 1888: Revd C E Storrs in Chair. Special appeal for funds for organ and choir. Subject of additional Curate due to growth of Parish. Decided two Curates to be funded from offertories. Additional Sidesman appointed. £1 granted to Iron Church. Remarked that communion had never been administered at Stentiford's Hill: a simple one to be provided out of Church expenses.

4 Sept 1888: Revd Hamlyn in Chair. Balance in hand £73. Mr Dodd had undertaken to print a monthly paper at 16/-d for 16vv copies. A room at the Conservative Club hired from Mr Churchward for rental of £10 per annum for Mothers' Meetings, Mens' Bible Class, etc. Vicar promised to write to rich residents in Torquay to assist financially. Number of Communion parishioners risen from 140 to over 300. Revd Hamlyn complained of very dangerous approach road to Iron Church. Referred to Town Surveyor.

Jamuary 1889: Balance of Church Fund £13:6:0d, but accounts outstanding for organ repairs, coal and draperies of £19. The deficiency would be met by Mrs Haliburton. Ellacombe contribution to Torbay Hospital Chaplain £5. Complaint that organ tuning not being done professionally. Vicar's Special Appeal allocated £50 to Curates' Fund, £26 to Scripture Readers, £4 for coal and £2:8:0d to Mission Church. Balance of Parochial Fund towards liquidating deficiency in Working Mens' Club account.

May 1889: Revd Jamieson in Chair. General Balance in hand £233:8:11d. - only fund in arrears Choir Fund. Increase in number of members in Council agreed and appointed. Vicar to produce plan for erection of a Choir Gallery at the West End to add to sitting room: cost of which promised by friend. Gallery to be erected during summer months. Scheme for enlarging Church by erection of a North Aisle to meet needs of growing congregation. Architect invited to prepare plan. Vicar to appeal for necessary funds. Vicar intimated that an Iron Church, costing about £170 be considered for Victoria Park. Mr Robinson made promise of £25. Subject dropped at meeting.

January 1890: Legal matters of Victoria Park Church satisfactorily concluded. Building so far advanced that seating could be installed . Possibility of purchasing the organ of All Saints, Tor for nominal sum of £50, which was accepted. Various adjustments made to subsidiary Church Funds. Local Board to replace lamp outside Church with another at public expense. Vicar to apply. Arrangements for opening New Church at Victoria Park discussed.

7 August 1890: Church Funds balance at £142. Mr S. given final warning over serious prejudice arising from 'a careless exposure of himself in the Church'. A proposal to erect a shed to contain spare chairs and objects of occasional use discussed. Cost to be advised. Mr Harris' stipend for professional services at Victoria Park Church discussed. Local Board did not approve a new Bray's Lamp near Church.

10 August 1891: Balance in hand £385 toward proposed new Parish Room. A small mortgage still existed on Mr Wyatt's land and in handing over this land Mr Wyatt expected to be the builder employed. These problems altered the complexion of matters with regard to total cost. Decided to use new site within the enclosure of the North of the Church. Suitability, access, dimentions, etc., fully discussed by all. Building Committee to get new plans drawn up. Mr S granted 20 shillings extra for remuneration as bell ringer. Mr S to be paid £10 a year for cleaning the new Parish Room and Mr Peek £2 as organ blower.

25 October 1892: Overdraft at Bank of £72 but Vicar confident of covering the discrepancies with his usual Autumn appeal.

13 January 1893: Chairman advised of serious danger to Church Funds to be faced following the death of Mrs Haliburton and loss of her legacy of £100. Possibility discussed of immediate reduction in staff and workers. Steps taken to dispense with Scripture Reader.

22 November 1894: Vicar proposed additional decoration to the Apse by suspending tapestry round the walls. Reference made to the unsafe state of St Barnabus Church by reason of Corporation having quarried too near. Deputation to 'wait' upon Roads Committee. Outlay required of £12 to equip Church Lads' Brigade - essential for spiritual training amongst youth. Rail to be provided on path to upper Parish Rooms and gateway proposed through wall on N. Side.

24 January 1895: Roads Committee declined to entertain any expense in securing the Stentiford's Hill Mission Church.

19 September 1895: Vicar explained proposal of a plan to light the Parish Church with incandescent burners which could greatly reduce heat at Evening Services and curtail the gas account by many pounds. The cost of the fittings would amount to £40:10:10d. Vicar's proposal agreed and Mr Drake instructed to proceed with the work. Vicar dwelt upon desirability of increasing lay workers to assist clergy and encourage zeal and christian fellowship. It was proposed to enlist services of Church Army for Ellacombe. Particulars of salary for a Church Army Captain usually about two-thirds of offerings.

There is a gap in the surviving records until 1903 when the PCC minute books resume and continue until 1936. Concerns continue to be centred upon the upkeep of the building and finances:

18 March 1903: Plans for a large room to be added at the end of the present Parish Rooms carried. Building Committee appointed and an architect selected to draw up plans.

15 April 1903: Plans produced at cost of £5:5:0d. Tenders to be invited for the work.

30 April 1903: A Mr Blatchford's tender for £162 accepted. Building Committee reported fault in plans resulting in insufficient headway, but plans were passed nevertheless.

23 June 1904: Chairman announced that the Vicarage House had been sold to Mr Mosse. Several sites had been viewed for a new Vicarage House. The new Chancel scheme was discussed and the preservation of the organ from the heat and cold. Vicar also proposed scheme to place Church Finances on a sound basis.

30 January 1906: Chairman announced letter from Tramway Company who require a portion of land belonging to Schools and offering price for same. Company to be advised by Trustees of strong disapproval of scheme on grounds of public safety. Suggested alternative scheme on advice of Borough Surveyor. Draft 'Right-of-Way' to new Church entrance presented and approved. Chairman asked to point out to Council that Church not to be held responsible for damage to road by repairing drains - to be stated in Deed.

8 February 1907: Plans to adopt means to deaden sound by building up window in Parish Rooms and sealing the window on the platform side with matchboarding, etc.

2 February 1910: Defective drainage in churchyard rectified and alterations made to light at corner of Chancel.

26 June 1911: Vicar announced he had accepted the living of Charles Church, Plymouth and would be leaving Ellacombe in mid-December. The Revd F. Vivian Dodgson appointed in his place. The Revd E. G. Payne appointed the first Vicar of St James, Torquay. A testimonial to be presented to him.

7 February 1912: Reorganisation of subsidiary Church Funds to clear deficit. Mr T. J. Rogers defrayed cost of decorating the Chancel and great satisfaction expressed at beauty of result.

31 January 1913: Present: Chairman, Revd E. M. Davies. Revd A. E. Foster, Messrs Chudley, Easterbrook, Brock, Hosking, Knight, Roberts, Howard, Watson, Tucker, Smith and Gordon Murray (Secretary). Statement of accounts overall deficit of £89:12:1d.

21 April 1913: Proposed extension of St Paul's Church and enlargement of one side only giving an extra 12 feet and seating for 85 carried. Offer of Mr Moxhay to supply plans free of charge was accepted. Vicar to appeal for financial support for project.

1 March 1916: Estimates for insuring Church and Parochial Buildings against loss by bombardment and aircraft to be discussed in a fortnight, including what rate per cent under Government Scheme with Lloyds.

28 March 1916: All buildings to be fully insured under Lloyds and Vicar to appeal for funds for that purpose (about £23).

28 July 1916: Revd E. M. Davys accepted the living of Cromer. Windows darkened in view of lighting restrictions for winter.

12 January 1917: Revd H. E. Stuart's services terminated by Vicar after a statement given and the Vicar's action approved.

24 July 1917: Special Council called to debate on electing women members and the principle of so doing was adopted and maximum numbers specified for each Church. Meeting of all women in Parish called to elect representatives.

28 May 1918: Revd A. C. Stratton (Chairman), Revd T. Young, Messrs Chudley, Easterbrook, Tucker, Crocker, Bussell, Dark, Trehewey, Collihole, Peake, Howard, Smith, Hunt, Berridge, Beasley, Conybeare, May, Dimmock, Ferris and Zaple. Mesdames Crocker, Woodley, Watson and the Misses Davies, Towell, Peadon and G. Russell. Vicar gave outline of plans to celebrate the Golden Jubilee of Parish Church at end of July. The Bishop of Exeter would preach on Sunday, 28 July. A Garden Party was suggested with entertainment and tea. Entertainment Committee appointed. A Sergeant W. B. Watson, RAMC., reported killed in France and a vote of sympathy sent to his wife. Considerable opposition to the Garden Party at time of serious National danger. Resolved not to hold it. 1

17 June 1919: Chairman reported serious illness of Revd Ford. Letter of thanks sent to Miss Phillips thanking her and the Sunday School

Teachers and scholars for efforts at Broadlands whereby £51 raised for renovation of Parish Church. Verger's salary to be raised to 25 shillings a week carried, after discussion, and further to 30 shillings to cover caretaking of Parish Rooms, upkeep of garden, Verger's duty and Baby Welcome. 1

5 December 1919: £38:18:2d. raised , to date, for the War Memorial target of £50. Mr Terry and Teachers invited to assist in canvassing the Parish.

19 April 1920: It was suggested that a hut for Scouts would be a suitable War Memorial, but one in the Church was preferred. Estimates to be obtained. St Pauls Church entrance door required widening and the pathway from Derwent Road was in bad condition.

16 January 1922: Hon. Sec. of Social Club reported total profit of £15:14:0d towards Church Funds. Vote of thanks agreed. Rearrangement of psalms on Sundays agreed, as was revision of Electoral Roll.

5 April 1922: Work of preparing the stained glass for the East Window was under way and a drawing exhibited to the Council members. Agreed that the work should be carried out, together with a suitable memorial tablet. Annual Report for 1922 - Full report of previous year's activities as minuted presented. The Revd H. G. Philipps took the place of Revd T. Young. Hearty thanks expressed to Revd R. Ford for his services to St Barnabus' Church, especially for his extra work on the proposed removal of the building to another site. No further advice received from the T.C. Housing Committee on the subject since last year. Building now needs complete overhaul before removal. Increased charge of 2d a copy for Church Magazine agreed and circulation sought to be increased, if possible. Reports by Secretary and Treasurer presented and agreed. Mr J Moore and Mr F. C. Weymouth elected replacements for sidesmen - Mr Langford and Mr Hunt at St Pauls and Mr G Drake at St Barnabus. Main change of importance at Parish Church the resignation of Revd H. C. Ruddle, who left in October last to take up similar work in Durham. A great loss to Parish. During summer the War Memorial window, partly presented by Lady Mackenzie, was erected in the Chancel and dedicated by the Bishop. A list of men of the Parish who gave their lives was under preparation and would be soon ready to place in the Church. Serious loss to Parish Church sustained by the death of Mr J F Tucker - a long serving member of the Council, a Sidesman and Sunday School teacher, etc. Treasurer asked to be relieved of his duties as soon as a successor

could be found. Bank requested sureties to guarantee overdraft, and several Members kindly agreed at rate of £20 each.

Annual Report for 1924: Great regret expressed at loss by death of Mr W. G. Dimmock of the Parish Church and Mr J. Tyson of St Pauls - Mr Tyson's experience as a practical builder being of much assistance to the Council when dealing with repairs. Average attendance well maintained (over 26). No change in services at Parish Church, but loss felt by reduction in staff. Felt essential that steps be taken for services of a second Curate at earliest opportunity. Finance Committee to consider implications. Mr Cole obliged, from domestic reasons, to resign from post of Verger. Mr J. Matthewson took his place. Treasurer pleased to report year 1923 ended with small balance of funds in hand. But in light of heavy expense forecast for 1925 a Bazaar and Garden Fete was to be held at Hatfield House on Wednesday, 3 June. A similar one for St Pauls arranged for June 27. Thanks expressed to Day School teachers for special efforts to obtain funds for repairs and alterations to Schools, and Sunday School teachers and friends for collecting funds for SS Annual Outings. Special thanks to Mr Beazley and Mr W Roberts for attention to Church Bells. It was found necessary to paint and re-letter Church Notice Board of St Paul's Church. Good progress and congregations reported, showing signs of new vigour after appointment of Revd Fanshaw, and various alterations and repairs to interior and choir stalls carried out.

4 April 1925: The Ellacombe Parish Rooms were crowded on Monday, 27 July 1925 on the occasion of a presentation to the retiring Vicar, the Revd A. C. Stratton and Mrs Stratton, the former having occupied the living of Ellacombe for 12 years - the longest of all past Vicars.

6 April 1926: Annual Report for 1926. Council regretted that, owing to sickness, attendance at Council had dropped to an average of 21 Members, although general interest had been well maintained. Regret was reported of the resignation of Mr Conybeare as Treasurer, who was succeeded by Mr L G Chudley. The installation of electric light was successfully completed and appreciated, and the outside wood and iron work repaired and repainted. A Garden fete, with assistance given by the Day School teachers was arranged and over £200 realised. The Missionary Committee, under Mrs Watson, was again active, as was the new Girls' Social Club under Mrs Higgins. The Revd F. S. Ford reorganised the Boy Scouts and Mr P. Dimmock appointed

Scoutmaster, assisted by senior members of the Troup.

10 April 1927: Annual Report for 1927. An Average of 21 Members attended 9 meetings held during the year, the same as previous year. Efforts to obtain the services of a second Curate proved unsuccessful. Owing to illness, the services arranged for Holy Week could not be conducted by him, so his place was filled by the Vicar. His suggestion for out-door evangelistic services to be held in the Parish were considered but not found practicable. Due to storms work has been necessary to the roof during the past year. The coloured design on the West Window is to be replaced in the near future. New surplices have been supplied to the Choir.

2 April 1929: Annual Report for 1929. Seven meetings only held and attendance of 21 maintained. Council placed on record appreciation of long services of Mr and Mrs Gordon Murray prior to leaving the Town. Number on Council reduced to 25. Regretted no increase in Congregation reported and collections very low. Mr S. A. Bryant appointed to post of Organist, replacing Mr Macey, deceased. No Sale of Work held in year. No renovation of the Church and Parish Room was considered and it was subsequently decided to make an appeal for £500 for this purpose. As a result, and with a contribution of £30 from St Paul's Church, this sum was raised - £200 of which went towards Church ordinary expenses and the balance to the renovations. An electric blower was suggested for the Church organ, but the subject postponed due to expense involved.

12 January 1932: Vicar stated that he had received a number of resignations from members of the late Council, which were accepted. Treasurer submitted accounts showing debts of £76.

16 January 1934: All three Church Accounts in credit. Following recommendations approved:- 1) Scheme to heat Parish Church - enquiries to be made plus an appeal for funds: 2) Revd Ford reported that more funds were needed for St Barnabus Church repairs. Parish Rooms to be used to raise funds: 3) Repairs also needed to St Paul's.

20 November 1934: Vicar reported new standardised Deanery Quota of £70 for next three years and at least £35 must be sent to qualify for grant. Agreed that Mens' Club can hold Whist Drives, if run in proper manner. No cash prizes - only ones 'in kind'. Proposal to change to a 'philosophy of greater unity' to uplift spirit of congregation. Title of PCC to be changed to Parish Family Council (PFC) and the 'Family' title to apply to various funds and gatherings to inspire a 'family spirit'. Ellacombe Old Boys' Association to reform a club at Victoria Park Schools.

22 January 1935: Ellacombe Argyle Football Club applied for permission to use the Victoria Park Schoolroom as a Committee and Recreation Room. Request referred for further consideration. Proposed that small repair work be given to unemployed in Parish. Scout Committee asked Church for advance to pay Messrs Wilkins, or would have to wait 18 months for it. Scouts to pay it back.

The last entry of these Minutes held by DCRO were signed by the Vicar, Revd Leslie St Aubrey, on 21 January 1936.

THE ELLACOMBE YOUNG PEOPLE'S FELLOWSHIP

This Fellowship was first formed in 1935 by a group of young people who were Confirmed around 1934. The adults who were principally involved with its formation were: Mr Walter Wyatt and Mr Reginald Ebdon, churchwardens; Mr Reg Hayman, a chorister, Misses Ethel Hansen and Lynda Sercombe - Sunday School teachers. The current clergy (besides the vicar - Revd Leslie St Aubrey) were: Revd Llewellyn Owen-Williams (curate) and Mrs Williams; Revd Lionel Lawrence (curate) and Mrs Lawrence and Capt Massey (Church Army). Among the early founders were: Joyce Greenfield; Doris Atkinson; Mary Helmore; Margaret Harris; Bert Langmead; Margaret Mairs; Clarice Fletcher; Stuart Bond; Harold Arnold; Leslie Bartlett; Colin Frost; Derek Shauler; John Brewer; Arthur Ebdon; Harry Powell; Bertie Chalker; Ray Skinner and Sydney Langmead. Later, Barbara Sloggett; Christine Harris; Mary Hyne; Kathleen Hooper; Doris Wakefield; Pat Snelling; Betty Warren; Betty Heath; Bill Frost; John Harris; Archie Ffoukes and boys from St.Olave's Grammar School, evacuated from London, and girls from the Maida Vale Grammar School, also evacuated from London.

Activities which commonly took place pre-war; Wednesday Social Evenings in Winter - group games; ballroom dancing lessons and competitions; visits to and by other church youth clubs and badminton. In the Summer there were evening rambles; swimming at Redgate Beach; Bank Holiday outings and extended rambles to Dartmoor, Dartmouth, and Broadsands. Three evenings a week there was tennis on courts off Higher Downs Road and Hampton Avenue.

ELLACOMBE CHURCH CHOIR 1952-53

1. Walter Wyatt; 2. Tony Moore; 3. Reg Wilton; 4. Percy Dimmock; 5. Len Harvey; 6. Nicky Cooper; 7. Graham Rawle; 8. David Olding; 9. Peter Young; 10. Wilfred Weaver (organist); 11. Alan Rawle; 12. Revd E. Robinson (vicar); 13. Paul Young; 14. John Rowse; 15. Keith Metcalf; 16. Cyril Watts; 17. Reg Hayman; 18. Alan Frayne; 19 ?; 20. Herbert Davey; 21. Ernest Walker (lay reader); 22. Tony Potter; 23. Dereck Collier.
Photo by kind permission of Graham Rawle

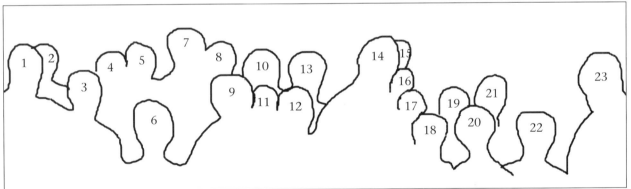

WILFRED WEAVER'S ELLACOMBE CHURCH ORGANIST'S LEAVING PRESENTAION 1955

1. Walter Wyatt; 2. Derek Collier; 3. Tony Potter; 4. Alan Rawle; 5. Graham Rawle; 6. Tony Moore; 7. Peter Young; 8. Percy Dimmock; 9. Nicky Cooper; 10. Reg Hayman; 11. Paul Young; 12. Alan Frayne; 13. Len Harvey; 14. Wilfred Weaver (organist); 15. John Prowse; 16. Cyril Watts; 17. David Olding; 18. Reg Milton; 19. Keith Metcalf; 20. Ernest Walker (lay reader); 21. Herbert Davey; 22. Revd E. Robinson (vicar). Photo by kind permission of Graham Rawle

Ellacombe Church Young People's Fellowship, 1948. Both pictures courtesy Graham Rawle

Ellacombe Church Young People's Fellowship members on Dartmoor in 1947. The fellowship members around this time included: Jean Boyd, Frank Skinner, John Powell, John Whitford, Ken Powell, Raymond Skinner, Mary Trump, Jean Taylor, Nena Dunlop, Ted Bragg, Jean Gillard, Jean Cooper, Peter Carrick, Graham Rawle, Sheila Allen, Ken Spruce, Revd G. R. Morgan, Edna Morgan, Jean Harris, Cynthia Heath, Barbara Taylor, John Bragg, Bill Newton and Jean Brewer.

At the outbreak of the War various members joined the armed forces, but membership was re-inforced for a time by the evacuees. Raymond Skinner joined the RAF in February, 1941, so activities after that date are not known. He re-joined the YPF in October 1945 and shared the leadership for many years thereafter with the late Miss Jean Brewer.

THE MISSION CHURCH OF
ST PAULS, PLAINMOOR

The Mission Church of St Pauls, Plainmoor, within the Parish of Ellacombe and under the jurisdiction of the Mother Church of Christ Church, Ellacombe, was opened on 28 January 1890 by the Bishop of Crediton, before a packed congregation. During the process of building the little 'tin' church, many local men and women had given many hours of voluntary labour in order that the project could be completed. Agreement was reached in 1890 providing for a 'right of way' from the Mission Church (the 'Iron Church') to St Marychurch Road, in consideration of the sum of £5.10s. per annum. The parties concerned were - on the one part, Robert Shedden Sulyarde Cary of Torre Abbey, and on the other the vicar and churchwardens of Ellacombe Parish Church.

In 1914 there was a further agreement between the parties concerned for a 'right of way' between the Mission Church and Broadmead Road. In 1907 a 'Deed of Gift' provided for a moveable church room to be used in connection with the work of St. Paul's Mission Church - the parties being, on the one hand, Miss Florence Skirrow of Bellair, Torquay and, on the other, the Revd Percy Baker, George Drake of Leighton, Torquay, a builder, and Thomas John Rogers of Shenley, Ash Hill Road, Torquay, Esquire as trustees. These trustees were later changed to include Arthur

Carruthers Stratton (replacing Revd Baker as vicar), Lewis James Chudleigh of Studland, Windsor Road, accountant, and Thomas Henry Easterbrook of Market Street, jeweller. In 1915 a conveyance was signed between the Revd John Percy Baker of Charles Parish Vicarage, Plymouth, and Thomas John Rogers of Shenley, Ash Hill Road, Torquay, Esq., on the one part, and the Trustees of the Exeter Diocesan Trust on the other, covering land fronting Broadmead Road in the Parish of Ellacombe, together with the Mission Church Parish Rooms and other buildings standing therein (subject to a mortgage in favour of the Revd John Percy Baker). Additions to the Church, building agreement and specification of works and plans were filed in 1914. In 1928, a Financial Statement and Solicitor's Bill relating to part payment of the mortgage was issued.

Extracts of an Annual Report of the St Paul's Church Hall 'Our Welcome', made in November 1910 by Miss F. Skirrow, the Secretary and Treasurer, make interesting reading:

President - Revd F. Vivian Dodgson
Vice-President - Revd E. M. Davys
Date of a Bazaar to be held on Saturday, 20 May 1911 to raise money for 'Our Welcome' Reserve Fund. A Mrs Spragg thanked for work on two social evenings and one spent at 'Belmont'. An outing for the men and lads in a drive to Exeter. A visit by a 'dearly loved friend' Mr Kember. who gave a fascinating talk about his work. Some disappointment reported over the fact that many who enjoy the games facilities do not remain to take part in the Service Hour. The Misses Bousefield and Mrs Dodgson thanked for taking the Bible Class in the absence of the Secretary. Miss Phillips thanked for her musical help; Miss Durrant for a handsome gift of books for the Library; generous subscribers for their gifts of money; the mens' Committee; the Women for their Bible Class Collections; the Caretaker and all others who have done little acts of kindness. Note is made of the Passing of the saintly Archbishop Maclagan, who, in the midst of his past busy life, found time to take an interest in the Mission and 'The Welcome'.

The following announcement was inserted in the local press by The Friends of St Paul's in 1967:

In 1966 St Paul's Church was closed (and demolished). Those responsible have merely issued a statement dealing collectively with all the Torquay Churches involved, although the position of St Paul's was very different to the others concerned. It had an enthusiatic congregation, an ardent band of workers and no financial worries, yet a really satisfactory explanation for the closure of this 'live' church has not been given. Most of the congregation still meet together and remain united and organised, awaiting the day when they will again worship together under one roof. The building may now be locked and empty but the Church lives on!

Ellacombe in the 1890s - a picture taken from what is now George Road. The building in the foreground, a former brewery, still stands, along with part of the imposing steps. The houses in the background were new when this picture was taken but all can be identified today. The wide street curving into the distance is Woodville Road. THE

Chapter 8 - Some Eminent Figures

This chapter sets the scene for the reminiscences that follow which, I hope, will recall for many readers the community spirit, the pride and the high standards of the residents who were, in the main, relatively poor working folk. Few Ellacombe (even Devon-born) residents remain domiciled in the parish, but many of its sons and daughters have, from humble beginnings, become prominent businessmen, or have risen in the ranks of politics, joined the senior ranks of the teaching profession. Others have built substantial careers in the public and civil services, and become renowned names in sport at county and national levels.

Ellacombe School can boast a proud record of the achievements of many of its young pupils launched into the tough working world with an elementary, but very sound, education, and who were encouraged by this to make their way upwards in the 'outside' world. There were few scholarship awards to the local (then fee-paying) Torquay Grammar Schools in the '20s and '30s., but of those that did win them, many became high achievers through the benefit of secondary tuition. And there were others who extended their education through the medium of the old Torquay Commercial College and the Central School at Plainmoor. Some late-developers, with the encouragement and support of many good, local employers, attended day release or evening classes at the South Devon Technical College in an effort to further their future careers.

Among those of note are: **Doctor Kenneth Briand**, who attended Ellacombe Elementary School as a youngster, has fairly recently been awarded a PhD from St Andrew's University for his historical research. Dr Briand, who now lives in St Andrews in Fife, worked in Torquay as a shop assistant before joining the Cameron Highlanders in 1937. He later joined the Royal Signals and saw war service in the jungles of Burma. After being demobbed he studied at St Luke's College, Exeter. He ended his teaching career as the headmaster of a large primary school in the north of England.

Bertram Arthur William Chalker, who now lives in Paignton, was born on 8 August 1920 and educated at Ellacombe School. He won a scholarship to The Torquay Commercial College, and continued his education at The Management College, Henley-on-Thames. He was, before retirement, an Associate of Corporate Company Secretaries, and a Member of the Institute of Marketing, the Institute of Personnel Management, the Institute of Travel and Tourism, and of the Royal Economic Society.

He joined the Territorial Army and became a member of the Royal Devon Yeomanry, Royal Artillery from 1939 to 1946, serving in Ireland and the Far East. He was awarded the Territorial Decoration.

As a sportsman he was Captain of the Regimental Football Team (winners of the Malayan Championship) and selected to play for Malaya in several International games (the only European to achieve this distinction). Following the cessation of hostilities, he was a member of the St Marychurch Spurs Football Team for several years. In 1952-3 they were Herald Cup Finalists, and in 1954-5 and 1955-6 South Devon Premier Division Winners and Herald Cup Winners.

He joined the Renwick Group (Torquay) in 1934 and served in most sections of the business - later in management positions. He was appointed a Director in 1963. In 1968 he became Managing Director of the Travel Division and Chairman of some of the Division Subsidiary Companies. He retired in 1975 (because of bereavements) but remained a Non-Executive Director/Consultant until 1984. Other activities included appointment as a Justice of the Peace in 1972, attending the Torbay Court and the Crown Court at Exeter. He was appointed a General Commissioner of Income Tax for the Paignton Division in 1976, and a Member of the Department of Health and Social Security Appeal Tribunal in 1984.

Lt-Col. W.J. (Bill) Elliott MBE, now residing in Torquay, was born in Ellacombe on 16 August 1916 (Dr Cooke from Castle Circus in attendance - charge for services 2/6d!). He was christened at St Barnabus' (the old 'tin church') in the Braddons. He first attended Torwood School under the supervision of Miss Weatherlake before transferring to Ellacombe School in 1927. In 1928 he won a scholarship to the Torquay Grammar School, where his education continued until 1933. After leaving school he joined the Torquay and Paignton Gas Company where he later qualified as Chartered Secretary in 1938.

In 1939 he joined the Army as a private soldier, and was granted a regular commission in 1944. He attained the rank of Lieutenant-Colonel at 27 years of age. He saw service in Egypt, Palestine, Syria, Malta, Italy and Austria, was mentioned in Despatches and awarded the MBE.

Retiring from the Army in 1953, he became a partner in Tolchards, the local drinks firm, only to be recalled to military service to carry out special duties during the Suez crisis. Returning to Tolchards in 1956, he developed the Company from six to almost a hundred employees, and initiated the building of a new factory on the Woodland Estate.

After retiring as Chairman and Managing Director in 1985, he obtained election to Devon County Council on behalf of Ellacombe and Upton. He was successful again in 1989 but did not seek re-election in 1993. Whilst at Devon Council Council he was variously Chairman of the Finance, Economy and Employment, Tourism and Torbay Highways Committees: also a member of the Pension Investment Panel and Devon Highways Committees. Presently he is involved with Exeter Airport, the National Rivers Authority and is a Governor of both Ellacombe and Homelands Schools. He found one of the most rewarding of his efforts on the Devon County Council was to spearhead the re-building of Ellacombe School to ensure its future for many years to come.

A former Director of Torquay United Football Club, he maintains that interest and is a Vice-President of the Torbay Civic Society and several members clubs, particularly those of the British Legion. A sports and keep-fit enthusiast, he still pursues swimming, golf, skiing, walking and gardening.

Arthur Vine Ebdon was born in Ellacombe. At the parish church he was a choirboy while attending the primary school. There, one of his teachers was Charles Hoare, who much later, as Mayor of Torbay, was one of the governors who appointed Arthur to South Devon Technical College. At the Grammar School, Arthur was Captain of the Soccer First XI. As Head Boy he wished the girls well when they moved to Shiphay and addressed

the Old Grammarians. His last professional act was to take over the school buildings for the College.

In North Africa during the War, in the Royal Army Ordnance Corps he served in every rank from Lance Corporal to WO1. Granted a direct commission in Italy, he saw service from Naples to Trieste, being fortunate enough to meet Pope Pius XII in St Peters. Having determined to enter Technical Education, from Exeter University he undertook teaching practice at South Devon Technical College. After working in the Edinburgh Education Department, he established Havering Technical College in Hornchurch. Returning to South Devon College as Principal, and implementing building plans devised by George Mackay, he introduced career courses for school leavers with or without entry qualifications, for those with special needs, for the unemployed and for adults. After retiring, on behalf of the Civic Society Arthur re-introduced the 'plaques of famous people' scheme devised by his grammar school history teacher Arthur Ellis.

As Chairman of the Brunel Trust, with Geoffrey Tudor, he prepared a scheme based on Brunel's projected country home at Watcombe. Following studies of the work in South Devon of the painter J.M.W. Turner and of the Carys at Torre Abbey, he hopes to look more closely at the famous builders, engineers and scientists who have lived in Torbay.

Archie Victor Skinner MBE, now living in Alfriston, Sussex, was born at Laurel Cottage, Lisburne Square in October 1927. When about four years old his family moved to 23 Congella Road, Ellacombe - to a newly-built house his parents bought for £775; the builder being a man called White.

With his sister Diana and brother Brian he went to Ellacombe Church School and then on to Audley Park. But his sister Diana went to the Torquay Grammar School. In those days they all walked to school regularly. Archie left school at fourteen years of age. He left on a Friday and started work on the Monday at Ebdon & Graham's shoe repair workshop in the basement of Mr Graham's house, next door to Mr Percy Bragg, then the manager of Shapley's Removals. He had worked for them for three years before leaving school during the evenings and on Saturday mornings. His main job was to take repaired shoes to Stead & Simpsons in the town, and return from them with further supplies needing attention. At eighteen he received his 'call-up' papers on Christmas Eve in 1945, and joined the

Sussex Regiment at Chichester. After initial training he was posted to, and spent the next three years with, the 1st Regiment of the Royal Horse Artillery in Italy, Trieste, Egypt and Palestine. During this time Europe was disturbed with the activities of the Stern Gang and the Irgun.

His army service completed, he had a desire for a different occupation, in the open air. He had always loved flowers and gardens and this led him to apply to the Parks Department of the Local Authority. The Parks Superintendent at that time was a Mr McCready, and Archie started work at Sherwell Park, Chelston, over the years gaining experience in all the different spheres of horticulture, finally spending seven years as propagator of trees and shrubs. He was then put in charge of the nursery at Cockington. During this period he attended evening classes at the South Devon Technical College in order to study botany and horticulture.

In 1971 he was appointed to the post of head gardener and administrator at Sheffield Park Gardens by the National Trust, and left the Torbay Parks Department to live in Sussex with his wife and two children - retiring in 1992. In 1985 he was awarded the Royal Horticultural Society (RHA) Waley Medal for the cultivation of rhododendrons and particularly for the conservation of the Ghent azaleas. In 1988 the RHA made him an Associate of Honour (this Honour can only be held by one hundred people at any one time) awarded for distinguished service to horticulture in the course of his employment.

In 1994 he was awarded the MBE for services to the National Trust and to horticulture. During his time at Sheffield Park he won four gold medals for exhibits from this garden staged at the Royal Horticultural Shows in London. In 1990 he was invited to lecture to the American Rhododendron Society at their Annual Convention in Hyannis. He is still an RHS judge and a judge at the Chelsea Flower Show, at Hampton Court, at Harrogate and at County Shows.

During his career he has continued to keep in touch with the Torquay Horticulture Society and particularly with Don Cockman, another Ellacombe boy who has made such a great contribution to that Society, and to local radio for so many years. Archie still lectures and since his retirement he has written and published a gardening book, *The Stream Garden*.

Stella Margetts (née Coombe) was educated at Homelands School at Plainmoor and later Westlands School, and lived in retirement, until her recent death, at Walnut Road, in Chelston, Torquay. For some years she lived and worked at her father's cafe and ice-cream business premises, situated in Princes Road, Ellacombe.

Throughout the continuing life of the Torquay Leander Swimming and Life Saving Society she has become a cornerstone in the history of swimming activities in Torbay. She joined the Society's committee at the age of 16, in 1930, and became the Devon County Ladies Free-style Champion in 1931. For 28 years she held the post of the Devon County Competition Secretary and, following this, honours were heaped upon her in recognition of her dedication to swimming.

In addition to being made a Life Member of the Western Counties she became President of Leander in 1973, President of Devon County in 1958, President of the West in 1972 and acted as International Timekeeper for 20 years. But the crowning achievement came when she was appointed President of the Amateur Swimming Association and inducted into that Office at the Annual General Meeting and Banquet held at the Grand Hotel, Torquay, in February 1984.

During her year of office Stella flew half-way around the world, travelled thousands of miles by road and rail, and as head of an organisation with more than 1700 clubs and half a million members, presented scores of trophies, including a presentation of medals at the Canadian trials for the Olympic Games which she attended as head of the British A.S.A.

Even at the age of 72 her work has not been confined to administration and teaching, for she has remained a very active and successful swimmer. In October 1984, in the Sun Life English Masters Championships at Weymouth, she won the 70-74 years age group 50 metres freestyle.

There is no doubt that it has been her organising ability, her inspiration and personality that has kept Leander to the forefront of continuing success (*TLS&LSS Commemorative Booklet* by Frank Pearce, 1987).

Edward (Ted) Bragg was born at 17 Princes Road East, Ellacombe, in October 1932. In due course, he attended Ellacombe Primary School. Later, he took and passed the scholarship examination - joining his older brother already at the Torquay Grammar School. As time went by he sat the School Certificate, did reasonably well, and then it was time for him to go out and earn a living.

His first job was with GPO Telephones. Starting at the Chelston Telephone Exchange, he became a Youth in Training. The training was thorough and divided into four parts. In each part he worked in a different section of telecommunications. During that training he was required to take several City & Guilds examinations at the South Devon Technical College. At the end of the training period he successfully qualified as a GPO engineer.

The Ellacombe families he recalled during that time were Mr Fowler (a former Torquay United player) and an overhead GPO foreman, the Bartlett family (a father and two sons) all of whom were senior technicians in the GPO, and George Seely, one of the most able engineers in the Torquay Telephone Exchange.

At the age of eighteen Ted was required to register for National Service and joined the RAF. There he met many similarly qualified GPO engineers. After a variety of postings, all in the United Kingdom, he completed his two years. The time was not wasted. He had seen many parts of Britain, met a wide range of people, learnt a lot about life and gained a few more City & Guilds Certificates.

On leaving the RAF, he returned to his job in the GPO and worked in a number of places - at Trelever in Cornwall, Dartmouth, Brixham and Shiphay. He also worked in the Westhill Exchange, next door to Westhill School, where his Aunt Ethel, Miss Baker, taught, enjoying her reputation as a martinet.

Although this moving around was very enjoyable Ted felt the future held little for him in the GPO so he then looked around for other jobs. In November 1954 he obtained a job in the BBC. He was appointed to the post of technical assistant on the newly-formed Wales/West television Unit. As a rather nervous recruit he entered the portals of Broadcasting House, Whiteladies Road, Bristol, on what was the start of a career that would last thirty-eight years.

From the start he enjoyed the work. In those days there were no set hours, no overtime, no five-day week, but the place was such fun, and so rich in humour and enthusiasm. One of the very early Outside Broadcasts he worked on was the Tall Ships race, starting from Dartmouth. On that occasion the Torbay *Herald & Express* printed a photograph of him at work. At the time he was deeply embarrassed.

His career with the BBC progressed steadily and the advent of commercial television gave many opportunities to the younger qualified engineers. He recalls that it is easy to forget now that when he joined the firm there was no Hessary Tor, indeed there were only seven transmitters throughout the country. He was and still is very fond of Bristol and made many friends there, so it was a serious decision to apply for a job in London. He was appointed Engineering Manager in Television Outside Broadcasts in January 1964, working on a variety of programmes, and then in January 1965 was made responsible for the television operations at St Paul's Cathedral for Sir Winston Churchill's funeral; a significant milestone in his life.

Then he became involved in the televising of many football matches throughout the country and was put in charge of the World Cup matches to be played at Wembley Stadium in 1966. At the time of course he could not know that it was to be the venue for England's victory.

In the course of the next year or so he was responsible for the first Grand National and the first Open Golf Championship to be televised in colour.

It was during this time he married Lillian Lake, whom he first met in Bristol. She had become one of the top make-up designers in television. In 1977 he was promoted to Head of Operations, BBC Television Outside Broadcasts and in 1980 he was given the job of co-ordinating the B.B.C.'c operational output from the World Cup Finals taking place in Spain in the summer of 1982.

His work in the United Kingdom involved him in Royal Weddings, a State Funeral and a couple or more General Elections. In 1989 he was promoted to General Manager, Television Outside Broadcasts. Although this meant being tied to a desk a great deal, he was involved in the transmissions of the Ryder Cup competition from Kiawah Island in 1991 and the broadcasting from St. Louis of the USPGA Championship in 1992. In that year he went to Spain again for the Olympics in Barcelona shortly before retiring in October 1992.

Donald J. Roberts was born at 23 Berea Road, Ellacombe on 5 August 1930. He began his primary education at Babbacombe C of E School in January 1935, transferring to Ellacombe School in the September of the same year. He remained there until 1941 when he left to take up a scholarship at the Torquay Boys Grammar School. In July 1946 he gained eight passes at School Certificate, with distinction in chemistry, and in July 1949 four passes at London Advance Level, with Grade A in pure mathematics, chemistry and geography. Having been awarded a Ballard Scholarship to the University College of the South West, he left school to read chemistry at the

UCSW, later gaining a distinction in subsidiary pure mathematics. In June 1952 he was awarded an Honorary Degree as BSc (London) in chemistry and granted a teachers' certificate in education in 1953.

Donald was called up for National Service and initial training with the Royal Corps of Signals at Catterick, Yorkshire in the September of that year, and was later commissioned as a 2nd Lieutenant in the Royal Signals, serving in Germany. He was promoted to Acting Captain there before being demobilised in 1955 and made a full Lieutenant in the Territorial Army.

After demobilisation he took a post of junior chemistry and mathematics master at Trowbridge High School, in September 1955, and was later appointed assistant chemistry and mathematics teacher at the Torquay Boys Grammar School in September 1957. The previous year Donald married Jane Marilyn Salter at All Saints Church, Babbacombe.

In 1983 he was appointed Head of Gilbert House at the School, finally retiring from full-time teaching in December 1990.

Swimming has been, and remains, an important part of his life. He first joined the Oddicombe Swimming Club as early as 1938, became a school junior breast-stroke champion in 1942 and a Devon County ASA junior breast-stroke champion in 1945. In 1977 he was appointed chief coach of the OSC and elected chairman of the management committee of the new Plainmoor Swimming Pool. In 1984 he was elected President of the Devon County ASA. After 50 years membership he was made an Honorary Member and in 1991 appointed coach to the TBGS swimming and water polo team. Finally - in 1995 he was appointed England Coach to the National Schools under-17 water polo team.

Don Roberts is still actively engaged in the activities of the Torquay Old Grammarians Society, being elected Vice-President in May 1991 and President in November 1993 - later being elected an Honorary Life Member.

Dr Ronald W. Truman was born on 6 January 1934 at 141 Ellacombe Church Road, known as 'Guest Houses', and attended Ellacombe School between 1939 and 1945. His father worked as a compositor on the *Herald & Express*. Ronald won a Scholarship to the Torquay Boys Grammar School in 1945 and, following National Service, took a place to study modern languages at St Edmund Hall, Oxford. He obtained a First-Class Honours Degree and lectured in Spanish at

Birkbeck College, London, for two years before being recalled to Oxford as a Fellow of Christchurch where he is a senior don to this day.

Ronald relates how he used to look over and admire Jack Lark's garden on the corner of Carlton Road from his home. He remembers visits by the French onion boys and their bicycles laden with strings of onions; also the lamp-lighter with his long pole and the man with the 'Hurdy-Gurdy' and monkey.

Philip Wade was born on 23 November 1933 at Pinewood Gardens, Ellacombe - houses built by Cruse & Bridgeman - and attended Ellacombe School between 1939 and 1944. His father worked for Hardings in Market Street. Philip remembers Miss Packe's country dancing classes - recalling the tune of 'Bonnets So Blue' to this day. He won a Scholarship to the TBGS in September 1944 at age 10 - entering Form 2X (an express Form) and proceeded to 4X after one year, missing out Form 3, and was in the last class at the Grammar School to take the old Higher School Certificate in the upper-sixth form.

Philip obtained an early call-up for National Service and served as a clerk in the RAF before taking-up his Open Laming Scholarship to Queen's College, Oxford, to study Modern Languages in 1950. At the end of three years he gained a degree and followed this by gaining his Diploma in Education at Oxford to become a teacher. He taught at Monks Park School in Bristol before returning to the TBGS where he rose to become Head of the Spanish Department. He lives in retirement in Pine View Gardens.

Peter Stotereau was born on 9 February 1963 in the USA and, at the age of ten, with his mother, came to live in Dunmere Road, Ellacombe. He attended the top class at Ellacombe School, where he soon demonstrated his academic ability by passing the 11+ in the July of 1974 to the TBGS. At that School he had a brilliant career, and gained a place to read Natural Sciences at Corpus Christi College. He obtained his degree and followed it with a PhD, and is now continuing his researches in Inorganic Chemistry at Glasgow University.

E.G. Fogwill, son of Frederick George Fogwill, was born on 2 September 1927 at 19 Princes Road West, Ellacombe, and commenced his education at Ellacombe School. He passed the scholarship to enter the TBGS and took his place there on 15 September 1938. He stayed on in the sixth-form and gained a County Exhibition to read geography at University College, London gaining a First Class Honours Degree in 1948.

Eric J. Easterbrook lived at 19 Victoria Road, Ellacombe, where his mother and father had a coooked-meat shop. He attended Ellacombe School and was a member of the school swimming team. In 1942 he won a scholarship to the TBGS, where he had a spectacularly successful academic career. A string of form prizes in the lower school was followed by a special fifth-form prize for obtaining seven distinctions in the School Certificate - the Bruce Paine English, Chemistry and form prize. In the Higher School Certificate two years later he gained distinctions in Physics and Chemistry and was awarded the W. H. Lord Chemistry Prize.

Eric gained a Devon County Exhibition to study at Imperial College, London, which was deferred until he had completed two years National service in the RAF. Returning to academic life in 1951 he graduated at Imperial with a First Class Honours, BSc(Eng.) and became an Associate of the Royal School of Mines. He was also awarded the Bessemer Prize and Medal and the Edward Ernest Glenny Scholarship for the best student.

Eric then spent six years doing industrial research before taking up an appointment as lecturer at St. John Cass College, which was part of the City of London Polytechnic - a post he held until his retirement in 1986.

He earlier had married Rowan Wills at Cockington Church. Rowan's parents owned Wills' cake shop in Woodville Road, and the couple are now happily retired in Shute, East Devon.

Henry Robert Rooke was born in 1902 at 16 Wellington Road, Ellacombe, where his father was a grocer's assistant at Slades on the Strand. He began his education at Ellacombe School, where gained a Scholarship to the TBGS. On leaving in 1920, he entered the Town Clerk's office and rose to chief clerk in 1946. In 1924 he was appointed to the responsible post of Mayor's Secretary, in which he was essentially 'the right man in the right place'. He served in this post for 43 years under thirty-eight different mayors, arranging all their public engagements and ceremonies with tact, diplomacy and patience.

On his retirement in 1969, when the Torbay County Borough was inaugurated, he became the twenty-third and last Freeman of the Borough of Torquay. His immense store of knowledge of the people and affairs was not wasted, as he continued to act as a consultant to the new Authority for the first years of its existence. His vast knowledge of local authority precedure was of great assistance when giving lectures on the subject at the South Devon Technical College and other local organisations during his early retirement.

Although not a pupil of Ellacombe School, the author feels it would not be right to close this chapter without mentioning one of its longest-serving teachers and civic dignitories, **Henry S.B. Hoare**, who has contributed so much to the school, the parish and Torquay. Harry was born at Dawlish in 1880 - moving when young to Kingsteignton, where he was apprenticed as a pupil-teacher at the village church school. Later, after three years in West Somerset he was appointed as an assistant master at Ellacombe Boys School, where he served for thirty years.

Keenly interested in every form of school sport, he founded the Torquay Schools Swimming and Rowing Association and was chairman for many years. During the First World War he became chairman of the newly-formed Torquay Allotment Association and played a leading part in extending the movement. He was also involved in the inception of the National Savings Movement, becoming a member of the South West Regional Committee.

He was awarded the MBE for his services to the War Weeks of 1939-1945. Mr Hoare was also a prominent member of the National Union of Teachers and treasurer of the Teachers Provident Society. He was a churchwarden of Cockington Church, president of the Torquay Corinthian Cricket Club and a former president of the Shiphay Horticultural Society and Chelston Allotments Association.

As far as his civic duties were concerned he served as an Independent member of the Town Council for Cockington-with-Chelston and was vice-chairman of both the Parks and Housing Committee and representative on the Torbay Divisional Education Executive, vice-chairman of Torquay secondary school governors, chairman of Torquay county primary school managers, a governor of the South Devon Technical College and representative of the Borough on the Education Committee of the Association of Municipal Corporations. He became the first president of the Association of Retired Teachers. He died a few days after his ninety-second birthday in 1972.

Chapter 9 - Family Beginnings

Although in many ways, and perhaps sadly not so today, working life and social activities in the early 20th century were well and truly centred within the boundaries of the parish and the local school. Belief in the religion of one's parents was deeply ingrained. However, improved education began to make the established order of things more open to question: more interesting social and athletic activities were found to be often available outside the confines of the church and chapel halls. Better wages and working conditions brought more opportunities within the grasp of individuals, breaking the chains of Victorianism and paternalism.

I was born at 5 Mount Herman Road, off what is now Windsor Road. My father, having joined the Royal Navy in 1894, retired after 25 year's service, and returned home just before the Great Depression - investing his retirement savings in both a house and a 'fish and chip' business at the rear of the building abutting a back lane. This was destined to fail before long, due to the post-war Depression, and to his unbusinesslike principle of helping the unfortunate with 'tick'.

The author's boyhood home at Mount Herman Road. The family fish and chip business was situated in the lane at the back of the houses.

He had been born in the Barbican area of Plymouth, and baptised in Charles Parish Church (now just a shell, after the Plymouth blitz), in 1874. The family, as far back as 1808, when my great-great grandfather was married at the same church, were all seafaring folk. Three of his brothers were all master mariners. His son William became a master mariner too, and was listed in the Plymouth 1851 Census as 'Master of a Smack'. He later became owner of a ketch which he named *Rosa Maria*, the christian names of his eldest (living) granddaughter, which he worked on the coastwise traffic trade. Unfortunately he died at the age of fifty of gangrene, after a leg amputation, leaving my great grandmother a working owner, and her eldest son (my grandfather) its master.

The whole family moved to Torquay in the late 1870s. My grandfather, himself a master mariner, carried on the family business, mainly conveying sand, gravel and stone, etc. from various local quarries (including contracts with Messrs Webber & Steadham in Albert Road and Grant's Marble Works at Watcombe).

One of his eight sons (he also had three daughters) was born in Bridport, Dorset, where a contract to provide building materials for the construction of West Bay Harbour was being completed, and my grandfather and his wife were staying at a local hostelry. The family business also provided building materials for the construction of the Royal Naval College, Dartmouth and other local public works.

In the late 1880s my grandfather obtained 'rights' to dredge the River Dart, and founded a sand and gravel business there, later based at Galmpton, where traces of the old weighbridge and the track for the steam crane still remain visible on the 'sand quay' to this day. The Business was to last nearly ninety years - finally going into voluntary liquidation in 1969-70.

When grandfather retired (he died at the age of 93) the business was left in the hands of three of his sons - William (the Eldest), Edwin and Ernest, together with their sons and grandsons. William, my uncle, was at one time master of the SS *Start Bay*, owned by John N. Philip of Combeleigh, Dartmouth, at the time operating locally as a passenger steamer.

Old Torquinians will certainly remember the family fleet of ketches - the *Hope*, the *Effort* and the *Mizpah* which were for many years used as

A watercolour of the Hope, *one of the Langmead Brothers' sand barges c. 1910.*

committee boats for the Torbay regattas. One was usually berthed at South Pier, and another by the old diving board off Princess Pier (swimming and diving events) in the Outer Harbour.

Photographs of these ketches in Torquay Harbour, and under repair at Philip's Yard on the River Dart in the early '30s, are on display at the Maritime Museum at Greenwich. Remains of the ribs and keelson of the *Effort* can still be seen in the mud at low tide in Galmpton Creek, and the wreck of the *Mizpah* lies up Mill Creek, Dartmouth, with a rusty iron barge moored along-side. Both vessels were built by Wm Date's Shipyard on the upper reaches of the Salcombe Estuary near Kingsbridge, in 1898 and 1880 respectively.

My mother had been a pupil, pupil-teacher and teacher at St James' School in Upton. She is recorded as living in the Local Board Buildings in Market Street in the 1891 census, where family

Bill Langmead and Stan Martin (of Galmpton) on the sand quay at Galmpton c. 1960. The steam crane is unloading sand from the river, with the grader and washer standing behind. Later the sand was loaded on to lorries at the weighbridge on the quay.

The Mizpah *and* Effort *in Torquay Harbour, 1935. These two vessels operated on the tides, dredging sand on the Dart and delivering to Torquay Quay. Later the business was operated from Galmpton, delivering sand and gravel using a fleet of lorries. The business closed in 1969-70.* National Maritime Museum

Unloading a sand barge at Torquay quay in the 1930s. At this time sand was offloaded by canvas bucket and derrick. National Maritime Museum

'lore' has it that her father drove the six or eight horses of the old fire engine, stationed in the rear yard. My father, then aged 17, resided nearby in Queen Street, above the rear of Pimlico, and earlier (1881 Census) in the Madrepore Road.

Later in this chapter I record my early recollections of this aspect of my family history. But here I record my memory of my old grandfather living with my mother and father in our house in Princes Road East during his last years of retirement. I recall how, in his early nineties, he would walk all the way from Ellacombe to the Fish Quay and back for his daily 'cuppa' at Stockman's Cafe. All fisher-folk and longshoremen will surely remember this cafe. The Stockman brothers, after destruction of the old buildings on the Fish Quay, continued a similar business at Beacon Quay, and later one of the brothers for many years ran a restaurant at premises under the Odeon Cinema, off Lower Union Street.

PERSONAL RECOLLECTIONS

I find the mind rather like the memory of a computer, in that I truly believe all our recollections in life, all our happy and sad times, are stored away in the recesses of the mind rather like a 'hard

William Date's shipyard, Kingsbridge c. 1890. This is the yard which built the Mizpah *and* Effort. Cookworthy Museum

disc', and it is a great pity we are not always able to access them easily without the benefit of the appropriate reference.

Many of the earliest memories of my childhood are vivid and permanent - others are simply hazy, but when put together with those of my brothers, they form a wide picture of our childhood.

Our home at Mount Herman Road was roomy and rambling, with a largish garden terminating in the specially-constructed fish and chip shop. This led to a rough back lane running diagonally from Woodville Road (then Higher Ellacombe Church Road) to Belmont Road above.

My very first friend was called Frankie Leach, who, along with his sisters, lived in the top house of Mount Hermon Road, where it joined Belmont Road. Sisters were 'unmentionables' to us boys at that age. We boys played in each other's gardens, in the back lane, and in the little park facing Windsor Road.

I recall never-ending mountains of potatoes turned into chips by a hand-operated slicer, and the all-pervading and deeply inviting smell of real beef dripping. The batter used by my father in his cooking was a very personal and private concoction. Fish came fresh from the quay, or packed with ice direct from Hull or Aberdeen by rail. I was always intrigued, as a child, to see barrels of fish packed in ice on the quay ready to be shipped up to Billingsgate via Torquay Station,

and on the down platform watching similar consignments of fish being unloaded for despatch to local fish merchants and shops.

My grandmother (on my mother's side) dominated the household, as did many old folk in Victorian times. She sat in a chair in the corner of the living room, where she 'held court', in severe black dress of the time, edged in white trim with a little white lace cap. She issued her instructions to all and sundry, particularly my poor overworked mother. Ill befell any who questioned her authority or opposed her will. Being the youngest of three sons (apart from a younger brother who died within a few days of birth) I was the 'spoilt child'. Later, I was to be known by my contemporaries as 'Ginger' for obvious reasons. I remember being photographed mounted on a lovely old wooden rocking-horse in the garden of No. 5.

From Mount Herman Road, after the shop business folded, we moved house to a small estate at the top of what is now Congella Road. At that time I can remember nothing but open fields reaching down to the pond that lay at the head of Lower Ellacombe Church Road, above the Brewery (Brewery Park). The pond lay within a small copse of firs - more a dump than any pretention of being a beauty spot. Certainly, when it was later dredged, a surprising variety of hardware, old bicycles, mangles, gas boilers, etc. came to light.

St James' School, Upton c. 1900. The author's mother was at the school as a pupil, pupil-teacher and finally as a teacher. THE

I recall some sort of pit in the centre of the field (Joy's Field?) below my new home, where I and our newly-acquired dog, Chum, used to play. From the woods above Congella Road (Warberry Copse) a footpath led steeply down through more fields (The Quinta) to Babbacombe Road, and thence across that Road to Walls Hill. This, in later years, was to become a favourite walk for Chum and I, leading to many great imaginary adventures into the then undiscovered delights of Anstey's Cove, Redgate Beach and Bishop's Walk.

These were the happy, indeed delightful, days when children could almost wander at will some distance from home, with no fear of molestation, and in the sure knowledge of refreshment and welcome from the houses of both relatives and friends.

The stately firs of Warberry Copse (so sadly recently devastated by storm), and its intricate network of pathways, was our 'Sherwood Forest', where our 'gang' fought many a battle with the soldiers of the dastardly Sheriff of Nottingham. Bows were made with string and local 'yew', while arrows were given direction and weight by the insertion of nails in the tips of thin saplings.

At the head of what is now Grange Road, there was a small pond where we slaked our thirst from a running stream, washed the mud from our knees, and made running repairs to our clothing in the hopes of avoiding 'boxed ears' on returning home.

The family were not very long at Congella Road before moving again - this time to an almost new house in the (then) recently erected bottom end of Princes Road East. These houses had been built by Heard, a local builder, good stone-built properties that have withstood the ravages of time with

The author's dog, Chum, who lived from 1922-39.

Fun and Games

Above: *Torquay c. 1898. Crowds throng the flag-bedecked harbour to watch the regatta in progress.* JP

Right: *Torbay Royal Regatta Fair c. 1890.* THE

Below: *All the fun of the fair! The reggata fair in the late 1890s. The steam-powered roundabout, stalls and sideshows, annually attracted huge crowds.* JP

Above: *Regatta Fair in 1954 when it was still held along the harbourside.* THE

Left: *Haldon Pier at regatta time. Passngers are disembarking probably from the pleasure steamer* Duchess of Devonshire. TNHM

Below: *The diving stage at the pier during the regatta in 1959.* THE

Above: *Diving Championships 1959. Stella Coombe presenting prizes.* THE

little or no damage or deterioration. They will remain so far longer than those put up in the post-war era that transformed and urbanised this area of Ellacombe

This was to be my home until 'called to arms' as a young Territorial at the tender age of seventeen. My mother, who died away from Torquay at the wonderful age of 93, would often recall me sitting at the foot of steep steps leading up to our front door, ice-cream in hand and Chum at my side, little realising that whilst I watched events passing me by on the road, my old dog was greatly relishing the opportunity of an occasional or extended lick of my ice-cream cornet!

I remember, with nostalgia, Heard & Bentley's general stores in Princes Road East, particularly Miss Bentley, a rather forbidding lady with a twinkle in her eye, but one who nevertheless always welcomed children shopping for their parents or calling to purchase sweets, etc.

Some of the happiest times of my life were spent in this era, before the Second World War came to change our lives irrevocably. As we grew it was almost an essential to join one of the local 'gangs', not the young thugs, I may add, that terrorise local urban areas today, but gangs, nevertheless, who were not above the odd fisticuffs or rough and tumble with other gangs. This was an important part of maturing into a tough old world.

The most popular time of the year was the period running up to bonfire night, when each gang ranged the neighbourhood looking for inflammable material with which to build their own 'pyre'. There was plenty of open space available for this purpose in those days. We were known as 'Heard's Gang', and we built our bonfire on waste ground at the edge of Brewery Park, where Denys Road now stands. Our nearest rivals and bitter enemies were the 'Stentiford Hill Gang' and many a tussle took place during raids and confrontations on both sides. Tunnels were bored through to the centre of our big bonfires, and within them (dangerously), tactics and strategies were planned and formulated. Being a natural-born organiser, I would arrange firework parties in our back lane, even at an early age, paid for by parents and attended by neighbours and their children.

Another of my 'brainwaves' was possible because of the lay-out of the garden at the rear of our house. The garden rose steeply, via steps leading from the back lane, to what was then a large allotment, divided from our garden by thick brambles and stinging nettles. The garden was crowned by my father's small greenhouse and garden hut. On this hut I positioned a paste jar over a small electric bulb, ran a twin cable down the garden and over the back lane and yard to my bedroom. To the wire I attached a war-surplus morse-tapper and my pal, Richard Wills, set up a similar arrangement two doors away. From our bedrooms, after dark, we were thus able to transmit vital messages to each other, in secret code of course! This did not precipitate the Second World War, but it did wonders for our morse appreciation.

The garden hut was a real den of discovery for me. My father's career in the Royal Navy had taken him to many corners of the world, and mementos of those journeys were there in abundance, covered in dust. Among those I remember in particular (being the usual warmongering young firebrand) were an old Turkish rifle from the Dardenelles campaign; a Turkish shell (with contents removed, of course), and with a brass plate attached inscribed 'Dardenelles, Gaba Tepe April 25, 1915' (still in our hallway today); an old assagai blade to which I later fixed a long cane (more of this anon) and the remains of a Zulu fighting shield.

I was never happier than at my father's knee listening to his 'service' stories when he (but rarely) was in the mood for reminiscences. There were exciting tales of chasing pirates in the China Sea in a brass-funnelled steam pinnace, complete with a Maxim gun on the foredeck. He told tales of campaigning with the Naval Gun Brigade in the Boer War; serving as Coxswain to HRH Prince Louis of Battenberg who commanded HMS *Cambrian* 1894-1897; and recalled dangerous days ferrying Australian and New Zealand troops ashore in barges during the assaults on the shore defences in the Dardenelles Campaign.

And so I spent happy but somewhat dangerous days hurling the 'fighting spear' from one side of Brewery Park to the other until one day when the blade landed in the foot of one of my close friends, Bertie Chalker (later to become a Director of Messrs Renwick, Wilton & Dobson, the coal merchants). His mother was not pleased!

But there were other happy days with Bertie (who lived above us in Princes Road East). We were often in one another's houses playing mock 'battles' with regiments of toy lead soldiers and cannons that fired matchsticks. Or we would pump up leather footballs, with adapters on bicycle pumps, securing them with leather laces with a special tool before departing to the park to emulate Torquay United's talented footballers.

Games we played were many and varied, and most comprised of simple materials. Some you bought, such as thimble-sized cap bombs thrown high to land with a bang. Bowling hoops were fun, and if one could'nt afford to purchase a wooden one, then an old bicycle wheel would suffice. Of course conkers' and marbles were common enough as games of skill, and the collectors of cigarette cards of aircraft, footballers, cricketers, army uniforms, film stars and many other subjects, had their devotees. I was one, and still have an album. We often played games on the pavement with 'seconds' where those who flicked a card that lay across another collected 'extras' for swapping.

Girls, of course, had their own favourite games. Spinning tops of brightly-coloured metal, or small wooden ones whipped with string on a stick. They also played hop-scotch on chalked pavements, played with diabolos and yo-yos, and, of course, with the perennial skipping ropes.

My father, by then being retired and being an ex-seaman, was employed by Shapleys the Grocers, then in business at the bottom of Fleet Street. Part of his duties entailed looking after the owner's sailing boat. It was in this, and in my father's own dinghy, that I leaned to sail and fostered a great love of the sea and sailing. Many a happy hour was spent on the water, both with my brothers and on my own or with Chum.

Later my eldest brother joined the Royal Navy, and nearly every year a vessel on which either my father or my brother had served or had friends, would lay at anchor in the bay. I would then be a privileged visitor, taken below into mess-decks to be regaled with cake and chocolate, being instructed in gunnery(!) in turrets large and small, or allowed to clamber down a maze of ladders to see the great gleaming engines at rest. The Royal Navy was a close 'family'. Knowing many of the 'longshoremen' my father made possible supernumary 'crew' trips in the Bay's pleasure boats, speedboats and the occasional fishing boats. In between, my brothers and I would row out to fish for mackerel on a spinner or anchor for dabs.

The Torbay Royal Regatta was the highspot of the year. Across Torbay were sights I would remember all my life: row upon row of warships, from tiny submarines and torpedo boats to huge dreadnoughts, anchored in lines from Torquay to Brixham, 'dressed overall' for review by the King and Queen in the royal yacht. At night great searchlights criss-crossed the sky.

These were also the days of wealthy racing yachtsmen such as Sir Thomas Sopwith - the days of the superb J-class yachts like the *Britannia*, *Endeavour*, *Astra*, *Velsheda* and others, and the graceful steam and motor yachts of the rich and famous anchored in the Bay and outer harbour.

I recall one particular J-class yacht moored within Princess Pier in shelter from a violent summer gale. I stood with my mother in Princess Gardens watching a crew member at work high on the incredibly tall mast of this huge yacht, only to see him fall (with horror) to the deck, to lie injured or dead - I do not remember more.

The evenings of the regatta were a child's paradise. All around the inner harbour the annual fair was laid out, from circular stalls with 'hoop-la' and electronic 'rings', to those selling candy floss, toffee apples and the inevitable fish and chips. There were great roundabouts with their tossing horses, while music from their beautifully painted organs filled the air. The ferris wheel and helter-skelter both stood on South Pier, along with palmists, astrologers and boxing booths for the adventurous.

At the end of the day came the magnificent firework display on the Fish Quay, supplemented by water fireworks tossed on the water in the outer harbour on floats. Sheer magic, for young and old alike.

As mentioned earlier, my uncles' sand barges were used each year as committee boats for the yachting regatta and for the swimming and diving events which took place beneath the great diving board, then sited on Princess Pier.

Right up to 1867, when the old custom was abolished, Torquay from time immemorial, held an Easter Fair on Easter Monday in Lower Union Street, and at Torre Square and East Street. In 1878, however, there were rowdy and disorderly scenes in the Torre Abbey fields which the few policemen on duty were powerless to check, and it took heavy rain late in the evening to disperse the crowd!

The Torquay Regatta Fair dates from 1841 (firework displays commenced 1836), when the Strand appeared as a fair with many booths, a show of wild beasts, swings and roundabouts. There were rural sports 'above the turnpike' which attracted many who appeared to enjoy the donkey racing rather than the yacht racing! Another amusement was the 'Dittisham Women Pulling', and during that period, before the Crimean War, a 'breakfast was held at 1 o'clock as well as a Ball at night'.

There were many ingenious events in those days: a 'trades' rowing match - the entrants dressed in many colours using spades, shovels, scoops, etc. as allowable propellants. Aquatic sports included the 'great sheepshanks leg-I-see' (a greasy bowsprit walk for a leg of mutton), 'grand drive-in matches by grotesquely-attired swimmers, and a 'Mrs Neptune' with monstrous hoops!

In order to reduce the risk of cholera in 1866 the authorities forbade the entry of 'Fair People' and tried to remove them to Ellacombe Green and later to Daddyhole Plain.

The regattas would end with a garden Party at Torre Abbey and presentation of cups, etc. and a Ball at the Town Hall at night.

My uncles' sand barges were principally used, of course, for dredging purposes on the River Dart. This was the basis of the Langmead Brothers Sand & Gravel Business which operated from the Dart for some ninety years. In the early days the sand was brought up from the Dart by sea and landed on the Fish Quay for local disbursement. Later, the barges spent their last days on the Dart, landing the sand and gravel on Galmpton Quay.

It was to Galmpton that I would be transported from the Pavilion, early in the morning, in one of the firm's blue lorries, to spend a happy day aboard the *Effort* or the *Mizpah* dredging - often trying, hopelessly, to shoot a poor unfortunate heron or cormorant with an ancient airgun. I recall drinking mugs of steaming tea made with condensed tinned milk - so strong that the spoon would almost stand up in the liquid of its own accord.

Although we were not as poor as some, times were very hard in the 1920s and 1930s. But for those that could afford it, food was plentiful and extremely nourishing. I remember particularly Hayward's off-licence at the bottom of Princes Road, opposite Chave's Garage on the one side and Shapley's Furniture Removers' garage on the other. On the counter, in front of racks displaying barrels of cider for collection in jugs, and bottles of Guinness and other beers, were stone jars containing tongue, beef and brawn (made from sheep's heads). Ham was 'off the bone'. Little wheels operated a mechanism within the jars that lifted the meats so that slices could be cut off the top with long-bladed knives.

Next to the off-licence was a cool, inviting dairy. It was my mother's habit to have pineapple chunks for Sunday dinner sweet, and I was regularly sent down to the dairy in the morning to collect the Devonshire clotted cream. This was normally transported in a glass dish which was weighed on the shop scales before it was filled, and the cream covered with a square of grease-proof paper. With the promise of my mother that I could 'lick the paper' on return in mind, I would wend my way homewards slowly up Princes Road, alternately pressing the paper on the cream and pulling it off to lick it!

Sunday teas were a pre-church ritual and invariably included plates of 'tuffs' (small bread buns), cut in half, coated generously with clotted cream, with spoonfuls of home-made jam invitingly deposited on each. Homemade cake, always baked on a Thursday (coconut for my eldest brother, fruit cake for the middle one and plain Madeira for me) was baked by our thoughtful mother.

Then to church in our Sunday-best for Evensong at 6.30pm. After church began a further regular Sunday ritual, especially when the better weather arrived. All the young people, and the mobile seniors, would head down Market Street to the Strand. About this time, after the conclusion of their own evening service, the Salvation Army Band would assemble at their Citadel in Market Street, next to the old Police Station, and then - headed by a great local character known as 'Skimpole' - would, to the stirring notes of drum and brasses, march down through Union and Fleet Streets, to form a circle on the slipway of the Inner Harbour. Here they held an open-air service for the public at large.

On May 11 1888, an incident was reported in contravention of the Section of the Harbour Act which said that 'No procession shall take place on a Sunday in any street or public place in the district accompanied by any instrumental music'. This was the second of such incidents (the first at Honiton in December 1882), when the Salvation Army directly challenged the authorities on what was later to become their regular Sunday evening march from the Citadel Headquarters in Market Street to the Harbourside. On the first occasion the great Miss Eva Booth was present, who later was the subject, with other Salvationists, of a prosecution for taking part in an illegal musical procession.

In my day, all the 'young bloods', by then over-full with religion, would depart for the Sunday promenade along the sea front towards Torre Abbey, chatting up the girls (but with a wary eye open for their parents or friends) and back along shady Rock Walk, if you were lucky in love!

Many other highlights in my young life come readily to mind. One day, probably on the occasion of a birthday, I came indoors sensing excitement. Low and behold, entry into the living

Heroes of the Salvation Army at Torquay who were arrested and imprisoned for upholding their right to march on a Sunday, in May 1888. Photo by kind permission of Major Harvey SAHQ Torquay

room revealed a gleaming new bicycle in green, covered crankcase shining, complete with a three-speed Sturmey-Archer gear. The bike was built by Swifts, I believe made for the Co-op. I was over the moon! How my father and mother managed it I will never know - probably by going without some pleasures of their own as loving parents are wont to do. How I treasured that bicycle, polishing and burnishing it every day. Pennies were saved for many weeks to purchase a dynamo-powered lighting set - a very modern innovation at that time.

There was no National Health Service, of course, in those days. Every week I was sent to a private house in St Anne's Road at Babbacombe, there to pay a small weekly sum into what was then known as The National Deposit Friendly Society. This guaranteed a medical service through a 'panel' doctor and hospital treatment at the Torbay Dispensary - then situated next to the present Court House in Upper Union Street. It was to this establishment I was transported to have infected tonsils removed (one day and home again!).

Door-to-door services were provided for essential household requirements. Milk was delivered, in the early days, by horse and cart. Housewives or family would emerge with milk jugs, to have them filled from a giant metal milk churn, by means of pint or half-pint metal ladles with hooked handles. There were no refrigerators, and milk jugs were often stored in metal boxes or on slate-covered shelves in cool larders, covered with little bead-hung nets to keep off the flies.

Most Devon housewives made their own clotted cream in shallow metal pans with milk from pedigree South Devon cattle.

Many older Ellacombe residents will remember the Lander brothers who toured the local streets with their three-wheeled carts selling all types of fresh fish to the stirring cry of 'Fish - Fish Alive-O'. I remember, too, odd gypsy-like characters who ranged from road-to-road on three-wheeled bicycle carts, offering to sharpen kitchen knives and scissors, etc. which they honed on abrasive wheels operated by the cycle pedals. Similar three-wheeled bicycle carts offered Walls ice-cream and triangular water ices.

Bread and cake was also delivered by horse and cart. I remember stables where I used to visit working horses at rest at the corner of Lower Ellacombe Church Road and Berea Road, or being given fresh shoes by the resident blacksmith.

Certainly the Torquay Co-op had a large dairy and stables in the corner of the old Albert Road, next to Webber & Steadham's builders yard. My Uncle Jack managed a corn and flour shop called The Torbay Mill Co. Ltd on the other corner adjoining Market Street.

Regular sights on the roads were the French 'onion boys', with their bicycles hung with strings of onions for sale, and the Italian barrel organs operated by a handle, with little monkeys perched on top clothed in yellow jackets and capped with Egyptian fez.

Other characters in my young life brought to mind by my brother and others, was a man called Albert, whose job it was to operate the tramline junction of Market Street and Union Street, and, I believe, lifted the overhead power arm from one circuit to another and changed the points. Another local character called, appropriately, Charlie Chaplin attended, and often led, the Town Carnival Processions dressed and walking the part. There was also a certain lady, who shall be nameless, with a son who was a notorious poacher, and who would often have his poaching equipment confiscated by the police: this lady, known as Nell would often be seen staggering up Market Street 'in her cups', raucously calling upon the police to return her son's illicit means of livelihood and daring the constabulary to take hold of her without dire consequences.

Another revered gentleman, known as Doctor Dunn, of Castle Road, had a somewhat eccentric habit of insisting that his sons wore highland kilts and walk about the town in bare feet. However, he was manifestly kind to the poor. He was known to visit Washer's Dairy in Market Street daily where he would purchase a fresh egg, pierce its shell, and swallow the contents raw!

Although I had close friends, it would be fair to say I was by nature a 'loner'. Much of my young life was spent wandering the streets on errands, or delivering messages or 'goodies' to sick relatives or friends of my parents - invariably accompanied by Chum. When not on duty in this way, I would be, perhaps, down with my father in Shapley's giant storage warehouse behind (then) Rockeys, drinking in the gorgeous smells of oriental spices, coffee beans, hung sides of bacon, and the many aromas of the old-fashioned grocery store.

Summers seemed endless - dry and always sunny in those days - probably an illusion, of course. Chum loved the beach, the sands and swimming in the sea (after a thrown stick) as did all of us children. No pollution in those days! The dog would sit patiently until buried up to his neck in sand, and when the word was given, jump up and shake himself vigorously to the screams of delight of nearby children. He lived to a ripe old age of eighteen, so it had done him no harm.

We all looked forward to the regular Church Festivals of Christmas, Easter and Harvest. At Christmas there were the carol and midnight services. The choir would form a procession around the church singing carols, and lit by lanterns or candles, preceeded by the verger carrying the cross. At Easter the church would be decorated with bunches of wild primroses and daffodils and other spring flowers. And at Harvest Festivals the church would again be filled with the fruits of nature, corn 'dollies', shaped loaves and mountains of fruit and vegetables of all kinds. Afterwards the choirboys were given the privilege of choosing an apple or pear or other fruit, before the 'goodies' were distributed to the needy, sick and the poor of the parish.

Good Friday was an annual family occasion when my mother would take us to a cottage in Liverton, where resided an old naval colleague of my father and his rosy-cheeked wife. Here we spent the day visiting nearby woods to collect armfuls of wild daffodils and primroses for decorating Ellacombe Church the following day, and then being filled full of rabbit pie and home-made sweets topped with Devonshire clotted cream from the farm across the road, before returning home.

Social activities began at school and widened and developed, generally, through the voluntary work of members of Parochial Church Councils and their social sub-committees. There were no Borough Council leisure centres or theme parks. For the young, fun and games outside the home were organised and developed through the church (or chapel) Young Peoples' Fellowships, or similar organisations.

Adequate clubs existed for men and women of mature age and at work, although the parishes organised many activities of interest to them as well through the medium of the parish halls. There were certainly no rest homes for the elderly as such - only the occasional nursing homes for the terminally ill, if there were family funds available to pay for their keep. Married and unmarried sons and daughters were expected to look after and care for their elderly parents in the twilight of their lives. Today, many of these duties have been taken over by the professional social services.

ELLACOMBE CHURCH MEN'S CLUB OUTING IN 1936

The author is shown arrowed. Among the boys present are Arnold, Bond, Chalker, Cooper, Coppin, Ebdon, Gilbert, Langmead, Marker, Newcombe, Pugh, Powell, Skinner, Smith, White, and Watson. Billy Bond (dec'd) was later a police superintendant at Okehampton. Arthur Cooper (dec'd) was a builder. Arthur Ebdon was a Principal of South Devon Technical College, Percy Pugh a postal officer. Harry Powell was killed in action serving with the RAF. Other notables include Mr Corline (potato merchant), and Brian Tanner, still an active member of the church, with Derrick Collier. Photo loaned by the late Sydney Bryant

Ellacombe Church had, and still has, a generously-sized church hall, and it was there that most young people of the parish met to learn to dance, to play badminton, to have tea and supper parties, to act in plays and to plan rambling expeditions on the moors, etc. during Bank and school holidays, and to organise Sunday school outings.

Scouts, Guides and Brownie packs were usually based on churches. Church social activities were, of course, not the sole prerogative of the young, as all ages were catered for. There were choir outings and suppers, old people's teas, harvest suppers, Christmas Parties and, of course, whist drives and organised indoor and outdoor activities arranged throughout the year. More importantly, the vicar and his supporting curates regularly visited the elderly, the sick and the poor - so that the parish appeared, in those days, to be the cornerstone of one's existence, a warm and enfolding 'family' through good times and bad - and the 1930s certainly saw some bad times.

Church and school were closely linked - particularly in religious education, Sunday schools, confirmations, etc. and on public occasions such as Empire Day and Whitsunday Processions.

My brothers and I attended Ellacombe School, and my middle brother and I sang in the church choir. The eldest was tone deaf! All three rowed for the school in the annual Torbay Regatta - with some success, I may add, as various rowing shields will testify. My middle brother was quite a sportsman, being selected regularly for both the football and cricket first teams. My only claim to fame was to be reserve goalkeeper on an occasion when we beat Ipplepen by 14 goals to nil, and I scored one of them! However - I did aspire to become a manager of the school magazine, responsible for the collection of the fees for advertising in it. In those early days, the boys and girls' schools were quite separate, each with its own Head. Having no sports ground at Ellacombe, we had to walk all the way to Windmill Hill at Hele to indulge in our sporting activities.

Our Headmaster, in my day, was an ex-military man and a stern disciplinarian, and we dreaded being caught for an offence, even of a relatively minor nature, such as talking in class, which invariably led to welts on the hands from a thick cane, harshly applied. But we rarely returned for repeats!

Many readers will, I am sure, remember the names of fine teachers of these times and recall 'Charlie' Parr, Mr Cowling, Mr Tozer, Mr Tomlins and others. We were well and truly grounded in the three Rs. Religious instruction was mandatory, 'tables' were learnt by heart, and good handwriting and spelling was obligatory. Discipline was firm, and as extracts from the School Magazine will testify, we were taught to respect our elders and to work hard and industriously when we left school or we would not be given employment of any kind.

At lunch times, and after school, our parents expected us to help out financially and earn pocket money by undertaking odd jobs such as delivering boot and shoe repairs, medicine from doctors' surgeries and parcels from local shops, chemists, etc. Girls were expected to stitch and sew clothing their mothers had taken in for washing, and help to make their own clothes.

Jubilees and Empire Days were the occasions for important school celebrations, when we sang patriotic songs, and were addressed by important local dignitaries - occasionally being presented with individual mementoes such as Jubilee Mugs and Spoons. There was a high degree of inter-school rivalry in both sporting and academic activities and, indeed, within schools themselves between the various Houses.

Swimming training and competitions took place at the municipal swimming baths near the (then) Marine Spa. I remember one occasion of note when a young child was sucked into the drain pipe of the baths due to some administrative mishap - and the 'hue and cry' *that* caused in the local press. School 'crocodiles' took us to various sites of local and historical interest, such as the Torquay Museum, Kent's Cavern, Grant's Marble Works, Longpark Potteries and others - after which articles describing those visits would appear in the school magazine.

Playgrounds were at the rear of the school. They had tarmac surfaces, high walls and back exits leading to a rear lane (Garden Road). This exited at one end into Windsor Road, and at the other into Ellacombe Church Road. The occasional 'rag-and-bone' man waited in the lane with goldfish in jam jars in exchange for old clothing or rags, bottles, etc.

An equally high stone wall divided the boys from the girls, and prevented any fraternisation within school hours. Any innocent boy or girl liaisons took place on the way to and from the school, or away from its influence.

Chapter 10 - Fond Memories

The following extracts are taken from correspondence and interviews recorded during the early 1990s with people who have close connections with Ellacombe. They reflect the life and society of the area in times gone by and are a reminder that change is not always for the better.
The names of interviewees, and the dates the interviews were made, are as follows:

MRS CARRIE (NÉE PYM) 12.1.93
MRS NORA DOWELL (NÉE BLIGHT) 12.1.93
MRS AMY STEPHENS (NÉE FROST) 13.11.92
MRS DOLLY WEYMOUTH (NÉE ZAPLE) 8.10.92
MISS MARY CORLINE 28.1.93
MR KEN SELLEY 6.1.93
MR TED & BILL SHAPLEY 5.2.93
MRS WINNIE DYER (NÉE CASELY) 27.2.93
MR A A BASTIAN 24.6.85
MR STANLEY CROCKER 3.6.93
MR B A CHALKER 30.5.93
MR BILL ELLIOTT
MR ARCHIE SKINNER

MR TED BRAGG
MR & MRS LES GIBBONS 16.12.93
MR V FELLOWS 18.3.94
MR KEN GRAHAM 24.11.94
MR KEN LASSETER 15.12.94
MR PERCY DIMMOCK 11.1.95
MR & MRS STAN ROBERTS 24.1.95
MISS GWEN DOWNEY 21.9.95
MR HENRY HANSON 31.9.95
MISS LILIAN BROWN 15.2.95
MR & MRS GILBERT FURNEAUX 12.5.95
MRS STELLA MARGETTS (NÉE COOMBE) 6.9.95
MR DON ROBERTS 10.1.96

MRS CARRIE PYM

My early memories were intensely sad ones, as both my mother and father died when I was about eight. I was born in 1905 in Braddons Street, next to Andrews' shop. We were to move to Melville Street, but my mother died first, and then my father two years later. This was in 1914, just before World War One. I had to look after my mother during her illness and also my father after her death until his. In between this I attended St John's Church School in the Braddons.

My mother died singing 'Rock of Ages' and I hid under the bedclothes until someone came to help me. Looking back I recall a so-called Relieving Officer calling at Braddons Street, a man with horrid eyes, who gave my mother a 2/6d grocery ticket and told her that that was all he could offer, except a consignment letter for the Workhouse at Newton Abbot. My father was a fisherman with his own 'crabber' and also a member of the lifeboat crew who then operated from Beacon Cove. He was a wonderful swimmer and would often appear back home just in his trousers. His boat was later sold to Mr Kent in Ellacombe to whom he would earlier sell his crabs and lobsters. One day, walking backwards against the wind during a visit to my uncle's in Alexandra

Road, I ended under a horse and felt its hard knees pressing into my back. My uncle worked as a horseman for Grist's Riding School in Wellswood.

I recall shopping for my mother at Reads, the butchers in the Market. Sixpence would purchase enough breast of lamb, stewing beef and suet for a stew in a large saucepan (white inside) with suet dumplings my mother called 'dough boys'. In the stew would go 2lbs of leeks, carrots, onions, parsnips and other vegetables bought for 2d at Stamps garden shop at the bottom of Market Street. Often families would have no funds for fuel, and would rely on the generosity of one who was able to cook. Jordans, the bakers, would offer cooking facilities in their ovens for 2d.

I was baptised at the St Barnabas 'Tin' Church and was made to attend St John's Church Sunday School punctually. The Vicar of St Barnabus was the Revd Ford - a very kind man who would invite children to his home for tea and to play croquet on the lawn. I loved music as a young child and would dearly have loved a piano to play. Miss Harkney was my school Headmistress in the little Church School in the Braddons. Although a stern and frightening figure, she turned out to be kindness itself. She said 'you've lost your Mummy and have nowhere to go. Would you like to come and live with me?' So I did - to Marnham Road, near Plainmoor, where the soldiers in training would march on Boston Fields. I remember how she used to wash my long hair in bay rum and taught me the skill of cooking meals in hay boxes.

Later I moved to live with my sister in Alexandra Road near the Ellacombe Post Office where I then attended Ellacombe School from about age 12 to 14. I can remember only two teachers, a 'Maggie' Churchill and a Miss Toll. We were taught the three Rs of course, but also darning, cooking and all forms of housewifery. I was the star pupil at buttonholing and a form of embroidery known as 'gophering' (to make wavy, flute, crimp-lace edge trimming). We were also taught ironing, etc. on periods at Homelands School at Plainmoor under a Miss Dutton. I was picked out to stand in front of class to demonstrate the art of the iron as my mother, a laundress, had taught me well.

I was a delicate child to rear - my mother thought I would not reach maturity (here I am 88!). I remember often going to Burgoynes, the chemist opposite the School, to obtain a potion for my headaches called 'Dr Jones' Headache Powder', which the School doctor warned 'would eventually close the valves of my heart'. After leaving school I went to live with a school friend as I did not get on with my sister, who was ten years older.

My friend lived behind and next to Rockeys in Fleet Street. I first worked for Frank Callard, the bakers, as a scullery maid, scrubbing all the cake racks, drain boards, etc. in all his shops in Belgrave Road, Torwood and Fleet Streets. I remember him as a bow-legged gentleman who would walk every day to work from his home near Torre Station. Equally I recall driving a splinter from the wooden draining board under my finger nail, and having to go to the Hospital in Union Street to have it removed. I still have a remnant embedded in my finger today.

From my friend's home I then became a junior nursemaid, looking after a little girl. When her parents left for Bournemouth I was asked to accompany them and did so for some years. But I was homesick. Then a lady called Irene Watkins was murdered on Fisherman's Walk and I became rather frightened as well, so left Bournemouth and returned to Torquay to live at Spring Place off Pimlico.

From there I went to work at the Devon Steam Laundry until I married. There I worked from 9.00am in the morning until 9.00pm at night, six days a week for the princely sum of 15 shillings a week. There was no half day, no electricity or gas and tea was made on a fire stove. Later I was offered a job of forewoman on the machine, but adamantly refused to support the sacking of the current foreman, so left to work at the council toilets next to the Pavilion Theatre. From early memories of the Braddons I remember 'Hancocks Roundabouts', which used to operate in the quarries where the council houses were later erected, after blasting in Alpine Road. Mr Hancock walked stiffly with an artificial leg. I was fascinated by this, as a child, and volunteered to clean his caravans for him.

I remember the cinema in the Market which was known to the youngsters as the 'Flea Pit'. I especially remember one occasion when I observed a strange elderly lady with a peculiar bead shawl looking straight at me in a rather strange way. I was 15 at the time and found the stare intimidating. Later, outside in Abbey Road, the strange lady approached me and asked if I recognised her. I answered, rather tartly, that I did not. But found, to my astonishment, that I had been recognised as her niece. It seemed I was the image of my uncle Charlie, her husband. He had earlier been a captain of the steamer *King Edward*, and had later emigrated to Canada. His wife, my aunt, had returned to visit her sister at Brixham, called Cameron.

Further early recollections of events are the annual regatta and fair around the harbour. I particularly liked the cake walk, and the dancing on the green which took place at regatta time on Torre Abbey Meadows.

I also recall school trips to Bradley Woods, and on the trams to Paignton, and going to 'Valleys' in Union Street for a 1d hot drink.

We played often in the Warberry Copse with little but a bottle of water and broken biscuits (7lbs for 1d) to sustain me, and old rope from my father's boat with which to fashion a swing.

I rmember buying regularly something called SP from Edwards the Tobacconist for an Annie Lear and being in trouble with my mother when it turned out be snuff!

I would love to sit on a bin in Andrews' shop in Braddons Street happily swinging my legs whilst sucking the contents of a halfpenny bag of sugar knobs.

Characters that also remain prominent in my mind were a rag and bone man called Dicky who travelled regularly through Ellacombe. He limped with one short leg and (I remember) embarrassed the Church at St Michael's in Market Street with references to his children having 'no drawers' until he obtained (proudly) 'combinations' for them.

I recall Easter Days when the 'Hot Cross Bun' man toured the streets with his popular product, and Addison's son and a Mr Bowden of Pennysylvania Road (cornet) who played in the Salvation Army Band. I recall finally leaving my mother one day at Torre Station when a kind lady riding in a carriage gave me 1d and a little lace hanky. I was so entranced I walked behind the carriage all the way in to Torquay, until brought home by a policeman to face a very angry mother who proceeded to 'forke' me! I have in my mind also, Lady Singer riding in her carriage with a face so white with powder I thought her head had been dipped in a flour bin.

MRS NORA DOWELL (NÉE BLIGHT)

I first came to the UK at the age of 2, having been born in 1898 in Ireland, of an Irish mother and an English father. The latter spent 41 years of his life in the Royal Navy, and after leaving, joined the Coastguard Service. He died, later, in Torquay at the age of 80. My mother died when she was 42. She was his first wife. I believe the early days in England were spent in Teignmouth, but I clearly remember celebrating my eighth birthday in Carlton Road - which (as in every house in which we lived) sported a flagpole - an obsession of my mother. I can remember little of my school days, as my mother had what I called an 'itchy bum' and was forever moving house. It follows that we did not spend long at Carlton Road, before moving to Derwent Road and then back to Teignmouth where I finished my schooling and went into 'service' there.

I certainly remember a happy period spend in Coastguard Cottages at Penzance, sitting as a young girl in the window watching the sea traffic movement below. The memory was enhanced by a sting on the backside by a wasp or bee and my tears being stilled by my father by his ministrations. On returning to Carlton Road from Teignmouth I became a housemaid and then an upper housemaid at Ridgehill in the Warberries between Barrington Road and Middle Warberry Road. Other staff working there I remember as the Misses Allison, Graham and Shaw. My employers owning the property were related to the Guinness family and they constantly visited a Mr Hooper, a Solicitor who lived at 'Ardvar' between Cedar Road and Higher Warberry Road.

There was much entertaining. Although work was hard and the days long, I was very happy there. I had to be on call and work from 7.00am to 9.00pm every day of the week, with only one half-day off a fortnight, which was usually spent playing cards in the servant's hall. There was nothing else to do!

We were usually 'stood off' for one week in winter. No dole money (no stamp). I had to be on duty at all times - woe betide me if the bell rang from upstairs and I was not immediately available to answer it. Nevertheless, we were fed very well and there was plenty to drink at Christmas and other festive occasions. There were two regular butlers, two drawing room staff, two housemaids and lady's maid, apart from outdoor staff. I remember the 'lady of the house' constantly grumbling at the price of meat - in those days (with the family, the staff and the entertaining) costing her from £20–£24 a week!

For this job I received the large sum of 10 shillings a week! Walking-out was restricted because one found it difficult to afford 1d for a tram journey. At this time my niece (already working there), advised me that Marks & Spencers, who had recently opened in Union Street, were recruiting staff. After being interviewed by Mrs Davey, the secretary, I went to work in the shop, where I remained for 25 years. I take it as a mark of great respect for staff relations that the company presented me with a gold watch in 1988 to celebrate my ninetieth birthday.

I met my husband (who died 12–15 years ago) at a dance at the Town Hall at Christmas time, which I attended with two girl friends. At the time he drove a taxi for a firm by the name of Dells. Later he became a driver employed by Devon General. After marriage we lived with my mother and father happily for five years in Park Hill Road. My strongest memory was of the many trips my parents arranged for family groups through the hire of 'brakes' from Mr Cordell's Stables at the top of Market Street. A 'brake' was a coach which could carry about 15 people.

Often a smaller 'brake' carrying 8–12 people would be hired, as well, for a day's outing and would follow behind the bigger vehicle. We would leave at 6.00am in the morning and always return before dark - travelling quite far afield. There would be no change of horses - only stops at farms to water them or to purchase eggs and other farm produce. Often there would be other emergency stops when, for example, wheels would catch fire - say going down Watcombe or Shaldon Hills!

Other little memories that come to mind are purchasing cooked pigs trotters for 2d from Pascoes in Market Street. On being questioned by my mother about my whereabouts I often replied 'on Ellacombe Green, eating pigs trotters'.

I can remember once being on a tram at the top of Market Street when the vehicle went out of control and careered backwards down the Street until 'bottoming-out' near Union Street. I was so scared I jumped off, awkwardly, at the bottom whilst the tram was still in motion and injured my arm and leg. There were sparks flying everywhere and the driver had to climb on the roof to deal urgently with the problem at the overhead wire junction.

AMY STEPHENS (NÉE FROST)

I was born in 1909 in one of three little cottages which then overlooked the present Coach Station in Lymington Road, Torquay. My father was born in Ellacombe Church Road, near Ellacombe School - where he later became a pupil - and my mother in Broadhempston, near Totnes. His parents were also born in Ellacombe Church Road, opposite the School. Later my mother moved to 215 Lymington Road. She was 'in service' at the Livermead Hotel, where she met my father.

The Season, in those days, extended from October until May - not a summer one as today. My grandfather was head gardener at a house called 'Hove' in St Marychurch Road. I remember him telling me that the owner ran into financial difficulties over stocks and shares, and had to dispense with one of his staff. But rather than sack his junior gardener (granddad's son-in-law, married only 12 months before and expecting their first child) my grandfather offered to resign in his place. Such was the generosity of his employer, my grandfather was given two cows as a retirement gift. With these he rented a field at Cockington, leased 'Long Field' at the top of Windsor Road, and opened a dairy in Victoria Road (Frost's Dairy).

He told me that when he worked at 'Hove', one young lady married at Upton Church, and gardeners made an archway of greenery and flowers all the way down St Marychurch Road to Castle Circus (then only a lane). Sunday School parties were held in grandad's rented field (where Ellacombe Vicarage was later erected). The curate,

at the time, left to become a chaplain at St Barnados, and the vicar - the Revd Percy Baker - (who christened me) left for Plymouth to become Bishop there.

We moved from Lymington Road to Carlton Road to live next to my father's brother, who had purchased his house there in 1886. My sister was born there in 1911. The houses were built by a Mr Tozer, and first named 2 and 3 Goodwin Terrace, becoming Carlton Road in 1906 (first as New Road). Windsor Road was then called Lower and Upper Bronshill Road.

Mr Tozer built a few houses on one side with a shop, stopped building for a period, and then began again opposite. The houses were sold for £150! Numbers 13 and 15 were offered at £200 the pair! I believe Painters built the houses at the bottom of Windsor Road and first called it Painter's Road.

I first went to school at St James', Upton: the teachers were the Misses Pratt, Spurr and Beddow. I remember our house in Lymington Road in 1915 was condemned because of water from the River Flete under the floorboards. We children were banned from Parkfield Road, across the road from us, which we knew as 'Italian Street' because of the Italian community that lived there. I recall the Speganias, and the very skilled marble masons called the Yardellas.

My father had an allotment where the Coach Station now is. He used to grow lovely carrots which we girls used to 'appropriate', wash and clean in the nearby stream, and eat without his knowledge. Being ex-army, he would complain to my mother (in army language!) that 'Somebody's pinching my — carrots. Just wait 'till I get hold of 'em.... I'll have a word with the Constable.'

Twas us, of course. Being caught by the local Bobby in those days meant a very painful flick on the ears with their white gloves, and a 'leathering' by one's parent when caught and reported.

My father did not enjoy good health after leaving the army, and had to work at the gentlemen's toilets in Castle Circus because asthma and bronchitis prevented him from taking manual work. Times were hard, having to rear four girls, but we were happier than children today. My mother washed for six policemen at the Market Street police station when we moved to Carlton Road, and I attended Homelands School. We girls had to go down to the Station each day to collect the washing and then walk to school afterwards. After school we had to darn the policemen's socks (which was a particular hardship, as they walked on duty most of the time - when not using a bicycle - and that was particularly hard on the socks!), and sew on missing buttons on shirts. On top of this, we had to darn our own stockings and mend our own clothes. In our early days of darning we were rather slipshod, until our mother would say 'Wait until your heels rub and then you will darn them properly!'.

We had no time to be bored. We would play 'paper chase' in the streets or follow arrows on walls. When the water carts sprayed water on the streets or roads in the dry summers we would take off our shoes and stockings and run after the carts barefooted. When we first started school, it was at Victoria Park Infants, under a Miss 'Lottie' Phillips, Headmistress. A Miss Dyment kept a little shop opposite the school where we children would buy a halfpenny-worth of biscuits to eat. We would ask her to to pick out those with little stars or alphabet letters on them, which we loved. I remember my sister Eva was a very naughty girl, constantly in trouble in class. In those days we girls wore embroidered aprons to school. Eva, as a bad girl, was made to stand in the corner with orders to cover her head with her apron. But she was irrepressible, and would shout to Miss Phillips 'I can see you through the holes!'

My father's sister lived opposite Cuss' Post Office. Mr Cyril Cuss, with whom I went to school, has sadly died only recently. My Aunt Polly's sons, Bill and George Easton, used to play football for Torquay United, and we would take refreshments over to them at their ground. I remember the Emmett brothers, also a very sporty family. Alf was a gardener and George worked on the quay.

Later I went to Homelands School, where Miss Collihole was a teacher and where I was caught climbing the school wall and punished. Next to it was the Open-air School for sick children, where they worked mostly outdoors, gardening, etc. in between periods of rest. Homelands was a private house before being turned into a school. I remember the Whitsun Walk, as a child, when we would dress in white silk frocks, assemble at Ellacombe School, walk down Victoria Road carrying flowers, and then back to Ellacombe Church for a special Whitsun Service.

Earlier I recall my sister (the naughty one) being sent to buy cream from a dairy called (I believe) Bollettis, opposite St James' School, and spilling it all over her new poplar, biscuit-coloured dress, grease and all, and being chastised severely: especially as all frocks were handed-down to younger sisters. One day my mother, being busy laundering, sent us to Corbyn Beach in our best

clothes, with old ones in a string bag to change into. This we did, tucking our dresses into our 'drawers' (no swimming costumes in those days!), to paddle. I placed the string bag on a nearby rock whilst searching a rock pool, only to turn a find someone had cut the string on the bag and stolen all our best clothes. We were in terrible trouble when we got home!

My naughty sister Eva had exceptional talent as a singer in her younger days - this being first identified at singing lessons whilst at Upton School. I remember a particular talent competition at the Bath Saloon when mother entered her name, only to find she had a bout of influenza at the critical time. Nevertheless - she was confined to bed on the Monday, turfed out on the Tuesday, on Wednesday was walked up and down the road, and on Thursday she competed with this disadvantage. She still came third! The first prize was awarded, at 93 points, to a young lady whose family were Salvationists; second was a Cornishman with 91 points and Eva equally 91. First prize was a twelve-months stay and instruction at the Royal College of Music in London, which was turned-down by the winner on religious grounds - a total waste. However - Mr Twining (then organist at St Mathias Church) was so taken by Eva's talent that he took her 'under his wing' for singing instruction. Eva was later to take 5 silver medals for her singing.

On one occasion Mr Sermon (a local Jeweller and one-time Mayor of Torquay) told her father (in the gent's toilets at Castle Circus) that he should listen to this talented young lady singing in the Town Hall, unaware of the relationship. When told he was her father, Mr Sermon not only 'stood-in' for Eva's father temporarily, but later gave Eva a silver pendant, this in addition to the gold watch she had received as a prize at the Town Hall.

Later my sister was to perform at places like the Grand Hotel, the Torbay Hotel and at Sunday performances at the Pavilion - often for a guinea, which was a substantial sum in those days.

I recall, when living at Carlton Road, the big houses in Bronshill Road. A Mrs Coogan lived at 'Henbury' (next to Hatfield House), which she later rented to Dr Simpson, the Medical Officer of Health. She died during World War Two, specifying the house should go to a male member of the family (Mr Coogan was a POW in Japanese hands).

'Bythorn', next to last on the north side near Windsor Road, belonged to Eric Perry, and 'St Martins' (opposite) to the Martin Family. Mr

Perry was to later marry a Miss Martin at St John's Church.

I first went to work for a Mr Murray at No. 5 Windsor Road. Mrs Murray was born at Windsor Castle and often entertained, as guests, friends and colleagues from the Castle. I worked there for five years, until the Murrays moved to Bovey Tracey. Mr Murray was a great benefactor and supporter of Ellacombe Church, despite the grievous disability of having had both legs amputated. Mr and Mrs Murray both served on the Church Committee, with a Mr Conybear, a Mr Smith and a Mr Collihoe (father of Miss Collihole the teacher).

The Christmas dinners for the senior members of the church choir were the most memorable occasions of the year (the boys were given a tea), and I was one of those who served at table. Usually Mrs Perry and Mrs Martin would preside on two big tea urns at the bottom of the table, which would be loaded with turkey, ham, fresh cooked beef and tongue, followed by Christmas pudding, etc. All the smaller churches in the Parish would be represented. Mr Murray and other ladies and gentlemen of the Parish were most generous.

After supper the men would sit around the two blazing fires on either side of the Church Hall, and each would have to sing a song. Poor Mr Murray would offer his 'Road to Mandalay', but this was suffered rather than enjoyed, as his singing was certainly not of choir standard!

Ladies and gentlemen I remember connected with Church affairs were, of course, the Revd Higgins, the Revd Leslie St Aubrey and a curate called Mr Stratton. There was a blind organist called Mr Bailey at St Pauls and Sydney Bryant at Ellacombe Church: a Mr Farley, with hearing problems, who had a shop near the corner of Highbury and Ellacombe Church Roads; a choir member called Mr Prowse (a lovely singer) who lived near a barber's shop at the top of Alexandra Road, opposite Highbury Road, and other choir singers and Church members, such as the brothers Percy and Stanley Dimmock, Harry Hanson, Derek Collier, Leslie and Ronald Thompson, Eileen Clark (later to be Matron at Hatfield House and who married Bill Blackwell), and Wyn Gibbons, the wife of Percy Gibbons, a Salvationist. Les, Fred Weymouth, and Eileen, were brought up in the same house in Dunmere Road. Leslie Weymouth had the most superb alto voice in the Choir.

I remember also Donald Sercombe, whose father had one arm and played the organ at the

Communion Service on Sunday mornings to relieve the organist. My aunt, Annie Tucker, lived at and managed the off-licence next to Selleys the butchers, in Hoxton Road. Later, Mrs Ethel Lowe (whose mother was a Tucker) took over the premises from my Aunt. Her brother lived in Braddons Street. When Ethel was 9, and her brother slightly older, their parents sadly died. Grandad Tucker was most concerned about the children's welfare, so my aunt Annie took them in. Ethel later married Ernie Lowe (who worked at the Ellacombe Brewery) and purchased the off-licence from my aunt.

I do not know how many are aware of the fact that that Torquay's first TB hospital was at a house called 'Smyrna' on the corner of Bronshill Road and Windsor Road. The hospital was later tranferred to Whitecliff. I remember a school friend called Norman Fursdon, who lived in Woodville Road, whose father died in 'Smyrna'. Patient's beds were often set out on the lawns and I would wave to old Mr Fursdon in passing when a small girl.

My father's sister, Daisy, lived in Kenwyn Road before moving after marriage to Princes Road East. His brother Jack lived at No. 17 Carlton Road. The Torquay Co-operative Society had a shop on the brow of the hill near them, built in what was once a quarry. I remember clearly Dr Dunn and his children, who went to Homelands School. I have a photograph of Cicely, and remember one boy named David who was killed in the First World War. Grace Washer, whose parents owned the dairy at the top of Market Street, and who was a geography teacher at Homelands, married a Mr Blake. I recall Ethel Blackmore (who married a Mr Chalker - a company secretary and later a director of Messrs Renwick, Wilton and Dobson, Coal Merchants), and Alfie and Sam Blackmore - a lovely family that lived at 13 Carlton Road: their father was a gardener. Also the Hookways that owned a bakery opposite Ellacombe School and a hairdresser named Coombes, also near the School, whose father was killed in First World War and whose mother worked for the Millbay Laundry, and used her front room as a receiving office for the laundry.

Finally - I remember vividly the annual Torbay regattas. Often we would be on the big wheel, which would be stopped for us to sing 'God Save the King''. And my mother would take us up to Warren Point to watch the firework display on the quay below. All our fun, in those days, was good clean fun. Youngsters of today seem to have great difficulty in finding enjoyment. We had no time to be bored, or to find mischief for idle hands. I was 17 when I met my husband - Reg. We courted for eight years before being married at Upton Church. Sadly, when he died, he did so suddenly, on a bus.

DOLLY WEYMOUTH (NÉE ZAPLE)

I was born in Cavern Road in 1904, in a house opposite to Freer's grocery shop. As a baby I looked so much like a toy doll that I acquired the name 'Dolly', which I kept all my life. For a while we lived first in Alpine Road and then in Lower Ellacombe Church Road, at the time that the brewery was operative and where I remember that large bonfire-night parties were held annually in the park opposite.

We moved to 84 Carlton Road when it was first built. My father was offered the house for £180 leasehold, but thought that sum would be a millstone around their necks - too much - so they decided to rent. My youngest brother was born there, and I remained in the house for 68 years. The property was part of what was first known as Minna Terrace, and was built by Mr Brock. He had a daughter called Milly, who worked in Crossman's timber yard below Carlton Road. There was an annual ground rent of 30 shillings, paid to the yard. Later we bought the lease.

I was a Zaple before marriage and had a twin brother and sister. My brother joined the Post Office as a messenger and served with them for 41 years. His twin sister married a Fred Sweetman and worked for Wicks. My father worked as a printer/compositor for the *Torquay Times*, where he set the type for the story of John Lee - known as 'The Man they Could Not Hang'. When not at work by night, as a professional musician/drummer he performed at the Pavilion and Royal Theatres. He would also play at Babbacombe Church services.

I spent my school days at Ellacombe School, where Miss Phillips was the headmistress and a Miss Matthews a teacher. We entered the school from a lane at the back (Garden Road). Often I would tell my mother that I was kept late at school for naughtiness, but in fact I would be playing with boys on Ellacombe Green. I remember the superintendent at Sunday School was a Miss Firth, and another sister a teacher. They lived in a big house in the Warberries called

'Sorrento'. I have a bible presented to me at the age of eight for Sunday School attendence, inscribed 'Presented to Dolly Zaple by the Revd Stratton'. There was also another big house nearby called 'Villa Languard' that had a plaque fixed to the wall outside.

I left school at fourteen to work first at a draper's shop where Mogridges once stood (later Menzies) and then as a trainee at Torre Post Office for two and a half years at 10 shillings a week. From Torre I moved to Bute Court, and it was there that I met my future husband - a Brixham man who was employed there as a chef. He purchased his working clothes at Cheffers(?) (Colliers?) in Union Street, and would also look very smart when dressed in a silver-grey fox trilby. I remember a jeweller's shop next door.

Adjoining Bute Court was the Windermere Hotel - then a hostel for girls. After courting for some five years, we were finally married at Ellacombe Church in 1926. For a period after our marriage we managed the Devon Cafe, next to Quants the chemists and a basket shop on the Strand. The owners of the cafe were 'The Cosy Corner Cafe Group'. We managed the cafe until the outbreak of World War Two in 1939.

From there I was to work for some time at the United Yeast Company, opposite what is now the County Court (previously Upton School). We retailed and wholesaled bakers' sundries, but principally yeast by the hundredweight. A Mr Lewis was the manager. I left this employment when I became pregnant.

The old Torquay Infirmary and Dispensary was across the road - later re-named the Torbay Hospital, until the new one was built at Lawes Bridge in 1928. In the early days, the garden opposite was retained for the use of patients. After leaving the company, and following the birth of my child, I worked first at Lipton's grocery stores in Union Street and then for 30 years for the Co-operative Wholesale Society in Albert Road - first as a cashier, later promoted to chief cashier. The Society had extensive premises in Albert Road - a tobacconists, butcher's shop, dairy and coal office. In the corner next to Webber & Steadhams builders' yard was the Co-op's main dairy and stables. As an employee I was expected to move to other Co-op premises in the Torbay area, including those in Carlton Road.

My recollections of life in Ellacombe in the early years of the century are many and varied. I was told that the name came from a wealthy lady who lived in Ellacombe House and owned land in the parish. Later she went to live at the Palm

Court Hotel, on the sea front, and was remembered locally for insisting on the enforcement of strict rules for men and women to bathe separately on Torre Abbey Sands. I was a member of the YWCA, and can remember Mr Rooke (the mayor's secretary) giving talks to the girls on the YWCA's premises, next to the Post Office.

Shops I remember in Ellacombe were Mr Low's the watchmaker in Carlton Road, and the Carlton Stores at the corner of Kenwyn Road: Len Harvey's (who was the verger at Ellacombe Church) grocer's shop; Savages off-licence in Ellacombe Church Road - opposite Mt Pleasant in Highbury Road (his two sons were in my age group); Miss Berry's dairy in Carlton Road (where I would be sent to purchase fresh milk and scrumptious clotted cream made on the premises), and Gagg's fish and chip shop in Princes Road. In Market Street were Hardings the ironmongers and further up Kitto's. Next to Hardings a grocer's shop by the Church of St Michaels and All Angels - a High Church where Father Peter Clynick and Father Absalom administered the sacraments at an altar approached through beautiful brass filigree gates - complete with swinging incence burners and servers.

I remember the old Fire Station and the Corporation Buildings that had a blue light on the wall outside. This was lit when an air-raid was imminent during the war. There was, of course, the Health Bakery further up Market Street - owned by a Mr Masters, who once had another shop in Fleet Street making rock in a two-armed machine in the window. And Easterbrooks, the jewellers, who would present teaspoons to prospective brides buying wedding rings at the shop; Routleys pram shop, and the Post Office garage.

Above the garage was Washer's Dairy, where one could watch homemade ice-cream being prepared in a large cannister packed with ice. Inside one would see a 'fishbone' metal handle with prongs, which would mix the ice with custard and dairy products, and was operated by staff turning the handle.

There was also Pristons the tobacconists, newsagents and confectioners, and, of course, the Primitive Methodist Chapel. It might be appropriate here to recall the age-old problem of the River Flete and its continual flooding effect upon the Town. I remember the river ran underneath Mogridges, Johnsons, the public house (the Union Hotel - which had an alleyway at the side) and the old Burlington Cinema, all of which were subject to flooding many times, and in the case of

the latter I have known the water up to the level of the seats.

Torquay being built on seven hills, tributories were often troublesome: one such stream ran down from Warberry Copse, through the fields and Congella Road, to Ellacombe Church Road (where a tree was once struck by lightning), causing foundation dampness to a number of properties in its path.

I believe that Warberry Copse was left to the people of Ellacombe to enjoy in perpetuity. Below Gagg's fish and chip shop was a building called the Labour Club, where Wilf Creber (the Head of the Co-op Funeral Service) ran whist drives. Nearby, at the back of Warberry Vale, in what was once a quarry opposite Ellacombe Church, Messrs Whiteways had a cider and mineral works and bottling plant.

At the foot of steps leading from Ellacombe Church Road to Woodville Road was Sellick's garage, and across the road Len Brown's electrical shop - still in business today. In the rear of houses at the bottom of Princes Road was a chapel where, again, I believe whist could be played in the chapel hall. Finally - I recall a doctor's house where the Regal Cinema used to stand before recent demolition. I believe he moved to Honiton when the Cinema opened in 1912.

Many other memories come to mind. Like other children, I loved the regatta and the fair around the harbour. My favourites were the chair-o'-planes and spending a penny for a mat on the helter-skelter. One could have one's fortune told, or play hoopla - with the prize of a goldfish in a bowl for a winning 'ring'.

One could buy nougat or ice cream at Forte's on Cary Parade. Boys would chase the girls with 'tickling sticks' and attempt to force confetti down the necks of their frocks. Regimental bands would play during the summer at the bandstand in Princess Gardens - the most popular being the Scottish regiments, with their kilts and busbies, who would perform Scottish reels and sword dances.

Many soldiers would lodge in Ellacombe, and I would often see them at Washer's Dairy purchasing junket and ice-cream, topped with clotted cream, for 4d a time. Most local families made their own cream from the rich milk of the pedigree South Devon herds. The American naval vessels would also call into Torbay during fleet manoeuvres from time to time, and all the local girls would be after the sailors! Not me, of course! We would watch the naval police, in their white helmets and gaiters, swinging long truncheons

Torquay GPO Indoor Staff, Christmas 1948. Back row l-r: *K. Opie; W. Murch, N. Dashper; B. Harding; ? Bond; G. Eden.* Third row: *S. Langmead; G. Milne; W. Hulme; E. Horswell; F. Harding; J. Mudge; ? Purdy.* Second row: *T. Kerslake; W. Durepaire; A. Hunt; W. Pillar; J. Lack; C. McMenemy; S. Bowden; A.W. Langmead; G. Burleigh.* Front row: *S. Hawkins; E. England; L. Hingston; A. Grimmet (Assistant Head Postmaster); G. Tickner (Head Postmaster); H. Toms; H. Cummings; M. Martin; B. Pane; M. Williams.*

looking for the troublemakers and drunks, and watch them throw the latter into the huge picket-boats lying alongside Haldon Pier.

I also recall the early fetes at Plainmoor, when children were given, as treats, rides in horse and carts near Jubilee House. The Revd Leslie St Aubrey was vicar at the time and the Revd Llewellen Owen-Williams curate. My brother, as a Post Office messenger, joined when standards were very high and hours were long. Every morning the boys would stand in the Post Office yard where Mr Clancy (the inspector) would examine hands and nails, the polish on boots and leather belts and the cleanliness of collars and smartness of ties. If these things were not of acceptable standard, the luckless offender would be sent home forthwith. On late shift, until 9 pm. boys would often be sent off to cycle to (say) Ilsham Marine Drive or Maidencombe with a late telegram to deliver after close.

My brother told his father once he was afraid to go alone, because he was too frightened, but he received little sympathy from that source, as his father told him he would just have to get used to it! Finally - I remember with affection Sunday School outings to Lustleigh and Chudleigh Rocks, where tea would be laid out on trestle tables after games in the fields.

MARY CORLINE

I was born at 20 Victoria Road in 1918 - eleven days after the First World War ended, and moved up to No. 21 when five years old. My family moved to Ash Hill Road, where I have lived thereafter. My mother and father were both born in Torquay: my mother was a Skinner and her father a cabinet maker, living in Hoxton Road.

My father boasted that he never went out with another girl and, on a visit to the Conservative Club in Hoxton Road, had to ask my mother's father for permission for them to walk out together! Grandad lived in Ellacombe Road, and was also born in Torquay. My father first went to a little school called St Winifreds, then to Ellacombe School as a child. At fifteen he was apprenticed at the Swindon Railway Works, training to be a qualified engineer. I remember his mother went to visit him in lodgings in his early days as an apprentice. He valued his new-found independence so much he purchased a clay pipe and an ounce of shag tobacco, and was terribly ill overnight from the experience. Nevertheless - he smoked a pipe throughout his life thereafter, and lived to a ripe old age of 99. My great grandfather started the potato business with premises in Albert Road before moving to the building behind the old police station in Market Street. Later, my Uncle Sam took over the business - but retired early in his 40s. During the Great War he came back again temporarily.

My father served his country during the Great War by travelling all over Great Britain, using his engineering expertise in the maintenance and repair of ships' and other engines. He was given an early discharge on 22 November 1918 in order to release Sam and take over the family business again.

I remember, vividly, during the Second World War when there were serious potato shortages, and queues stretched from the Primitive Methodist Chapel to the back of the police station waiting to collect a ration of 2lbs each - some with tears in their eyes with big families to feed. Stocks of potatoes were collected from storage in caves in the Totnes area. We were both a wholesale and a retail business, and in the early days serviced all the big houses and the hospitals in the Warberries (Rosehill and Whitecliff), and the old Torbay Hospital. Our two horses were stabled off Victoria Road. Alf Perry looked after and drove the horse and cart on deliveries. Roads were quite bad, in those days, and one horse was worked one day and was rested the next. Frank Conway worked in the stores with Tom Gatting, who lived in Warberry Vale.

My best friend was Joan Clements, whose father was a police officer, but lost his foot in the 1914-1918 War. I remember the police superintendent then was called Eddy: there was an Inspector and his wife who lived on the premises - occupying a flat attached to the Station.

I went straight to school at Ellacombe at three years of age, and left at twelve, finishing my education at the Torquay Commercial College which was then occupying the premises of the old Upton School. I recall one fellow pupil was Leslie Goodrich, the solicitor. My memories of Ellacombe School are sparse: Miss Phillips was the Head, and teachers were Miss Fairbourne, Miss Collihole, Miss Blackler and Miss Eggford. We had Miss Terry for physical training. My older sister was a school monitor. Eileen Mayo was another of my school friends, and a Norma Prowse. The three Prowse sisters lived together in Hoxton Road, next to the Conservative Club.

I recall some episodes of my childhood days vividly: for example - I was given a singing doll for one birthday and a pram for it at Christmas. I remember playing on Ellacombe Green one day when a horrid boy snatched the doll out of the pram and smashed its china face on the ground. I remember the Primrose League, with a Miss Gooder prominent in its activities. There was also a lady called Mrs Gay who lived at the top of Victoria Road and taught us ballet dancing. One day she organised a ballet show at the old Picturedrome in the Market (the 'Flea Pit' as it was commonly known). All the children wore little satin ballet costumes with thin shoulder straps. I remember the occasion particularly, as my mother, always terrified I would catch a chest infection, made me wear a woolly vest under the straps. I was mortified!

Sunday School was held at Ellacombe School. At Whitsun we would parade outside the school, dressed all in white and carrying flowers. We would march down Victoria Road to the Green, where the vicar would hold a short church service. I can remember, on occasion, being selected to present bouquets to prominent guests at church fetes and at the opening of Ellacombe Bowling Green. I presented one to the Mayor when I was 9 or 10 years of age. The Revd Higgins was the vicar in those days - a rather strange man. He would allow no dancing between boys and girls in the Church Hall. I remember one occasion at a Christmas Party when a little girl would not do her forfeit, and Mr Farley (a jolly school superintendent) said 'Never mind, darling, give me a little kiss instead'. This was instantly stopped by the vicar! I don't know what would have been made of this little episode in today's thinking? The Revd Owen was the curate, who later left for Southampton.

I recall a week of events at the Church Hall in aid of the Church Missionary Society. We girls had to dress up in saris, for some reason. Ruth Davey, who had a superb singing voice, took the lead part. Miss Bulleid was there in charge of a unit of the St John's Ambulance Brigade.

Percy and Stanley Dimmock would organise moonlight swimming dips at Redgate Beach. As a young child I particularly remember church services when Ellacombe was the religious centre for the gentry in the Warberries. We children would stand agog watching the coaches and horses, with liveried coachmen in powdered wigs and breeches and wearing hats with feathers on the side, drive up to disgorge their distinguished passengers, and wait at the back for the service to end so that they could drive them home again. In those days Ellacombe Church would be packed, with additional chairs set out in the aisles. I remember

Miss Friendship, whose grandfather donated money towards the new chancel, and Dr Dunn, whose verse over his front door was well known to all 'Let not thy sorrows cause thee to forget the greater harm from which thou are kept secure'.

MR KEN SELLEY

My father came from Sidmouth, when quite young, and worked for Eastmans, the Butchers (43 Union Street). The Manager was a Mr Berry. When my father left to start his own business there was a pending threat that he would find his shop surrounded by horses and carts in an attempt to upset his trade. But this, of course, did not happen. He would travel regularly to Newton Abbot Market in a pony and trap to purchase his own cattle until the Second World War started. He also owned his own pig farm at Barton, and was a qualified slaughterer, horsedealer, cattle dealer and butcher. His first butcher's shop was in Pembroke Road (1923) and he moved to Hoxton Road in 1936.

He would walk to the 'Klondyke' for a drink and always arrived home whistling. Ned Avery was the licensee at the time. Sometimes my father would visit the Country House Inn (Jim Tonkin). I remember clearly during this period a coal merchant in Potter's Hill by the name of Jack Fagin, and also recall seeing his horse puffing and blowing up Potter's Hill - ending up exhausted at the top. My father was very fond of fat, and would send me to Easterbrooks for quarter of ham - but I was to specify it should be 'mostly fat'!

I spent my early school days at Ellacombe School. I remember Major Collett was the headmaster, and Charlie Parr and Mr Cowling teachers, and a Miss Blackler the music mistress. At times I played in the school soccer team, and was certainly caned by Mr Collett a number of times. My sister also went to Ellacombe School. She took up singing professionally - later to perform at the Royal Theatre in Abbey Road (now a cinema). She also sang regularly with the Torbay Operatic Society and the Newton Abbot Local Operatic Society after moving to the area following her marriage. Certainly Ellacombe was known for natural springs - in fact one ran consistently under my father's shop in Hoxton Road. Even during droughts it ran freely.

Personalities I remember were: Albert, who operated the points at the tram junction at the bottom of Market Street, and often had trouble re-connecting the overhead cable when it would fall off the wire, and Skimpole, who had a three-wheel 'kit', would start in St Marychurch and run all the way down to Union Street, using his foot on a block of wood as a brake.

I also remember a Sergeant Bolt, a huge policeman. We boys were terrified of him. I had my ears boxed by him and by my father afterwards for some misdemeanour. The local police used Ellacombe Green for drill purposes. When I left school I studied accountancy at college. At the age of 17 years and 8 months I threw this up to join the Regular Army (February 1943), transferring later to the Paratroop Regiment. I was captured and imprisoned in 'Little Belson' (Stalag IIB). When the War ended I did not wish to return to office work, so joined my father's butchery business, where I became a recognised judge of cattle at Newton Abbot Market, Totnes and the South Hams. I feel I have 'done my bit' for Ellacombe as a Counsellor for some sixteen years. The parish will always a permanent part of my life.

TED and BILL SHAPLEY

I believe my grandfather may have been born in Torre, where he had a grocer's shop, and my great-grandfather married a Tully girl from Galmpton. I remember my father would spend summer holidays at Elberry Farm, Churston, and Tully was his second christian name (The Census Records for Churston Ferrers 1851 confirm that a Mary Tully Shapley lived with her grandparents in Alston Farm Lane, aged 2 - born at Newton Bushel).

My father was born in Torquay, also, one of twins, with two more brothers and one sister. Before the First World War he worked in the shop fronting Hardings Ironworks in Market Street. He returned from war service to find himself jobless, like many others. His eldest brother was a director of an ironworks in Birmingham called Edwards, and was able to provide him with a job there until the 'slump' of the 1920s. During his time at Birmingham he married my mother. I was born in Birmingham, in a nursing home which exists to this day. My father moved back to

Torquay about 1921/22, and we lived for about five years at the rear of the Conservative Club in Torwood Street. The old GPO was nearby and Eric Perry's garage in the rear of the Royal Hotel. Not far above Southlands House lay Braddons Cliff where Lillie Langtree was reputed to have stayed when the Fleet was in Torbay with the Prince of Wales aboard.

My uncle ran the sub-post office at All Saints Road in the First World War. As the Post Office paid for lighting, heating and rent of the premises he was able to run a van delivery and taxi service at the same time. He declared that horses required too much attention and had to rest unproductively at weekends, so he decided to buy six Model-T Ford vans from the USA. Three of these were used as taxis. He would take my father with him in the evenings.

After returning to Torquay my father worked for his uncle and Aunt Lillie at the W. J. Shapley furniture removers business in Princes Road, driving lorries and running the office. But after some personal disagreement with the aunt left to start his own removal business in 1931, garaging his lorries below Princes Road, and living at number 36 above. In the early days, he did a laundry round, collecting and delivering baskets from as far afield as Warren Road to Warberry Road West and the big houses in the Warberries. I believe one of the early Shapleys of Devon was an Assistant Abbot at Torre Abbey in 1542. There is certainly a Shapley Tor and a Shapley Manor known on Dartmoor. The family seems always to have been in the grocery and provision business - viz. Shapleys on the Strand.

My grandfather had a grocer's shop at Torre, and another relative a shop at Newton Abbot. The latter recounts delivering groceries by horse and cart over the South Dartmoor area, going out one day, sleeping and resting at a farm overnight, and completing his deliveries and returning home the next day. I remember he had six children - all girls! No son to carry on the business.

I was at Ellacombe School from the age of five until leaving at fourteen. Names of teachers during this period, I recall, were Miss Collihole, Mr Tozer, Mr Parr, Mr Cowling, Miss Blackler and Mr Tomlins. Memories of my schooldays are vague. Those that do stand out are the almagamation of the boys and girls schools, when Mr Parr felt the girls were marked unfairly high for tests in needlework, cookery and home management, and the boys conversely so at the handicraft centre at the bottom of Rock Road. He therefore imposed a 10% uplift on the boys' marking to compensate. I also recall the 'gang warfare' that broke out between the boys when Boston Fields School was closed and half of the pupils came to Ellacombe (the other half to Westhill), and when the Braddons School also closed, and half were similarly transferred to Ellacombe (the rest to Meadfoot). It seems the Ellacombe boys felt somewhat superior to the others - some of the poor children wearing shoes without socks!

Empire Day celebrations were sometimes held at the Recreation Ground, and I remember feeling sorry for the poor policemen in their heavy uniforms in the extreme heat of those summers. Some would be overcome and faint. One I recall was a Sergeant Pack who lived in Ellacombe Church Road, and had a parrot on the lawn! The policemen would parade on Ellacombe Green for drill, and on a Friday for pay. Often identity parades would be held at the police station. One poor unfortunate boy was picked out for stealing apples. I was given sixpence for attending the parade, and another sixpence for the best handwriting. Why the latter, I can't recall. Men were invited to attend for a similar purpose, from the nearby Palk Arms, for which they received a shilling.

Most boys did not mix with the girls at school - the latter were considered noisy and rather uninteresting. It was only when we left school we found their company attractive and productive! I remember one or two by name - a Margery Elliot from the Braddons area and a Mary Venables, whose father had a dairy in Victoria Road.

I can recall the shops in that road clearly. Starting with the Ellacombe Post Office, there was a haberdashers, a cooked meat shop, a dairy, a general store and a greengrocers. Opposite the School was Wyatts, the chemist, a tobacconist and another greengrocers. I believe the lady in the last shop married one of the schoolteachers. I also remember one of the Hookway girls fell, and drove a knitting needle right through the palm of her hand. The most athletic girl at school was Ethel Blackmore, who ran like a hare, and won almost all the races in her class.

Competition for scholarships at the Torquay Grammar School was severe. I think there were three types of scholarship - admission passes (a form of entrance examination) where entry was allowed, but no provision made for the costs of uniform, books and equipment; assisted passes, where some financial assistance was given, and a full scholarship (the most highly contested). For the working-class poor the full scholarship was the ultimate goal, but the opportunities were few and far between as most places were fee-paying. If memory serves me aright, this was about £4.50 a week. Uniforms were obligatory and purchased, in the main, from Pickards in Union Street, although Costers were stockists. Entry to the Central and Technical schools was conditional upon the provision of complete school uniforms likewise, and even Ellacombe School had its own uniform.

I sang in both the school and church choirs until leaving to go to work in the Post Office. I particularly remember children from St Pauls and St Barnabas joining with the Mother Church for cream teas, where quite a number of children had never seen meat in sandwiches before - being more used to bread and dripping - and would spread mustard on bread on its own!

Characters I can recall in Ellacombe are a milkman by the name of Bowditch, who would operate late at night in the Hoxton Road area from a steel milk churn on a three-wheeled truck; and Phil Read, whose garage lay at the rear of the Chapel in Market Street and a shop at the bottom of Ellacombe Road. 'Rolly' Read's favourite party trick was to lift the front end of a Baby Austin up with his hands - engine and all!

I remember being sent to the basement to find, to my amazement, a pile of sand with a potted palm tree in the centre, and seaside paintings on the walls - his children's play centre! I further recall the older boy in the Powell family, a non-commissioned corporal bomb-aimer, being one of the first casualties in the Second World War, being lost on a flight over Germany simply dropping leaflets! I recall another boy from St Olaves/St Benedict School (evacuated from London) with a voice like an angel.

I have often wondered who, in my early days, owned all the houses in Ellacombe, as almost all were rented?

MRS WINNIE DYER (Nee CASELY)

I was born in Rattery in the S. Hams on 19 June 1897 - the youngest of eleven children, four girls and seven boys. My parents lost three children in one week, of diphtheria. Both my father (James Casely) and my grandfather were born in Rattery and my mother (I think) was born in Harbertonford. Granny, on my mother's side, came from Harbertonford also, and was a Grant.

Her mother came from a family of business people in Buckfastleigh by the name of Mann. She was well brought up at a boarding school, and came into money at 21, but sadly died at 44. Her husband had a shoemaking business, employing 9 men and a number of apprentices.

In my early years I lived with my father and mother outside the village on the Marley Estate, which was owned by Sir Robert Crews whose family seat was at Haccombe. Resident at the Marley Estate were the Misses Elizabeth and Beatrice Crews. We would regularly see the two sisters drive to church on Sundays in their pony and trap.

Father was a carter on the estate - driving two beautiful horses and a cart on shopping trips to South Brent. With the coming of motor vehicles he carried out general labouring duties until deafness overtook him. I went to the village school, as a child, with sixty other children. The headmaster and his wife looked after the education of all the children, of all ages, in the essential subjects, in handicrafts and especially religion. He was a very good teacher, as well as an amateur photographer - not backward with the cane, and very strict: but this did us no harm at all.

Two of my brothers left the village later to join the Metropolitan Police in London. Times were very hard, but we kept our heads above the water. We were always well fed and well clothed. We had special clothes for school, Saturday clothes for working about, and Sunday bests.

My father grew all his own vegetables from a large garden in order to help feed his family. He had a good education - attending nightschool. His mother was district visiting nurse/midwife, working under the instructions of the local doctor. This was a common arrangement, in all areas, at the time. The Vicar called regularly - twice a week - on a Wednesday and a Saturday.

All children attended Sunday School in the village. At Christmas time the vicar held a Christmas party for the children, with a decorated tree. One local farmer, I recall, always gave each child an orange and a bun on Christmas Eve. At all other times save Sunday School outings at places like Lustleigh, Chudleigh and the beach at Paignton, children made their own entertainment - this in any free time, as most had jobs to do after school. Boys would play marbles, and wooden hoops were common. My favourite enjoyment in the summer would be in simply gathering sticks in the woods.

There was nowhere to go in the village, but on occasions we would cycle all the way to

Kingsbridge. In the mornings the boys would walk half-a-mile to fetch two galvanised buckets of water for house use, whilst the girls were sent to the local farm for milk, cheese, butter and cream. One child would fill the coal scuttle from a bunker and another chop sticks for the fire. This was all done before walking a mile to the village school. There was no water or gas, and only oil lamps for illumination. There were no toilets and waste was emptied in the fields.

Social levels were fairly strictly prescribed. For example - the children of farmers were considered a class above that of the village ones, and youngsters of both rarely mixed. Farmers' sons and daughters tended to intermarry, as did those from trade. However - one of my brothers 'kept company' with a blacksmith's daughter from East Allington and I with her brother, but not for long.

Well known farmers in the area then were the Coaker (Coker) family. Provisions for the village homes came in by horse and cart. There were grocers and bakers twice a week from South Brent and Buckfast. I remember cream and butter then cost 10d a pound. Fishmongers came from Brixham and as far away as Plymouth - all the fish being very fresh and near alive.

I was kept at home until the age of nineteen. Between leaving school and then, I was sent to South Brent daily to train as a dressmaker. I was made to return home before dusk, or by 6 pm., or my father would be sent to look for me after he finished work. I journeyed each day by bicycle without any fear of attack. But having trained, there was little work for dressmakers in the village, apart from applying fancy brailing to long frocks, worn out by hard usage. So I, like many of my age group, looked outside the village for a career. Most girls had little alternative but to go 'into service' - my sister going up country for this purpose. But such work offered little reward. After much thought and discussion, my mother allowed me to go to work in Torquay - but only if I lodged with a Bill Parson's family, who's first wife had lived in Rattery and was a cousin of my father. They kept a careful eye on me!

My 'digs' were at 44 Ellacombe Church Road. I believe Bill Parsons was a waggoner. I started work behind the counter at the International Stores, at age 19, near the old Burlington Cinema in Lower Union Street - working 8am to 8pm daily and 8am to 1pm on Wednesdays and 8am to 10pm on Saturdays for some 10 weeks. Then 4 men working in Slades (the grocers in Abbey Place) left to go into munition work, and I was offered one of the vacant posts. The hours and wages were better - 8am to 7pm with half-days on both Wednesdays and Saturdays, and a tea break, for which I received the sum of 12 shillings a week. From this I had to pay 10 shillings a week for my lodgings (no food included), provide my own overalls, threepence for an insurance stamp and a penny a week for a postage stamp to write home (mandatory!). I managed most of my own washing and made my own clothes. Occasionally a local washerwoman would 'do' my overalls, nightdresses or summer frocks.

We had to walk everywhere , but there was just no time to be unhappy. I had to take hot water upstairs on a Sunday for a bath. On my half-days I would usually go for a walk, or cycle home to Rattery to see my mother. Very occasionally all the girls at Slades would save up enough to go in a party to Maidencombe for a cream tea. I was the first female to work at Slades. I remember Robert Rooke (later the Mayor's Secretary) I think was 15 when I started there, and he would come down to the shop on Saturdays with a clean coat for his father, a grocer's assistant there. Mr Peak, the Manager, was very strict, and would call everyone by their surnames only. When our hours were reduced to 8–6pm we were not allowed a tea break. Mr Rooke (senior) and I would slip out and go up the steps to Rock Road, where we would obtain tea which we would take back and drink behind the counter.

Some of the girls who worked with me, I remember, were Freda Niblin, who lived in the end house of Highbury Road and whose father drove a coal wagon for the Co-op, or worked in the store; Peggy Hunt, who lived opposite Ellacombe School and whose father worked for Avery the scales people - she was only about 16; a niece of James the greengrocers in Market Street; a girl called Lock, one called Woolacott, who married a policeman, and another who married a Mr Luxton from the Upton Vale Hotel. I remember one rather sad little maid whose father was a farmer in Abbotskerswell.

Christmas stands out in my memories of my days at Slades - or indeed of all butchers and provision merchants, when poultry and meat of all kinds hung outside the premises in the fresh air for all to see. There were no health officers to harass the tradesmen in those days - but no doubt the air was very much cleaner! When the lads came back after the War in 1919 and were given their old jobs back, I was made redundant. However, the manager at Slades was able to recommend me to a similar post at Harveys at Torre as an experienced shop assistant, where I stayed until I married in 1921. My husband was a Torquay man, born at Exeter Villas near Ellacombe Church. We were married at Rattery Church. As Princes Road West was erected, his parents rented one of the new houses there, and that is where we set up home until we moved to Princes Road at Christmas 1927. I have lived there ever since. His sister lived in Ellacombe Church Road and was a bit of an artist by the married name of Hodges. She had eight children in all, three of them in Canada before returning for more after eight years between.

My husband learnt his trade as a carpenter at Eales the builders, but was anxious to leave his employ and work on his own account. His love was principally for boats, both working on them and hiring them out during the summer with little real business success. Both our children were born whilst we lived in Princes Road West. My husband, unfortunately, had a serious operation in 1940. Being too old for military service in the 1939/45 War, he spent much of it building army camps at Brixham and at Perranporth in Cornwall.

Traders I recall from my young married days in Ellacombe were Tom and George Pearce, the fish-mongers, who lived at Camden Road, and would sell their fish from a pony and trap - first driving down Abbey Road, through the Town and Albert Road, and then up to Pembroke Road, where they would park near the Palk Arms in Camden Road. Then there was Mr Bradford, who brought fruit and vegetables up the back lane. He would employ boys to deliver his products to nearby houses on the promise of fruit as payment - but only gave them a stick of rhubarb!

And I remember Hookways, the bakers, as the twin girls were the same age as my daughter, Betty. My niece Margaret met Brenda Hookway when both were working away in Gloucester, and would travel home by coach together. They remained good friends thereafter. One local self-trained nurse/midwife was a Mrs Bishop, who lived in Ellacombe Church Road (Mount Pleasant). Her youngest daughter also trained as a nurse and married a man called Slack. Our own visiting nurse, who was certified but not regis-tered in those days, was a Mrs Berry, whose hus-band was a policeman.

I remember the police parades on Ellacombe Green for drill and pay days. The station sergeant, who lost an arm in the Great War, was Sergt. Mairs, whose family also lived in Ellacombe Church Road, and were regular church goers. There was also a security policeman named Geoffrey Gale, who lived in Bethel Cottages, and was a friend of my son Jack. I believe Mr Gale covered the security aspects of various social clubs and was based at Watcombe.

I have a friend with whom I correspond who is currently in a local nursing home, who is 96, and has a son called Derek, an inspector of police. I knew her before I married. She came, originally, from Brixham: her mother was a cook in one of the larger houses in Teignmouth Road, and she lived in one of the lodges. I believe she once did a short TV interview programme on BBC about life in the early 1900s. I only had two children. My son Jack, who now resides with his wife and children in Australia, and a daughter Betty, who died at the age of eight-and-a-half in Rosehill Hospital as a result of St Vitus' Dance. Both children went to Ellacombe School. Miss Phillips was the girls' Headmistress, and I remember a Miss Tremlett and a Miss Pack. My daughter was very keen to learn, but - sadly - had a health breakdown.

Jack, my son, was very good with his hands. I particularly remember a very religious woodwork master who refused to give him 10 out of 10 for his work on the premise that only God was per-fect! The Torbay Regatta was always the event of the year - the Home Fleet in the Bay, the great sail-ing yachts and the luxury steam yachts of the rich, like Sir Thomas Sopwith. The children loved the fair around the harbour, of course, culminat-ing in the firework display on the quay, and on the water. My husband's friend also had a boat, and we would watch the event from the water. During the the last War the ladies of Ellacombe formed a housewives' service in parallel with the Street Wardens. Mrs Dyment was our Leader: she always wore her uniform, but the service uniform could only be worn after twelve months in the unit, and had to be paid for by the individual herself. Armbands were, however, provided. We all attended first aid and other lectures. Our main purpose was to provide in-house refuge for victims of air-raid attacks - giving first-aid and succour until the main rescue services were able to cope. In between, we would darn and knit socks, etc. for the gun crews on Warberry Hill, and make goods for newly liberated countries. We worked closely with both the Street Wardens and the Fire Watchers - who would make tea in their little huts. We would pool our meagre rations to provide home-made cakes and biscuits.

I remember the Post Office, for which my son worked later, had its own Home Guard unit. My son married an Australian girl and left after the war to settle in that country. In later years I spent many a happy evening in the old Bowling Club hut behind Pembroke Road at whist drives and other social events. We would have lovely suppers. Mrs Stone, who lived above the pub, would cook potatoes, and we would add cold meats and trifles. I also belonged to the Co-op Benevolent Club, and have been a member of the Good Companions Club since the age of 60.

MR A A BASTIAN
(In a letter to Ellacombe School)

I was greatly honoured to receive your letters to me, its like receiving a Roll of Honour for Gillian and Lynsey - your handwriting is like mine used to be until they invented ball pens and old age gave me the shakes. In my days we had inkwells and pens with nibs, and some time you was honoured and went round with a big bottle of ink filling the inkwells: some silly twerps used to finish up with ink on their face, hands and shirt - an unusual way of filling the inkwells!

In the thirties the only bakery I knew was Hookways, just down the steps by your school - the top of Ellacombe Road. We didn't get school meals like you probably do, but bought hard bakes or penny sausage rolls. I lived at 57 (I think) Ellacombe Road and used to go home to dinner - if we could afford a dinner.

On the corner opposite the bakers was a barbers; he used to give us boys very short haircuts and smarm it down with haircream. I hated it and once I got outside I used to ruffle it up. Can you imagine your hair, boys, plastered down and parted in the middle, it looked real cissy!

My dad was the RSPCA Inspector, and he later moved into the Animals Clinic in Torre - I think it is still there. I lived above it. The playground in my days was full of holes. As you say, Claire, the boys were separated from the girls, very much separated, we hardly ever met up - more's the pity. When we went to 'Tanner Hops' (Dances at small halls at sixpence) half the boys would be wallflowers. They had not learnt to 'chat the girls up' as we called it. Nowadays they all know the answers - but there was more romance in my days. We went to Sunday School at Ellacombe School, and once a year we went on a Sunday School outing to Galmpton. We went in a big field near a farmhouse and drank lemonade, ate pasties and

ran round mad. Then the School went crazy and took us on a GWR steam train to Swindon for a day out at the locomotive sheds. I think our mums and dads had to fork out 5 or 10 old shillings for this, but it was very educational, although I wanted to be a cowboy and not an engine driver!

Yes, Claire, our clothes *were* different: I wore short pants until I was 12, and felt real proud and grown up in my first long trousers, grey flannels, etc. We also wore navy blue caps with a light blue motive and a school badge. Most kids' parents couldn't afford these things. Shoes had leather soles; when the leather wore down you had holes in them, so you stuffed them with cardboard.

I wasn't too bad off as my father had regular work, and the £4.10 shillings average wage he earned was pretty good in the '30s. We kids went to the Picturedrome (Millers) in the Market, since pulled down, and saw 2 big films, a comedy and a newsreel for 6d. There was also the Empire down the road from you, the Electric, the Burlington, the Regal, and the Tudor in St Marychurch. The Electric we got in for a farthing - the old man on the door was shortsighted and used to think it was a sixpence!

In the Market was a stall with a man selling second-hand comics, and we stacked up with Rovers, Wizards, Boys Cinema, Triumph, Gem and Magnets, and bags of broken toffee, tiger nuts, pasties, stale cakes from Wills the bakers (his son went to Ellacombe). You could do all this with half-a-crown - but 2/6d was a fortune to us kids.

I used to sell rabbit skins and jam jars to a rag merchant in Pimlico, off Market Street, to get my picture money. Gillian - I'd like very much to come to your Summer Fayre (excuse my writing, my hand are getting cramp), but London is still a long way from Torquay. I shall probably be down round October when the Good Lord fits my wings! So I won't be in time to be one of your ghosts. Thank you for your delightful letter - I hope your Headmaster gets this letter translated into English! I do apologise for my writing, it's not in the tradition of Ellacombe University!

Now Ned, yes I did play in goal for the school 1930-31 - the team in white (that's a red sweater I'm wearing). I must've been about 14. Some of the boys probably got killed in the War. I was in the Welch Regiment, and was captured by German parachute troops on Crete. I spent three years 329 days in POW camps in Germany and was rescued by Patton's Texas Rangers - sounds romantic, but true.

Serena, thank you for your letter. I am glad you do not get the cane any more - but it did not do us any harm, although it stung like a bee! It was more humiliating to stand in a corner with your back to the class, although they didn't supply dunce's hats. Being boys, we had all men teachers, the girls in the other half of the building (which, by the way, we never entered, being 'taboo') had lady teachers.

I left school when I was 15: I could have left at 14, but there was no work around except errand boys or hotel work, which was slave labour. My father used his influence and got me a plumber's apprenticeship at 6 shillings a week. I left that later and became a signwriter's apprentice at bigger money (8 shillings a week). We boys couldn't afford bikes. Although you could buy one 'mail order' for about £3 - or 2 shillings a week; £3 was a man's weekly wage in the 30s. We used to make our own bikes - bone shakers, we called them - out of old frames and rusty, tire-less wheels found on rubbish dumps. It was great fun - but we made a terrible noise.

Mr Cooper would have got frustrated teaching us lads cycling proficiency! There wasn't a lot of traffic on the roads though - horse traffic was still around, and we had a tram shed at Plainmoor. I lived at Daison Crescent, Westhill then - that was my third home in Torquay. I remember the airship R100 passing over Plainmoor.

We played our sports, Serena, on Windmill Hill: I don't know if it still exists. It was a long walk to get there - or maybe my legs were shorter! Best of luck at Westlands.

Thank you, Timothy, I cannot remember this garage - we probably didn't have cars around (pony express and stage coaches!), it must have been put up and pulled down again after I left. I did some painting when I left school - up a big ladder painting a drain pipe at the Imperial Hotel (is it still there?). I was very high up, but tried to be brave - all for 8 shillings a week.

Ellacombe School, Jenny, was a Church of England school in my days. We started our education there and finished it at 14, although I was 'thick' in arithmetic (all types) and stayed on to 15. We could pass our exams and go to Homelands School at Plainmoor - that was 'posh stuff'. I passed an art exam, but never kept the subject up - won a weeny little cup at Ellacombe for athletics. We kept it one year and handed it back - also a pair of spiked running shoes. We had PE or PT, we called it, every morning in the playground - no kit, come as you are rain or shine - flinging your arms about until Mr Cowling, our

master, got creaky bones and we slung it in. Or maybe you stepped in a pot-hole full of rainwater and got sloshed all up your legs. Mr Parr (affectionally known as 'Fatty' Parr) acted as music master, and we assembled in squares and sang songs 'Drink To Me Only' and 'What Shall We Do With the Drunken Sailor', etc. - we must have sounded horrible!

Talking of sailors - the Home Fleet used to come in, the *Revenge*, the *Hood* and all those great battleships when we had a real navy. The town was full of sailors, mostly drunk, sometimes foreign battleships. There were French and Italian, and just before the war, a German battleship. They were exciting days, Jenny!

Then there was the regatta, with roundabouts and sideshows all around the quay. We had great fun and no hooligans - even a drunken sailor was loved by the kids!

I saw pictures of the Ellacombe and Hayes match in the *Star & Sun* - that's why I wrote to your School, Alan. We never played Hayes - Westhill School was our big rival, and there was Torre School, Homelands and I forget the others. We were not that good either, although we had two or three good players including the Emmetts, who played professional cricket later on. Also we had 'House' teams Gilbert, Grenville, Drake and Raleigh. I played in goal for Drake and we were terrible! I let in 18 goals one game and next week I was picked for the school team. Apparently I made half a dozen brilliant saves and the rest of the team let me down - so our sportsmaster said. What a joke!

Sam, boy, I saw that 1930 clipping of the football team. Is that the one with the team in white shirts? The boy on the left in a suit is George Cook: he used to live right opposite the school. All the rest, including me in my red goalie's sweater are all pensioners or dead by now - so enjoy life while you can, young Sam. In the year 'dot-dash-dot' your grandson will look at your school photos and say 'Cor! didn't they look funny in those days?'

Thank you for your letter, Martin. I used to go to Plainmoor regularly when I was a boy. Torquay were in the old Third Division (South), we used to climb over the wall when we couldn't afford threepence to get in. The team wore black and white stripes and were called 'The Magpies'.

Angela, you have a majority of lady teachers: this is discrimination! Mr Cooper must get the backing of the boys and get some men teachers signed up. In my days we never saw the lady teachers. I think the girls taught themselves!

Sometimes the clergy came round from Ellacombe Church to lecture us, so we went to sleep or sucked on our 'gob stoppers' - penny each the big ones, and they changed colour as you sucked them. The school was Church of England, so we got a lot of visits....

And finally, Adam, the school has not changed on the outside - I know because I took a photo of it last year on a week's holiday. Ellacombe Green looks the same - in fact very little has altered - only people, the boys I ran wild with and the girl I secretly adored are no more!

Thank you Mr Cooper, and best wishes to everyone.

A. A. Bastian

STANLEY CROCKER, AGED 78

Ellacombe had always been considered the 'working class' area of Torquay, the exact opposite of Torwood - the place where the 'gentry' lived. The way to Torwood and the Lincombes was via the Warberries, the large residence area where servants and tradesmen had to use side entrances and not the main gate. I believe Lillie Langtry lived in one of the large houses and often had Queen Victoria's son to visit her. Many Ellacombe girls were employed as servants in these large houses, and washing was 'taken in' by many of them and their mothers.

Warberry Copse was completely overgrown and busy mothers used to send their children away to play 'Robin Hood' and 'Cowboys and Indians' there. Joys Field had a stream running down to the newts and tadpoles pond at the bottom. Standing at the top of this field the only sound that could be heard across the valley was the noise made by chickens at the bottom of people's gardens. At this time the Council were still using horses and carts, and waste matter was taken by this form of transport to a tip at the top of Rosehill Road.

Ellacombe Green, with its shed, was used as a meeting place for the old people of the area. At one time, the Green had a tented circus, and at other times was used for political speakers at election times. Noted speakers I recall were an H. M. Medland from Plymouth and an Alderman Scardifield from Dartmouth. There is still a reminder of the old horse and cart days at Ellacombe Green in the form of an old fountain trough, where tradesmen's and Council horses stopped to slake their thirst.

All children went to Sunday School in those days. The Revd Stratton was the incumbent at Ellacombe Church - Mr Hughes, Mr Payne and Sammy Maddern (the barber) ran the Princes Hall in Alexandra Lane, and there was, of course, the Methodist Church in Market Street.

There were fish and chip shops at Cavern Road (Martins) and one in Hoxton Road (Coombes) run by a lady from the Caribbean: a side street at the rear of Mount Herman's Road had Langmead's emporium. Cinemas were the Empire, opened in

Coombe's fish and chip cafe, c. 1933. Stella Coombe

1912, and the Picturedrome in the Market. The latter was the first Torbay cinema to show double feature films and had a coloured fountain shining above the lady at the organ. The Empire had Saturday shows with Pearl White tied to the railway lines - a 'See Next Week' episode! This cinema also screened Torbay's first 'talkie' in September 1929. Shops in the area were Maunders, Dykes, Weddens and the Vectis Steam Laundry. Hookways the bakers did a good trade with their penny meat pies and six-a-penny hardbakes.

Ellacombe School had a number of schoolteacher characters - Headmaster Mr Collett, Mr Tozer, and 'Charlie' Parr: Harry Hoare, Councillor for Chelston, taught there.

The Market in Market Street was a source of second-hand books. Two Billy Bunters could be exchanged for one that you had not read before. This was also true of the Funny Wonder, Sexton Blake and The Triumph. Climbing the cliffs at Stentifords Hill was always a 'dare' for small boys. One boy from Warberry Road West fell off and was badly injured: his name was Wannell. Ellacombe's claim to fame might be as a warning spot for the onset of danger. Sirens on Warberry Hill warned of approaching bombers during World War Two, and a bonfire was lit on the spot to warn Sir Francis Drake that the Spanish Armada was approaching in the Channel.

Mrs Muriel Sellick, a lifelong Ellacombe girl, is a Freeman of the Borough of Torbay. She used to play, as a child, in Warberry Copse.

B. A. CHALKER

I attended Ellacombe School from 1925 until 1931, and left to take up a scholarship at the Torquay Commercial College. The Headmaster, at that time, was Major Collett. Teachers I remember were Mr (Charles) Parr, who also was the choir master; Mr Tozer the sports master and Mr Tomlins.

Both Mr Collett and Mr Parr were cricket enthusiasts and were Somerset County Cricket Club supporters. The school Houses were known as Drake (blue), Raleigh (yellow), Grenville (red) and Gilbert (green). Football, cricket, athletics, etc. took place at Windmill Hill, Hele - participants walked from school to and from the playing fields.

Swimming lessons took place at the Marine Spa Baths on Wednesday afternoons. Woodwork lessons for boys took place on Friday afternoons at the Abbey Hall at the bottom of Rock Road, under the supervision of Mr Stan Gorvett. The premises are now the headquarters of the Deaf Club.

At Ellacombe Church I can only recall that the incumbent was the Revd Higgins, followed by the Revd Leslie St Aubrey. The organist was Mr Sydney Bryant and the Church choir used to sing annually at the Exeter Cathedral Choral Festivals. I can remember the names of the following local boys: Harry Powell, Bert Langmead, Bob Marker, Norman Heath, Ron Chudleigh, Francis Annear, Terry Crudden, George Perrin, Gordon Chalk, Cyril Smith, Vic Hunt, Jack French, Eric Waldron, Mervyn Davey, Arthur Ebdon (later Principal of South Devon College), Ken and Cyril Lasseter and George Pearce.

All local games were played in Ellacombe Brewery Park. Football coaching was occasionally given by Jack Fowler (Captain of Torquay United). His sons, Derek and Jim, developed into good footballers. During cricket a hit into the brewery earned six runs, but the batsman was out (for losing the ball!).

I remember particularly Miss Bentley's small general store in Princes Road East, used by the children for the weekly purchase of sweets. One penny purchased four different choices - each separately wrapped! At the top of the road there were no houses or buildings. A stile gave access to fields (buttercups and daisies) and Warberry Copse. In the vicinity of Princes Road were a number of small shops and businesses. There was Mrs Crisp's fish and chip shop, visited on Saturday lunchtime by the sometimes muddy and tired footballers from Brewery Park. The attraction was a twopenny 'Chelsea' (fish, chips and peas), and a penny 'Monster' (bottle of lemonade). At end of the session Mrs Crisp used to distribute 'scribbles' from the morning's frying - a very popular event!

Mr Maddern the barber was well known to locals. The cost was threepence, and you requested which famous footballer's hairstyle you wished to copy. 'Cut mine like Tommy Lawton please'. Other businesses were: Shapleys (haulage and removals), Selleys (the butchers), Lacey the chemist, followed by Knapman when he retired, Watkins the grocers, Tozers and French (butchers), Smerdons (general stores), Haywards (off licence), Len Brown (radio and electricians), Sellick (hauliers), Coombe's fish and chip shop (family renowned for swimming - particularly Stella) and Hookways (the bakers). There was also R. Kirksopp, who later became Mayor of Torquay, who owned the dairy.

There were two 'Ellacombe' cinemas - the Empire and the Picturedrome. At the latter, on Saturday afternoons, there were thrilling serials - silent films with piano accompaniment. Entrance fee was two or three pence. Finally - I can remember that the trams finished running through the parish in 1934. For the full circular route on the bus the fare was one penny.

The development of Ellacombe began with the opening-up of Market Street and the Ellacombe Valley in 1853. Mr Lawrence Palk was largely responsible for the promotion of schemes for low-rented cottages which were necessary to house the large number of working men needed to build the hundreds of houses and villas in the Warberries for well-to-do families.

'BILL' ELLIOTT

Whilst attending Ellacombe School, I played football for the school team and also for the Torbay Schools' eleven. At that time the Emmett brothers were at Ellacombe School and were prominent in all the sports. George, the eldest, subsequently played for Gloucester and England. In those days the Empire Cinema was 3d on a Saturday afternoon and the Picturedrome, in the Market, 3d on a Saturday evening. Being silent films, the organist at the Picturedrome was a Mr Sparrow, who on Sunday played the organ at the Abbey Road Congregational Church which I attended and sang in the choir.

A Mr Shinner from Chatsworth Road in Ellacombe was a pillar of that Church and its Sunday School. After transfer to the Grammar School - to which transport was by tram from Market Corner to Brunswick Square, and cost one penny - I played football and cricket in the school first eleven and was awarded my 'colours'. I became a violinist in the school orchestra and leader of the second violins.

With three other contemporaries - Grute, Williams and Pugsley - we formed a dance band, which was quite a financial help to schoolboys at £1 an hour. I was also a coxswain for the Torquay Rowing Club - trained by Charlie Pratt - and proudly display the silver medal awarded to the

senior fours in 1929. My years at the Grammar School included a cruise on the *Nevasa* and a trip to Paris with 'Mousey' Martin as the master in charge. Life was quite demanding! Later I found relaxation as a member of the Paignton Operatic Society in Palace Avenue where, in addition to taking part in the 'Arcadians' and 'Hit the Deck', I achieved a one-line part in 'The Maid of the Mountains'!

ARCHIE SKINNER

My brother Brian Skinner joined the Gas Board, starting as a fitter's apprentice, and rose to become a manager before retiring in 1994. My sister Diana married another Ellacombe boy, Bill Horwill, who before retirement a few years ago, was head of the Pensions Department of the Prudential Insurance Company in London.

Boys who were my contemporaries in Ellacombe were: Arthur Prowse of Egerton Road, who was a carpenter with P. W. Wilkins, and married my wife's sister: the Fowlers - Jack, who played for Torquay United AFC, Alan who joined the Royal Navy, and Jimmy, who worked for Post Office telephones: the Underhills - Derrick, Bunny and Jimmy(?): Jim Higgins - who held a good position at Sifam Electronics, and his brother Clifford, who was also known as 'Giggy': (all the three families above lived in Berea Road - as did Don Roberts and his brother. Don became a teacher, and came back to Torquay to teach at his old school, the Torquay Grammar): Ken Selley (whose family were Ellacombe butchers) became Mayor of Torbay: the Tozer brothers.

Another boy who lived in Lower Ellacombe Church Road, just a few doors from the Old Brewery, was called Packe. He later joined the priesthood. His sister emigrated to South Africa. And there was Dennis Penny - a local signwriter who achieved so much with the St John's Ambulance Service.

Our lives centred around the Church, the Sunday School and the Choir (then boys only). The vicar was the Revd Leslie St Aubrey, and the choirmaster and organist was Mr Perrett. When we boys were not engaged in church activities we played football in Brewery Park, Lower Ellacombe Church Road, or played up in Warberry Copse or The Quinta - or went swimming in the summer at Redgate Beach. The two churchwardens at

Ellacombe Church were Mr Ebdon and Mr Wyatt the chemist (opposite Ellacombe School). Of the men in the choir, I can remember Mr Dimmock, also two of my uncles - Bob and John Prowse - the latter also for many years secretary of the Parochial Church Council. Incidentally, they were both gardeners. The two brothers Hayman were choristers, one an alto and the other an excellent tenor. Harold always sang the tenor solos for the 'Crucifixion' and the 'Messiah', which was sung regularly in church. The bass solos were performed by a Mr Life.

The boys practised on a Tuesday and the full choir on Thursdays. The hall behind the church downstairs had a billiard table and a table tennis table, which we were allowed to use. Other names I recall were: Ruth Davey, who lived opposite Brown's radio shop and was a well-known contralto: Mrs Ebdon, wife of the churchwarden, was a Sunday School teacher. I still have a book - a Sunday School prize for good behaviour and attendance: Gordon Hooper who, although having a leg in irons, was always playing football. He lived opposite the chemist in Hoxton Road and later became a dental mechanic: (the son of the chemist, Mr. Knapman, became a well-known London coroner).

Two doors from the Church, in Ellacombe Church Road, lived Arthur Parsons. He did well in the Police Force, and I believe became a police inspector. The three brothers Powell lived on the terrace opposite Sammy Maddern, the barber, in Princes Road. Harry, the eldest, was killed in the RAF while Frank became the manager of Leonards shoe shop, in Union Street, and Ken of Hodges, the Outfitters at Exmouth.

Brian Leaman lived in Princes Road East. His sister died at an early age, but I think he became a schoolteacher. Denzil Nenner (who lived opposite Arthur Prowse in Egerton Road) also joined the police force and moved up in the ranks.

In Warberry Vale lived Ernie Wyatt, who made a career, too, in the Royal Navy, serving in submarines. Bill Shapley, who lived two or three doors below Sammy Maddern, followed his father into the removal business - later in his own right.

In Ellacombe Church Road lived the Popes - Ken, Alan and Doreen - and opposite them, the Rookes, who were all in poor health.

The shops I remember, apart from Browns already mentioned were: Heard & Bentleys in Princes Road East - general stores; Smerdons - fruit & vegetables; Haywards - the off licence - who often had salt cod hung up outside the shop and this was known to us as 'toe-rag'. The Cabin (next

door) was a tobacconist, Bennets, a shoe repair shop further down from the Cabin, and Mr Fearn's dairy. He always gave the customers on his 'round' a present at Christmas - a jug or a cream dish (All the above five were in Princes Road).

Hookways bakery was near the School while Ernie Lowe's off licence was next to Selleys, the butchers, in Hoxton Road. Ernie always had trouble sorting out the sweet coupons - especially from my brother(!).

There were two fish and chip shops - Martins, in Cavern Road and Willets, opposite Chave's garage. Across the road was Allinson, a butcher. A business, which always drew the attention of the boys on the way home from school, was Mr Lark's, the blacksmith, whose working premises were at the top of Lower Ellacombe Church Road. Mr Lark's brother Jack lived on the corner of Carlton Road, and as a young boy I walked past his house on errands to the Co-op (in the same road) on many occasions. I always stopped to admire his immaculate garden even then. I wonder if that helped to influence me in my future career? There was a barber's shop next door to Knapman's the chemist, in Hoxton Road. It was run by a Mr Hughes, whose daughter married an American soldier - as did Beryl Blackler, who lived in Florida Road.

During the War, our football ground in Brewery Park was taken over for military purposes by the American Army, and many young boys were given the occasional doughnut by the soldiers. I remember St Marychurch being bombed. I was going down to Redgate Beach for a swim with Bill Shapley, Ken Powell and Arthur Prowse, when this happened, and we quickly took cover from the German aircraft we saw coming over the sea to carry out that tragic attack. Twenty-one children and three Sunday School teachers were killed and many others injured in that bombing raid. When I left Ellacombe there was still some evidence of canon shell attacks in the pavement in Berea Road. It was such a steep hill that I remember the Co-op horse-drawn milk-floats and bread-carts would use the kerb as a brake on that hill.

Re-reading what I have written illustrates that all the people I have mentioned lived on the side of Ellacombe between the Church and Warberry Copse. We did not know the people who lived over the school side very well - but then we did not go very far from home as few people had cars in those days.

TED BRAGG

I have no memories at all of living at 17 Princes Road East because, before I was two years old, my family and I had moved to 43 Princes Road. My father was Henry Percy Bragg and my mother's maiden name was Edith Mary Baker. The house in Princes Road was next door to Ebdon and Graham's boot and shoe repairers. Their workshop occupied the cellar of the Graham's house. To the rear was the Liberal Hall, much used at the time for whist drives and jumble sales. Further to the rear and below was Shapley's garage where my father worked.

I remember my first day at Ellacombe School - attending in the company of Bobby Lear. Bobby had the most exciting address I could think of: he lived in the Fire Station, Market Street. The family later moved to Florida Road. The teachers were the Misses Kirkham, Blackler, Packe, Mudge, Crocker and Collihole. Mr Parr was in charge of the fourth form, and Mr Collett was the Headmaster. The teaching staff at the Torquay Grammar School were led by J. Harmer. Due to the war, the age range of teachers was very wide. Some had recently qualified and others brought out of retirement. I remember one or two in particular: Mr Wheeler (Woodwork), Mr Cooper (Eng.Lit.), Mr Pearson (Maths), Mr Ellis (History), Mr Dutton (Geog.), Mr Martin (French), Miss Evans (Biology), Miss Slater (English), Mr Jones (Chem.) and Mr Burns (Geog.).

One particular teacher who was probably the eldest, Mr Tom Lovett, lived with the apocryphal rumour that he had in earlier years won a fortune on 'Tipperary Tim' in the Grand National. This story gave him considerable kudos with the boys. We usually walked but sometimes cycled to the school, which was shared with the evacuated St Olave's School from London. This necessity led to shared equipment and form rooms, with an integrated timetable. The day sometimes started at nine o'clock and on others ten-thirty, finishing at three-thirty or five.

The Ellacombe boys I remember at Torquay Grammar School are: Derek Slee, Alan Palmer, Tony Holloway, David Down, Roy Backwell, Peter Collier, David Gutsell, Graham Rawle, to name but a few. Having remembered some of the boys it is only right to recall some Ellacombe girls. I wonder where they are now: Jean Taylor, Hazel Nenner, Mary Trump, Peggy Brown, Pauline Bevan, Marie Skinner, Anne Langdon and Doris Dare. This list could go on for some time. There were also the Harris sisters, one of whom, Jean, married my brother.

Evacuees were very much part of our life. In the early forties many homes had a small child billeted with them. We had a little girl called Shelia Shelvey from Fulham. She stayed a year or so and kept in contact with my mother until the Sixties. After that American soldiers were billeted in people's homes. We had a soldier from the Bronx called Tom Giangrasso. After he left he sent my father cards from various parts of Europe.

The Americans ate in a large field kitchen erected in Ellacombe Old Brewery Park. This park had played a big part in the lives of the young people of Ellacombe. Many important football and cricket matches have been played there; the stars being the Fowler family, 'Ginger' Spagania, 'Gigi' Higgins, Denzel Nenner, the Bowden family, the diminutive Bobby Thorne and Gordon Hooper whose disability hampered him not at all. There are many others too numerous to catalogue here.

During this period I did a Saturday morning butcher's round for Charlie Taylor. He had taken over Tozer's butcher shop in Princes Road, opposite Haywards next door to the Wool Shop and near Smeardons the greengrocer. This earned me two shillings a week, better than a paper round!

During the wartime period the Home Guard were very prominent. They paraded in the Parish Hall and patrolled Walls Hill and other parts of the exposed coastline on a regular nightly basis. A number of my generation were messengers for this patriotic band.

The Young People's Fellowship organised by Jean Brewer and Raymond Skinner played a significant role in my and many other teenage lives. It met in the Parish Hall of Christ's Church Ellacombe three evenings a week. The vicar at that time was the Revd Leslie St Aubrey, the curate Revd Morgan. There was also a memorable lay preacher, Mr Walker, who had spent much of his life as a missionary in Japan.

The Warberry Copse, Walls Hill, Torquay Harbour, Anstey's Cove, Meadfoot Beach, Bishops Walk, Goats Path Watcombe all played an important part in our lives. On Bank Holidays we usually went to Dartmoor, to Haytor, Dartmeet or Hounds Tor. It all seemed quite an adventure.

MR and MRS LES GIBBONS

Les - I was born in Devonport in 1910. My father was first trained as a boot and shoe repairer and later employed as manager of Oliver's Boot Shop in Plymouth. He was later transferred to a similar post in Wellington, Somerset, where I lived with my parents until the age of 16. At that time we moved to Torquay, living at Princes Street, Babbacombe (destroyed in World War Two by bombing). Jobs were particularly difficult to find during the post-war depression and he found employment shifting coal for Renwick & Dobson (at 4d a ton!) at the old Torquay & Paignton Gas Works.

Phyllis - I was born in 1911 (one of ten children) at Bath Terrace in Belgrave Road, where the old Gas Board premises were situated, and later moved to Beausite Cottage in Hillesden Road, near the top of Braddons Street. My maiden name was Lear: my father came from Devon and was a regular soldier who had served in Ireland during the 'troubles'. My mother came from Torquay. I went to school at Braddons Street Infants where a Miss Harkney was Headmistress. I can remember the name of only one other teacher - a Miss Graham - who would sit in front of the class knitting a complete stocking each day! One school occupation remains in mind - we were given trays filled with sand, and told to make pictures or letters in it with our fingers. There was a shop known as 'Maudie Andrews' at the bottom of Braddons Street where one could purchase almost anything from specially-shaped loaves of bread and various jams to paraffin and salt fish.

I would often play by the bottom lamp, swinging around it on a rope, and my brother and I at marbles or with tops or hoops.

We were very poor. I was once sent to collect soup from a welfare kitchen in Albert Road, but found it mainly consisted of boiled pea-pods, so my mother threw it all away. Sunday School was at St Barnabus' (Tin) Church, and I remember attending a Sunday School outing from the Mother Church of Ellacombe, and came back to a magic lantern slide show in the Church Hall afterwards.

On Saturday mornings I would be sent to the Corporation Buildings in Market Street, with a can, to collect thick Jeyes Fluid provided free, for sanitary purposes, by the Board of Health.

Les - my first job in Torquay was that of an errand boy at Slades the Grocers in Abbey Place. My job included sweeping behind the counters and cleaning the overhead coin-transfer system. Part of being given employment was to survive an 'honesty test', which involved my employers leaving a 2 shilling piece on the floor behind the counter for me to find. My mother told me to be sure to take it to the manager, so I passed that test!

I remember during my time at Slades an old boy whose job it was to boil hams and roast coffee beans. I would go upstairs to his workshop for my dinner break, and sit on bags of coffee-beans with the rich aroma of coffee and hams to whet my appetite! I stayed at Slades for six months, and then left to work in Cann's Fish Shop in Babbacombe, near my home. But pay was very poor, so I decided to leave, bought my own 'kit' (a three-wheel barrow) and started my own fish retailing business at the tender age of 17.

I was known as 'the Boy' by the fish-selling fraternity, bought my stock at the Fish Quay (sometimes from Brixham) and would then depart to sell, where I could, throughout Ellacombe, Babbacombe and St Marychurch. Some weeks I barely earned 10 shillings. There were about twenty of us in this trade - fish retailing 'on the road'.

Brownings owned the Fish Quay 'franchise' in my time. There was Francis and his wife, and Edwin, George and Ernie (the auctioneer), who were his brothers. Another main dealer was a Mr Ching (not a Chinaman) - a farmer who lived in a big house at the top of Westhill Road. He bought up all the stocks of mackerel and spratts for resale, or for tinning. Rumour had it that he spread spratts over his farm fields as fertiliser, only to find next day that seagulls had eaten the lot!

There was also Johnny Uglow (a blind man rather well known for his strong language), who would walk unaided on the Quay ridge (edge) with a bucket on a rope, and collect sea water from the harbour for us to clean all our fish in wooden tubs for 3d.

Known to many Ellacombe folk was Phil Lander, noted particularly for his habit of wheeling down Market Street at speed on his three-wheeled fish 'kit', braking his progress with sparks flying, with a foot on a metal skid pad on the road. He was a regular on the roads and streets of the parish, and lived in Alexandra Road. He would also buy-up surplus stocks of furniture and household effects at sales and re-sell them. My wife and I bought a mangle from him for 10 shillings.

'Queeno' Martin was another selling fish from a cart. He lived in Queen Street and, I believe, had a family of some 21 children! Another was 'Cockney' Weiss (of German origin) and who lived at the top of Waterloo Road. Of particular note, because of his special 'Cockney' barrow with a slanting top, was Alfie Lyle - a well-known character, but a problem for his fellow fish sellers as his speciality was to buy in quantity and sell cheap, thereby undercutting his colleagues. Whereas they would sell mackerel at 1d each, Alfie would sell at 16 for 1 shilling.

The only fish that could be sold on a Sunday were mackerel, because they were known to 'go off' quickly - but they, and other cheap fish were the staple diet of the poor.

Next in retail 'stature' were the owners of horse and carts - the most well known being Frank Chick, Jack Dist and Jim Veale. These three were particular friends and drinking partners, 'hard cases' each. Their lovely high-stepping horses were stabled at Warren Road, and they traded all around the Town. When fish were in short supply at the Quay, they would race each other to Brixham for stock. 'Cosher' Pearce also had a horse and cart, stabled at the back of Princes Road. He lived near Franks, the Butchers, in a back alley by Hoxton Road and had a son in the Royal Air Force in the Second World War who was decorated for bravery.

And there was Billy Land, who lived at Plainmoor, and later bought a fish and chip shop at Hele. Lastly, were Tom and Jack Snell; the son lived at Lummaton Cross and the father at Kingskerswell. They were noted for the age of their poor old white pony (20 years).

'Top of the Tree' were the proud owners of motor vehicles, the most notorious being Bert Rendle who worked only on Wednesdays, loaded his van with supplies on the Quay, and had a lucrative business selling the fish at the Newton Abbot Market. From time to time, he would go out of business for a spell, and then start up again funded by the Brownings. Then there was Percy Gillard, who owned a 'Baby' Austin and sold in the Preston and Paignton areas; Fred Mayers, who did well in Chelston and Belgravia selling to the hotels and big houses, and Jack Nethercott, a Navy Pensioner, who owned a 'Bull-Nose' Morris and garaged it near Princes Street in Babbacombe. Also familiar in the fish retail trade were Fred Bond and 'Liza' Sparks, who held street-side stalls at the bottom of Market Street, outside the Ice Stores. All of us did a good trade with the Navy when the Fleet was in Torbay.

Phyllis and I first met when I called at her house on my 'rounds' in the Braddons - not a very successful courter, as I did not turn up on my first date! We courted for five to six years before marriage, as we could not afford to do so earlier. We married at the Newton Abbot Register Office on 20 February 1932 at 22 and 21 respectively. The fee was 7s.6d - being less costly than a church wedding. We lived for twelve months in two rooms in Berea Road, Ellacombe. After this, two (terrible) years in another cottage in Princes Street, then back with Phyllis' mother in Hillesdon Road.

From there we often looked at a neglected cottage belonging to Highclere House in Higher Warberry Road. It was owned by Mr Nesbitt, the Manager of the Tramways Depot at Plainmoor, who kindly allowed us to rent it at 16 shillings a week - not an inconsiderable sum in those days. But by then I was earning 30 to 40 shillings a week, so we managed. We were there for about seven years, until the outbreak of the Second World War in 1939, when I joined the Royal Navy for the duration.

I remember, particularly, a well-known lodging house called Hughes, in Braddons Street, which catered largely for the poor, the lame and the crippled from the first World War, and who numbered amongst the residents musicians and entertainers who would play and perform on the streets of Torquay. One I recall was an escapeologist with a difference who would, as a speciality, swallow pebbles and make them rattle internally. He performed outside the Marine Tavern, and was also a sword swallower! Others would sell postcards, matches and odds and ends on the streets to earn a meager living. They were rough lodgings, but it was shelter of sorts. We could see them, sometimes, in the yard below our home.

The character known as 'Charlie Chaplin' was also a resident. Another well-known family that lived in a Court off Stentifords Hill were the Browns, who were a family of musicians noted for their accordion band that played regularly in Castle Circus on Saturday evenings. I believe they were the same family that toured Ellacombe sharpening knives and scissors, etc.

'Skimpole' (or 'Skimpo') was another Braddons character - a 'man of all trades', remembered for his duties at Market Corner operating the tram points, and who would occasionally drive cattle to Newton Abbot Market.

A well-remembered sight of pre-war days was the chip stall of the Cavalier family - which was pushed all the way down Fleet Street, from Swan

Street where it was garaged, to the slip by the Harbour - with its chimney smoking away and fat and sparks flying, as it prepared for business. I believe the family lived in St James Road.

Nearby in the Madrepore Road were, I recall, a dairy, a German barber, and a family bakery noted for its owners who sold bread from baskets in the nearby streets, and who were always dressed in black - often covered in a dusting of white flour. I remember an Italian by the name of (I think) Percelli who, with his daughter, Polly, roamed the streets operating a barrel organ on a pole, by turning a handle. He also had a son who worked for the Gas Board.

At the top of the Braddons, at Grafton Terrace, was a wheelwright by the name of Brock, whose son played in the Grand Hotel Orchestra, and whose mother was a dresser at the Odeon Theatre (now a cinema). On a Saturday my wife and I would pay 6d for seats in the balcony of the theatre and enjoy music hall variety, which took place twice-nightly all the week and on matinée afternoons. At times, I would earn extra money as an attendant showing patrons to their seats.

The Fish Quay was always a very busy place. After the early morning landing of the catches, there would be the Langmead Brothers unloading sand, coal being shovelled into carts pulled by horses for unloading again into Messrs Renwick & Dobson's coal stores, and bundles of slates, for housing, being passed by hand, head over head, for stacking in piles ready for transportation elsewhere in builders' yards. Tea and buns, etc., were always available, at break times, in Stockman's Cafe nearby.

But always a joy for the locals was a visit to the Quay, at Regatta time, to marvel at the beautiful caravans of the fair people, which would be parked in lines across the unloading area whilst the fair was in full swing on Victoria Parade.

Nearer home, I recall (as a child) waiting for the milkman to fill my jug from his big churn with a tap at the bottom. He was so long in coming that I was persuaded by a lady to help myself (and save time) by filling the jug myself. But disaster! Despite every attempt I could not turn the tap off, and fled - leaving milk flowing everywhere on the road. My mother was faced with a bill for

A steamship unloading coal at the Quay c. 1930. Stockman's cafe lay at the right-hand end of the block of offices and stores to the extreme left of the picture. THE

30 shillings a disaster in those days. However, she refused the milkman's offer to forego the charge if she was prepared to beat me severely in front of him - preferring to pay up and do the necessary in private, in her own time. What a mum!

There was a music shop in Market Street I recall by the name of Moons, as I earned extra money in a loft upstairs over the shop chopping sticks for sale in bundles. Nearby was a second-hand furniture store, by the Green, where we bought our first furniture - a table and two chairs for the princely sum of 6 shillings. Next to the blacksmiths, and stables, at the bottom of Berea Road was a coal merchant who, in his spare time and with his son, was the conductor of the Town's Silver Band. A well-known bakery was Wills' in Woodville Road, where one could purchase the most delicious pasties at two for 3d on a Saturday night. They also had a stall in the Market. Our special treat was a block of chocolate for 4d, and an ounce of St Bruno tobacco for 8d.

Two also well-known and very severe gentlemen of Ellacombe were the School Attendance Officers - the junior of which (I believe) was called Mr Rooke: the senior was called Mr Jaggs, and had a hook in place of one wrist. Ill befell children who were caught 'playing hookey' - a caning offence in those days at the very least!

One of the best fish and chip shops in Ellacombe was Coombes', at the junction of Princes Road and Hoxton Road. Their daughter, Stella, was a superb swimmer and winner of competitions with the Leander Swimming Club. During the summer Coombes' superb ice-cream was sold at Corbyn's Head.

In the early 1930s I recall a very bad rainstorm that hit Ellacombe, and water poured down from the Warberries to flood all the houses adjacent to Brewery Park. This was well before 'global warming'.

MR V. FELLOWES
(transcribed from a letter to the author)

Many thanks for your interesting letter following the insertion of the photograph in the local press. This came about when my nephew and wife Ron and Jean Freer of Florida Road sent me a photocopy of an Ellacombe School Magazine of 1928. Jean knows Stan Crocker, the Editor at the time. I had left school in '26, but my brother Francis and his two pals Reg Lang and Louis Parnell were in the production team. Of my family, grandfather and grandmother both came from Topsham. After moving to Torquay they owned the single-storey grocery shop at the foot of Cavern Road, since demolished. Grandfather died in 1904 at the shop and grandmother in 1910. Many debts were left 'on the slate' when the surviving spouse died. I never knew them.

My father was in the navy at the time, being the yougest left at home: he walked to Plymouth as soon as he was eligible to join - brothers and sister having emigrated. Mother and two sisters and a brother settled in Torquay from Filleigh, near South Molton. The usual Victorian large family, worker-tenants of Lord Fortesque.

At that time Torquay was developing. As ever, people were on the move within the county. Our friendly neighbours next door came from Plympton - like my parents with one child and enlarged in time, three of us, six of them! A couple nearby came from Bristol, also one from Bath. As I remarked, father's three brothers and sister emigrated to Canada in turn - the eldest prospered there as a building contractor in Montreal.

Until 1927 we - father, mother, sister Daisy and brother Francis - lived at 32 Woodville Road, beyond the steps, before moving to No. 31 near Greek's Dairy. Nephew Antony, a widower, now owns the house on the demise of my sister in '93. Having lived in the road all her life, and with a good memory, you would have to go no further for information. I stay there when I visit - used to be twice a year; I must remember on my next visit to look in the Market to see the doors of the cabins I made when working for Mr Sture of Westhill as a joiner who built them. My employer had worked on aircraft for De Havilands during the Great War. Errol, the second son of Shapley, the grocer, was a pilot, keen on aeroplanes and had plans to build one.

My employer and I (whilst Mr Sture kept his other work going) finished the main parts for him, and Mr Shapley took it away to Plymouth for completion. I lost track of it until late 1936, when he came to me and asked if I would work for him on another larger aircraft, which I did. We built it at their stores behind Fleet Street, took it to Exeter for assembly and test flight, where the pilot let the tail clip a hedge and turned it on its nose. I was pointed towards Fairey Aviation at Hayes until 1946, when no longer require, but remained in West London until retirement. Marrying a Hampshire girl in '36, we moved to Knoll Cottage at the bottom of Barton Road. We moved to London in '38 (how naive!) to Ealing, moving again to Ewell to be near a daughter in '81.

Your name and address must be from from the Langmeads of Dunmere Road: would it be your father who owned the two sailing barges *Mizpah* and *Hope*, which drew sand from Galmpton to the Torquay Inner Harbour - wonderful Dart sand - and I believe crossed the Channel to the French coast bringing the onion sellers?

I remember your father moving to Mount Herman Road to open a bungalow fish and chip shop. Since again being in touch with you, it seems my recollection of your parents is at fault. I was sure they lived in the terrace on Dunmere Road, not below; the only family I knew there were the Drews: the two boys were my age, the father worked at Swaynes Brewery in Lower Ellacombe Church Road.

Reg the younger was one of our group of four choir boys, and in earlier times we would all go off on Sunday afternoon walks. Reg died not many years ago in a house on the same terrace as he was brought up in. Living on the upper terrace was Mr Windsor, who started a haulage business with a wartime lorry. That was the end house nearest the Church. At the same end was Mr Gibbons, coal merchant, who had two sons. One played the cornet, and would play solo at the Church social evenings. He also played in a band (cannot recall the name) in opposition to the Salvation Army! His older brother was a postman - a great friend of a friend in our terrace who was a GPO counter clerk and whose father was a chauffeur (the Downeys). I remember his car when parked on the Road - an upright ruby-red vehicle with steel studded tyres painted white.

Of Dunmere Road I remember the Clarkes, Clarence and sister; the Weymouths - two boys - father in a bath-chair (war casualty, I presume); the Pierces - one boy became a draughtsman at Jenkins marble works, later moved to London. Father was a tea taster and mixer at Shapleys, the grocers.

Of the ladies you mention, Amy Frost 'rings a bell'. The closest I came to one of you was sitting next in a double desk in Mr Hoare's Class II or III: that was a room off the main hall. In those days, the hall was divided into three by drawn curtains. During my time at Ellacombe School these curtains were replaced by folding screens as funds allowed.

My earliest memories, being scared with others when a 'blimp' came in sight above the Copse (a Zeppelin); trudging or being taken to the bakers near the School (later to be Hookways) to collect a bag of fancy biscuits for my birthday tea. It was March, and had to be after dark; going to the Police Station (in Market Street) to get a permit for potatoes which were duly served at Corlines at the rear.

As we boys of Woodville Road grew older, much time was spent up the Copse - thick undergrowth then, not cleared until after the Second World War. Each 'gang' had their own camp. Across Windsor Road was what we called 'Second Copse' - a flatter area covered by gorse, with a cleared area large enough to kick a football about. On the way up or back we would look in at the smithy at the rear of Ellacombe Church Road. Often a horse was being shod - I think the name of the blacksmith was Lock.

Later still we played football at Walls Hill - five pitches of a kind, and the cricket pitch which is still there. There was a nine-hole golf course and the quarry nearby was still in operation. I remember standing with my father on Castle Hill facing the Town Hall to see slides projected on a large screen of the proposed development of the Westhill Estate. I believe those were the first council houses built in Torquay.

We were all sent to Sunday School as children at 10 o'clock (Mr Farley, the grocer, midway between school and church). The Head would march to Church at 11 o'clock.

The annual treat was to Paignton - two hired tramcars. There was a required stop at Preston for photographs. When old enough we enrolled in the choir - 12 boys, 8 men: our treat was a trip up the Dart, and a dash to Merton's fish and chip shop on pay-day, once a quarter (sixpence my first payment!). We boys merged together as 'gangs', usually of 5 to 10 boys. The 'Heard Gang', an older age group from Hoxton Hill, was the one found to have a 'den' at Hopes Nose (what a way from home!) in which a few stolen goods were found (not serious for correction). These groups were usually older schoolboys, mischievous maybe, never any damage.

Reverting to people you have met - Gilbert Shapley's sons Ted and Bill were known to me. The family had a removal business - operating from the rear of Princes Road (bottom). I believe one of them was a great friend of my brother-in-law Sidney Freer. I believe they were apprentices at Shapleys on the Strand together and remained friends. Getting back to Berachah Road, one side is the terrace of outbuildings of Hatfield Road, tenements on the other side. Hookways, bakers, the corner facing Ellacombe Church Road and

Lock's Hill. At the foot of the Hill was Lock's the butchers. I can see him now, bustling about. In those days it seems with all these little family businesses the boss was always 'on the trot'. Prayers were always said before a shop opened.

The Hookways, as a young couple, took over an established business, moved down from Exeter somewhere about 1925. They had three girls and remained there until retirement. Mr Hookway used to deliver mornings and afternoons, had a 'hunter' between the shafts. He rode it at gymkhanas at times. Did you ever hear the horse once bolted? It was in one of these three out-buildings that the French onion sellers camped in when they were around (usually only for a few weeks).

Then there was Henry Blunt who had a couple of horses and carts. He had a long low loader which we often saw going down Market Street towards the Royal Theatre on a Saturday night. He seemed to have a regular contract to take the show's scenery and kits to Torre Station. Those were the days of variety on stage. Some were excellent.

I remember Charlie Bishop's car repair work-shop was next to the Ellacombe Joinery Works where I was apprenticed. That was an established concern when Edward Terry of Babbacombe, Bill Middleton of Ellacombe and Peter Winter of Petersfield - wartime 'buddies' - took over from Philips. Some of the machines were still in use when I last called in '91. Bill Middleton was on his own, with staff, when I visited about '49. His son carried on and extended the first floor work-shop, and his grandson was in charge when I last called. Going seemed to be tough then, like many other businesses and trades.

Reverting to names again: Bertie Chalker - I think he knew my brother Francis, two years junior. I think they were at Jenkins, the marble people, at their offices in Union Street. I cannot work out - your brother Harry sounds right, but I had left School two years before the magazine you mention which printed his rhyme. I recall visit-ing a pottery at Petitor, smaller than Longpark, next to Grants monumental masons - both now gone. Maybe the buildings are still there, on the bend in Teignmouth Road opposite the Golf Course.

On the boundary of Ellacombe - the Copse, Windsor Road, Bronshill Road, Chatsworth Road down the steps to the top of Market Street; a line up to the end of Pennysylvania Road across to the top of Hoxton Hill to the Copse. The area behind Princes Road East and West to the cart track which led to Ellacombe Church Road, and the rear of it to Windsor Road was open ground, allotments and Joy's Field. Joy was a Coal Merchant in Princes Road - the end terrace house near the slip road to Lower Ellacombe Church Road: open ground where Joy occasionally had a hurdler which was exercised there by a jockey called Kernick who used to ride for him.

Race tracks in those days were at Petitor, Haldon, Newton Abbot and Buckfastleigh. The terrace of houses, owned by Mr Cruse was sold in the early twenties to set up his son, who began by building bungalows in Windsor Road towards the Copse. He then built semis on the allotments to the rear - that was the beginning of the develop-ment of that larger area. Cary Park Road, between Warbro Road and Windsor Road, was cut with houses each side about that time.

Reflecting on those days, one did not have to travel far for the necessities. There was Pristons general store in Woodville Road near the Park, Greek's Dairy at the other end of the terrace. Tremayne would supply a bicycle from his front room: Bert Mitchelmore repaired boots and shoes in a shop. Page the bakers by the steps, Gibbons - coal merchants - at the other end. Another gro-cers - the Misses Green at the end of the road: greengrocers next, name forgotten. Pike's bakery down the road towards the Church: Tucker's off-licence at the bottom of Ellacombe Church Road, another dairy in Carlton Road - these dairymen did their rounds with motor-cycle combinations with box-cars - another general store corner of Carlton and Kenwyn Roads.

One could almost tell the time of day by trades-men delivering - horse-drawn milk floats, baker's vans, Mr Weiss with a three-wheel barrow selling fish; Valley's ice cream cart on Saturday after-noons on his way to Walls Hill from Union Street - always too expensive for us. Walls 'Stop Me and Buy One' ruined them.

The group of shops in Hoxton Road, and by the School were much smarter then, 75 years ago. Whyatts, chemists; Richards, saddlers; Weddon, newsagents and Hookways bakery, with Hatherley's barbers by the School. French, butch-er; Pike's dairy - he used to travel to relatives in North Devon every Wednesday on his motor-cycle combination, Mrs Pike installed, for butter and eggs. Their relatives had a smallholding near my grandparents in Filleigh, near South Molton: seemed to be dead-on-time coming down Woodville Road on the return journey.

Next was a grocer (name forgotten) before the days of packaged wares - everything weighed and bagged. Hayward's off-licence, and across the road Smerdon's greengrocers. Up Hoxton Hill was another baker, another small business, baking in the morning and delivering himself in the afternoon, carrying a large wicker basket - must have been hard times making a living.

Sammy Bowditch, a farmer from out near Scott's Bridge, used to deliver milk to one customer in Woodville Road early evening.

Sorry to be so long writing, and about the time taken to write this, starting and stopping as time goes by. I am now a widower, keeping house and chores. Keeps me occupied!

KEN GRAHAM

My father came to Torquay from Middlesborough and my mother from near Par, in Cornwall. My mother's first husband was called Smerdon, and had died. She then met my father. My three older sisters were Smerdons, and I was a Graham. The family of Smerdons were related to those that ran a confectioners shop and greengrocers in Princes Road. I do not know how my father and my mother met; nor do I know anything about my grandparents. My mother came up from Par to join her sister who lived in Seaton, and was comparatively well off. Again, I do not know why my parents came to Torquay and set up home in Pennsylvania Road, where I was born.

My father was earlier a merchant seaman, and when he left the sea became a steam engineer - servicing steam-powered machinery such as steam-rollers. I was born on 18 September 1920, and was the eldest son - having a younger brother called Frank and a sister called Ruby: she died during the last war. I lived in Pennsylvania Road until we moved to Berea Road - which was then just under construction. Ours was the second house built, next to the Rundles, who lived in the first. Nearby lived Mr Underhill, who was a commissionnaire at the Electric Cinema. Ron, his son (who died very young with diabetes), also worked at the Cinema. There were two other brothers called Peter and Derek.

Opposite lived a lady who was employed as Matron at the old Torbay Hospital in Higher Union Street. I remember she always wore a white apron. A few doors up lived Jack Fowler, who was a regular player for Torquay United. My friend Jack Drage moved, with his parents, near to

the top of the Road, next to Grace Redwood - a big girl. Up above them lived the Higgins family. One son worked in a factory at Shiphay and another one I knew as 'Greg' Higgins lost his eye playing snooker. Apparently he hit a ball which struck an electric light bulb, and fragments of glass did permanent damage to his eye. I remember Roy White (who worked for Renwick's Travel Agency) and his older brother, and the Shepherd family, the father of whom always walked the Town in a kilt.

Not many houses in this area were erected at this time (mid 1920s) - those that were, were 'Joy' built. The field adjacent was known as 'Joy's Field', just below Warberry Copse. Before the Joy houses were erected, a lime pit existed nearby. A boy from Congella Road, who later drove Devon General buses, fell partly in the pit and permanently damaged his hand (left crab- like). Because of this injury he could never join the armed forces.

I was educated at Ellacombe School, where Major Collett was Headmaster and Mr Parr, Mr Tozer and Mr Cowling were teachers. There were also two lady teachers - one of whom was called Miss Tiffany. I do recall the man who used to take the school photographs in the playground, because he had a prominent, rather bulbous, nose.

I was a regular player in the School football team with Fred Phillips, and Les Honeywell - who lived in Ellacombe Church Road, near to Browns, the Electrical Shop. We would walk all the way to Windmill Hill to play, or to take part in other sports. I was an 'unbeatable' 100-yards runner.

My wife would not believe this tale - but because we were nearly all poor, with little money to spare, one boy turned up to play wearing football shorts made up from his mother's cut down 'drawers'! Most could not afford shinpads, and had to 'make do' with rolled-up newspapers in our socks.

I joined the Sea Scouts as a schoolboy, and we used to meet at Walls Hill in a tin hut. A Dr Drake was the Scoutmaster. His father had a butcher's shop in Preston. I obtained the job of delivering meat, by bicycle, on a Saturday in the Preston area, which I enjoyed - especially the occasional 'tips'. Whilst at School I sang in two church choirs - with Geoff Drage at Upton Church (where a Mr Trotman was the Organist), and with Eric Waldron at St Johns: the latter Church paid higher choir fees! After leaving school I met Vera Stantiford at Upton Church, who used to attend services with her friend. We did eventually 'walk out' for a while, but then I went away into the Navy. Her mother ran the Burlington and then the Dorchester Hotels.

I can remember regular visits to Hookways, the bakers, on a Friday when I had my weekly penny pocket money. Then we could buy things for as little as a farthing. I used to call at Hookways for 'hardbakes' at a farthing to eat before starting school in the mornings, or call at Ernie Lowe's - a general shop on the corner opposite Ellacombe Church (near Selley's the butcher). Nearby was a grating in the road, where people sometimes dropped pennies in: we boys would try to recover the coins by means of magnets tied to sticks.

I was made to go to Sunday School. My mother was very religious. We were not allowed to play cards or do games on a Sunday. I was first sent to the Methodist Chapel Sunday School, in Market Street, and then to the one at Ellacombe Church. When later joining the Navy I never knew whether to describe myself as C. of E. or Chapel Non- Conformist! We would go on Sunday School outings to Dawlish, Haytor or Lustleigh - always by train. I remember being invited to sit on the lap of an older girl called Gwen Mudge on one outing (her brother was a Boy Scout), and I thought she was 'the cat's whiskers'!

This reminds me of an old saying (very true!) 'A man chases a woman until she catches him!' I didn't belong to 'Heard's Gang' because I did not like the boys who did. I was 'captured' by them one day and tied up. My brother ran off to tell my father, and he had to come and release me! We had a 'gang'` of sorts, up the hill above Brewery Park, with our own bonfire. 'Heard's Gang' would come and raid our 'brake'!

Frank Annear was my best chum. His father had lost both his legs whilst serving with the Torquay Fire Brigade. He ran a boot and shoe repair business in Woodville Road. His son, Frank, unfortunately, had a withered leg, but would not let the disability prevent him from playing football in Brewery Park. We would often play there with Vic Hunt, Bert Chalker and other 'soccer-mad' friends. Roy Hunt was Vic's younger brother. I used to go to Woodville Road nearby to my chum's birthday party, and I remember being given 'seedy cake' (made with caraway seed), which I hated. I would eat it quickly - which was a mistake, as Frank's mum then thought I loved it and would offer me another slice!

I worked at Waglands, a grocer's shop at Chelston, as an apprentice shop assistant at 7/6d a week, before joining the Royal Navy. Frank used to sleep in a shed at the back of his garden when his parents 'took in' visitors during the summer. We both had push-bikes. Frank would come to wake me in the mornings at Berea Road, as I was a heavy sleeper. You may not believe this, but I used to tie a length of string to my finger when going to bed, and dangle this out of the window. Frank would tug this to wake me, and we would then get on our bikes and go down to Torre Abbey Sands to swim before going to work.

On first leaving school my sister Margaret Smerdon, who was a manageress at Bobby's on the Strand, wanted me to apply for a job as a trainee window dresser. I went for an interview with another lad called Bobby Finn. However - I didn't really fancy the job of dressing ladies' models or wearing the currently-required striped trousers and black jacket. I therefore went to work at Shapley's grocery shop, at the bottom of Fleet Street as an odd job lad. I particularly remember the big cellar below the shop, where I would help to unload boxes of stores. In those days it was the practice to include gifts within the boxes, and often the shop girls would come below to see if there were gift stockings included! My job included polishing the brass signs outside the shop, going out on bike deliveries and taking messages to Shapley's big warehouse down behind Rockeys stores further up Fleet Street. Len Harvey worked on the cash desk, operating the overhead cash dispensers to and from the various counter sales staff.

Les Rowan taught us boys to box and was a scout leader. His father was the Chief Fire Officer, who tragically died in a car accident a long while ago. Freddie Combes was another local boxer.

I went, part-time to the Art School, in Braddons Hill Road West, after leaving Ellacombe, and also attended evening classes at the Technical College in Teignmouth Road to improve my education when I worked at Chelston. My mother helped with the fees, although she could ill-afford the money. My sister would recite poetry to me, although I was rarely receptive. She was, however, good enough to win several elocution contests at the Town Hall under the direction of Ernest Goss. My eldest sister, Vy, worked on the till at the Picturedrome Cinema in the Market. Her husband was, for thirty years, a gardener at Cockington. A woman played a piano at the Cinema to accompany the action in the silent films shown there. I remember an action-film serial called 'Wild Man of Borneo', which ended each week with the hero in an impossible situation, which was always resolved by next week's episode! The Empire Cinema, built later above

Ellacombe Green, presented the first 'talkie' film in Torquay, which was Al Jolson in 'Sonny Boy'. When I lived as a child in Pennsylvania Road there was a fish and chip shop in Cavern Road called Martins, and another in Princes Road, next to the dairy near Hoxton Road, called Coombes. The daughter of the proprietor, Stella, was a great swimmer - a member of the Torquay Leander Swimming Club and later a National swimming coach. I was a keen swimmer and a member, and recall that Monica Pearce was a superb swimmer also. We swum a lot at the Municipal Baths at Beacon Hill. A young girl nearly lost her life in the pool, being sucked into the drain pipe whilst the pool was being drained. Luckily she emerged at the sea end at Beacon Cove. Another lass wedged her foot in the grab rail at the side, I remember, whilst getting out, and was lucky not to break her leg falling back.

The Babbacombe Regatta was always fun for Ellacombe youngsters - as indeed was the Torbay one. I would take part in the sports games, and loved to attend the Fair at night on the Downs. We kids would go up there after the Fair had left and search for money which had fallen in the grass: we always found some.

Names come to mind as I talk: the police station, then in Market Street, had a station sergeant with one arm (lost in the Great War). There were also two police brothers (detective sergeants, I believe) who lived in Ellacombe Church Road. I remember them particularly as they were always accompanied by an Alsation dog. The Skinner family were well known at the Harbour - Keith and Maurice - all boatmen.

My wife came from Wales. She gave me five children - four girls and one son, and was an excellent cook. I met her at at a dance at the Co-op Hall - a favourite meeting place for us youngsters. She came up from Wales with a friend to work in Belgrave Road.

I joined the Royal Navy in 1936 with a Sid Hopkins, and trained (later as a gunnery rating) in HMS *Impregnable*, and at Whale Island, and came home to Torquay when my period of regular service was ended.

KEN LASSETER

My father and mother came to Torquay from Hayling Island in Hampshire. He was advised to go to Devon for his health - having been discharged from the Army in 1918 in very poor physical condition. I was born in Portsmouth, close by. We came to Torquay in 1924, when I was six and my brother Cyril between two and three years of age. Father was a monumental mason before the war, and worked extensively on the spire of Chichester Cathedral, at Goodwood House and other country houses. He was born in Shrewsbury, but had travelled, since birth, to various parts of the Country, following my grandfather's trade as a journeyman-chargehand wood feller. The Company for which my grandfather worked eventually opened a large factory at Chichester, and that was how father met mother, married her and settled in the area.

My mother was a tailoress and costumier (one of fourteen children), and came from the Hampshire–Sussex border area nearby. I remember attending a private school on Hayling Island, as there were no junior state schools nearer than Havant. The area was quite rural then, and we had a farm at our back, so I was brought up with farm animals and in an agricultural environment. When we first came to Torquay we lived in lodgings at the top end of Hoxton Road (No.69), and from there I would attend Ellacombe School. We journeyed to the town by rail: our furniture arriving later on a Lethbridge & Mercer pantechnicon.

Whilst working as general foreman for a local builder, my father bought a plot of land at the top end of Lower Ellacombe Church Road and built upon it three houses - one we retained for our own use and the other two were put up for sale. It was some seven to eight months before we moved to our new home, and there we stayed until I got married. By then my father had established his own building business, which I later joined as a partner. At the time we moved to our new home, other houses were being erected at the bottom of Berea Road and at Egerton Road.

Other builders were Heard (who made up all the nearby roads), White and Joy. I remember the latter as coming from Peckham's Copse, near Chichester. He came to Torquay and lived in a property with stables, garage, etc. on the hill between Lower Ellacombe Church Road and Princes Road - an area later to become known as Joy's Hill. It was from here he bought the land to build in Berea Road and nearby. I also remember, vividly, that Heard had a stone quarry at the top of Brewery Park, by the pine trees opposite our houses, and the stone was used for the road building.

An old quarryman I knew as Jim used to work the stone, and after dynamiting would scatter rubble and stones over the surrounding property. Heard became responsible for many light repairs as a result. Nearby was a blacksmith - a man who worked at his trade until he was around 90 years of age. My father and I would take our building tools to him for sharpening and repair. Around the pond, opposite, a Mr Jennings had his allotments. I remember he had a tarred hut for his gardening equipment, which one day caught fire and made a terrific blaze. I was about thirteen at the time. It was after the fire that the pond was in-filled.

I was a member of the infamous 'Heard's Gang', whose favourite pastime was to pick fights with neighbouring 'gangs'. I remember going into 'battle' with two lads (later plasterers) of German extraction near the local archway, and on another occasion got mixed up with 'Billy Bond's Gang' (later at the Grammar School with me) on the steps leading up to Kenwyn Road, where they had got themselves trapped! His 'lot' had a bonfire at Plainmoor, whilst our 'gang' had the same in Brewery Park. It was a common sight to see us boys dragging collected material for our Guy Fawke's Night celebration through the streets for the big event of the year.

I had a number of boyhood friends - Vic Hunt, Bert Langmead, Eric Waldron, Les Prior and Arthur Cooper. The latter got me into trouble at school and a caning from Major Collett, the Headmaster. It was so unfair, as I was only retaliating against the bullying of my young brother, and got caught and caned for my noble act!

Ken Prior, a lad who was tranferred from a Westward Ho! Grammar School to Torquay became a close friend. He lived nearby, in Egerton Road, and his father was a policeman - a big man, who could easily tuck a boy under each arm. Les had three half-sisters, with little in common with their half-brother, so he spent a lot of time in our house with me. There was also Ken Lander, who lived in the Corporation Buildings in Market Street, as his father was a fireman there.

Very little remains in my memory of my schooldays at Ellacombe School. I recall the names of most of the teachers, of course, in particular Mr Charlie Parr, who took music classes and trained the school choir for competitions at the Town Hall. I recall he tried to get me to join St John's church choir - in his view, the best in town, but I offended him by not choosing to become a member.

Woodwork classes were held in an old building at the bottom of Rock Road: the teacher was called Mr Gorbett. One job I intensely disliked was being called upon to take the hospital collection box around the School classrooms in front of the other boys.

I remember the school had a varnished 'Board of Honour', on which was inscribed the names of boys who had won scholarships and others who had accomplished acts of merit for the School. I also remember that discipline was very strict, with a stern Major Collett as the Headmaster. But this was accepted without question, and we felt no real resentment about corporal punishment, if it was justly earned.

Although I was fond of sport at Ellacombe School - particularly cricket - I never made the first team. I remember painfully pulling a hamstring at the Windmill Hill playing fields.

I was fond of fishing from an early age, and later joined the Angling Club, which had a clubhouse on the bend of Princess Pier. This was seaward of the concert hall that once stood there before the fire that destroyed it. Another pal and I (his father was a solicitor) would, when the fishing was bad, climb under the wooden floor of the pier to search for coins which had fallen through the planking and on to the concrete base below.

Holidays were carefree days for youngsters in those days. No doors were ever locked, or needed to be. Mostly we ranged over the area - fishing off the rocks at Anstey's Cove with bait collected from Torquay Harbour (mussels, etc.), or bought mackerel - or foolhardily rock-climb at Redgate. I remember on one occasion we climbed a narrow path with my younger brother, who suddenly froze after nearly falling off the cliffside, and I had to carry him back up. Another pal with us, called Maddocks, slid to the bottom on his backside - wearing out the seat of his pants in the process! Another common but dangerous climb was down into Long Quarry, where a young lad called Sonny fell to his death and drowned. He was a very good swimmer, and might have survived had he not hit his head on the rocks below.

At about this time my father brought home a dog who was about to be 'put down' for sheep worrying. The animal was truly vicious at first, but within two or three weeks became tame and affectionate, and took to me in particular. Later he would walk to meet me halfway from school, would take my books, and scamper back to the house - to await my homecoming, still with the books in his mouth, on the doorstep.

Another 'hairy' adventure I remember was riding Frank Pook's bicycle down Upton Hill - only to find the brakes failing at the bottom. I was very lucky not to catch my wheels in the tramlines - a common hazard during the days of the trams.

Trams were very popular - 9d (old money) for a circular tour from the Strand, via Ellacombe, St Marychurch, Babbacombe and Wellswood, and 3d from the Strand to Paignton, where the line terminated. I was told that, in the early days before overhead power it was not at all uncommon for horses to be electrocuted on contact with the electric floor studs. I spent much time about the harbour and on the water, as my father then owned a converted lifeboat which he moored in the Inner Harbour. I was very interested in yachts and yachting - in particular the beautiful J Class yachts and the luxury cruisers of Sir Thomas Sopwith, and Lord Runciman's three-master with solid teak embellishments.

I did not attend Sunday School, as a child, which was uncommon. My father had had a very strict upbringing, and therefore he decided to be more lenient with his children and would not force them to go against their will. During school holidays I worked in Oxley's Shop in Ellacombe Church Road (opposite Woodville Road). The owners were friends of the family. Part of my job was to weigh up and fill blue paper bags with rice, tea, dried fruit, etc., and was strongly told off at the outset, for making the contents overweight. I would also accompany the husband, in his big Ford saloon, on his deliveries of boxes of groceries to customers. On Sundays my family, and theirs, would drive out to the Moors - a great luxury in those days.

Milk was delivered to our doors by the dairy, and jugs were filled from a large metal milk churn, by measure. A man called Jan, from Hoxton Road, delivered our newspapers. I remember he later became a conductor on the new buses. Our groceries were delivered by van from the Home & Colonial Stores in Union Street. Once or twice my father would send me to collect delicious home-made faggots and peas from Easterbrook's shop in Victoria Road.

I remember a terrible flood about 1938, when the water rose at the bottom of Lower Ellacombe Church Road to the level of the Hoxton Road above. The flood water entered the basements of all the nearby houses up to ground floor level as far up the road as the Old Brewery.

My schooldays changed when I obtained a scholarship to the Torquay Boys Grammar School. I remember the 'fee-paying' boys were put into Class 2A and the remainder into Class 2B - although positions were generally reversed after the first year, and we moved up into Class 3!

There was an annual intake of 35 scholarship pupils from the Torbay area - Ellacombe School averaging two of these places a year. Necessary books and clothing had to be paid for by parents. Many children bought books second-hand from the class replaced in the ensuing year. To buy new from Jowetts, the printers, was expensive, for example Geography primers were 7s.6d, even in those days. Clothing and sportswear were generally purchased from Rickards the outfitters, in Union Street.

The Headmaster was Mr Jackman - highly respected by both pupils and parents, and in the profession. When he walked into a class there was instance silence and attention. I recall the names of some of the masters - a Mr Dutton (who lived in Cary Park Road) who also looked after the cricket teams, Mr Coates the gym master, Mr Martin, the French master, a Mr Edwards and Mr Ellis (the local historian) who taught history. In those days we had to study a minimum of seven subjects for the Cambridge Examination. I could not get on with history, an eighth subject, and was allowed to drop it on appeal.

My main interest in sport was the game of cricket, and I remember many nostalgic matches at the school's sports ground at Cricketfield Road. Part of the nostalgia remains over the memory of the home-made cake we could always buy from the groundsman's wife at the back of her cottage. Many 'old boys' will remember this mouthwatering cake she would sell to us at a penny a slice.

After leaving school I went to work at Crossmans, the timber merchants, whose imposing entrance in Union Street dominated Market Corner. I had first taken the Civil Service Cartographer's Examination, but was incensed when, having gained over 85% marks, others with considerably less marks were offered posts, and not I until the following year, which I refused. My career at Crossmans before the war was absorbing and satisfying. After a spell in the office and yard to learn the trade, I passed the Timber Trades' Federation examination in Softwood and Business Studies and 'took to the road' as a representative for the Company. Among the commissions in which I became closely involved were supplying shuttering to Laytons, who were contracted to burrow under Rock Walk in building the main town sewers, and the rebuilding of Messrs Bobby & Son's premises on the Strand after its disastrous fire. In those days, big cargo ships from Russia, Scandinavia and other countries would offload large cargoes of timber on Haldon Pier, which would then be transferred by lorry to Crossman's timber yard. I would be involved in dealing with bills of lading, invoices, etc. at the shipping agents, whose premises were situated off Union Street - all a-bustle with ship's captains loaded with the vessels' papers and cargo manifests. One particular commission I remember was to select special timber for Shapleys, the grocers, whose son was a keen aviator. When his personal aircraft was completed, I was invited to accompany him on his maiden flight at Exeter Airfield, but quickly declined the offer!

I remember the founder, Thomas J. Crossman clearly. He was quite a character, who would come into the office every day until of great age. At near 90 I recall him requesting his secretary to book him a tour of Canada! I worked for his son, Harold.

Colleagues in my time with the Company were Miss Hanson, the office manager, a Miss Browning, Kay Brooks and my future wife, who was a ledger clerk at the time. Amongst the yard staff was the senior, a Mr Peters, Sam Bowden and Fred Edgecombe, plus a junior. There was another traveller called Tommy Clarke. Overall, Crossmans employed a large staff. Shortly before the war I was called up for service with the Militia, with whom I trained for some months until enlisting in the Devonshire Regiment. I served in Belgium, at the beginning of the conflict, being part of a military force covering the retreat of the main army to Dunkirk. I was captured at the time of the evacuation, and remained a prisoner of war in Germany for five years.

Prior to leaving Crossmans for military service I became friendly with a young lady who corresponded with me for a period until the letters ceased, as she had found another boyfriend. In the meanwhile my future wife, who I remembered as a business colleague, would send me cigarettes. On return from the war I called upon her to thank her for her kindness over the years. She was called Betty Cornish. Her parents and grandparents were market gardeners from Maidencombe. In retrospect (and I'm sure my wife will concur), I was not a very romantic young man! Within some eighteen months we decided, by mutual consent, to get engaged, and married at St Marychurch (after the destruction of the Church in a German bombing raid) in the church hall, at the rear, on 22 November 1947.

At this time my future wife lived with her two sisters in a house in Compton Place: I later bought out the sisters' share. We lived there for some time before buying our present house in Pine View Gardens, where we have remained domiciled ever since. I did not return to work at Crossmans after the War, for a number of reasons including the offered remuneration, and finally went into partnership with my father in the building trade, where I remained until retirement.

PERCY GODFREY DIMMOCK

I was baptised at Ellacombe Church on 29 July 1906, and my brother Stanley 18 months later in 1907 - both being Confirmed at the ages of 15 and 16 respectively. We lived then at a house called Woodleigh, in Hatfield Road. My father came to Torquay from up-country - I believe in the London area - as I remember going on a visit to his brothers with him, there, when I was small. He started his own printing business in a shed at the rear of the house, specialising in engraved and headed notepaper and envelopes, with personalised crests - the business being supported at the time of the First World War by the many American and New Zealand troops who were billeted in the area of my home. All crests were done by hand, in colour, and embossed on the stationery. My brother and I would help with the packing and delivery of the completed orders after school. Sadly my father died when I was 15, so we remember very little of his origin.

My mother came from Five Lanes, Marldon, where she was born. Grandfather, there, had a mini-farm and smallholding, but had damaged his health with tree surgery. My early memories of grandmother were of bi-weekly or summer visits, and walking all the way from Ellacombe, down Upton Hill, across Cricketfield Road to Shiphay and over two fields to Marldon. There we boys would have to draw water, collect wood for the fire, help in the garden and with other chores, after which we would be refreshed with tea and cake. My energetic mother would then say 'Come on boys - it's a lovely day for a nice walk' and off we would go, down an old lane by the Smokey House Inn into Preston, catch a tram back to the Pavilion and then walk back to Woodleigh, Hatfield Road. Mother would then say 'What a lovely time we've had' and with much groaning we would agree!

My mother was a very strict disciplinarian. I remember clearly her birthday one day, and the birthday cards that arrived. I had the temerity to ask her age, and was told that 'little boys should be seen and not heard', and had my ears soundly boxed. On another occasion I could not resist 'sampling' a sweet from a tempting display in the Home & Colonial Stores in Union Street, could not hide it in my mouth and had another ear-boxing session all the way home to Ellacombe. And that was nothing to the punishment I received if marched home by a big, burly, six-foot policeman for some minor misdemeanour! Another punishment was received, after collection of cream from the local dairy one Sunday, when I dared to question the rule that one never shopped on a Sunday!

Living in Hatfield Road, Ellacombe School was but a few minutes walk away. Teachers I remember were 'Harry' Hoare, Mr Weaver, Mr Cowling, Mr Blanchard, Mr 'Charlie' Parr and the Headmaster, Mr 'Harry' Terry.

The Girls' School next door had two teachers I recall - Miss Blackler and Miss Collihole. My job every Monday morning was to fill up all the desk inkwells from a special watering can stowed away in a cupboard. I remember particularly a tough little lad called Harvey (who later kept a gardeners' shop opposite Upton Church) throwing a 7-inch blackboard cleaner and ink pot at Mr Hoare - smothering him with ink - and for which he received a caning of 'six of the best' from the Headmaster.

I also, being a bit of a 'lame duck' with ill health, was often called upon to look after other sick children, or the 'walking wounded' until they could receive proper attention from the staff.

We children looked forward to 'Empire Days' and other National celebrations - not, I feel, because we were very patriotic, but rather because we were given certificates and the rest of the day off school!

I was not a strong, healthy child - spending as much time being nursed at home as in being educated in the classroom. I suffered from a number of afflictions then such as persistent ear trouble, a damaged shoulder and other childhood complaints which needed special diets and nursing. To add to these I managed to splinter a thumb at cricket, damage a shinbone at football and receive a bad knock on a knee in the school playground - these entailing frequent visits to the school nurse in Pimlico for treatment with methylated spirits, etc. to harden skin and bone. I was also subjected to heavy bullying from a lad who lived in Windsor Road, so my schooldays were beset with problems and were consequently not very academically rewarding. All the children of my age group will remember the shops we used opposite

the school. The chemist before Walter Wyatt was called Burgoyne: next door was a saddlery and 'tack' shop and next door again a sweet and confectioners called Webbers. The last one was a flower shop, and underneath, at the back, Boon's boot and shoe repairers.

At the time I was at Ellacombe School, the baker's shop opposite (across the road) was owned - before Hookways - by a Mr Anderson. I loved to go down Market Street to purchase hogs pudding for my mother at Pascoes, outside the Market, as Percy Lee, serving, would always give me a little extra piece to eat for myself. Other shops I particularly recall were French, the butchers, at the bottom of Hoxton Hill, Martin's fish and chip shop in Cavern Road (where we choristers would happily spend our choir fees on battered fish and 'scribbles'), and Sammy Maddern's the hairdressers in Princes Road. He was a very religious man and, I believe, was relieved of a contract with the Hospital to shave and haircut the patients because of his efforts to get his 'patients' to 'confess to sin' or otherwise suffer 'eternal damnation'!

We young children were very militarised, living in the shadow of the 1914–1918 War. We held our sports games at Plainmoor before moving to Windmill Hill for the purpose. But Plainmoor, apart from use training and drilling troops, witnessed the daily drilling of little boys, marched there by Mr Terry to the command note of a whistle and (unbelievably) to exercise in trenches with wooden rifles and bayonets with which to attack and stab filled sandbags! Our stern 'drill sergeant', Harry Terry, would also march us down to the swimming pool at Beacon Cove where we would undress, swim, dress again and return to the school, all to order by whistle! I seem to remember the patriotic Mr Terry being 'mentioned in despatches' for his zeal in training and disciplining his diminutive 'troops'.

Whilst attending these same baths at a Swimming Gala, I remember taking part in a swimming event when I got severe cramp in my flimsy cotton bathers and had to be fished out with a long pole - so embarrassing!

My brother was the clever one, academically, and passed a scholarship with ease for a place at the Torquay Grammar School. But because my mother refused to let one son be treated less advantageously than the other, she managed (I know not how), to pay for me to go there also. And it must have been a hard struggle for her, as my father had died, and because he had not paid his 'stamps' she had the greatest difficulty in obtaining a widow's pension of 10 shillings a week and had to offer accommodation and lodging to clergy and others connected to the Church to makes ends meet. I remember a Mr Thompson and a John Hall as lodging with us at this time.

Almost all local children attended Ellacombe Church Sunday School. Two sisters, whose father was a local watchmaker and repairer, named Rawle, took the classes. Later I graduated to a bible class run by Arthur Smith, a good christian man, and because my brother and I had naturally good singing voices we later joined and belonged to the church choir for many years. Earlier I remember being paid a fee of 2/6d a time for operating the church organ pump for a Mr Macey, the church organist at the time, and a Mr Peek who used to play in the Town Band.

Each year the church choir would take part in the Annual Choral Festival at Exeter Cathedral, which, I believe, still takes place to this day. Later I was also to take a very active part in church affairs, being at times people's warden (church affairs - vicar's warden, services), a churchwarden and a sidesman. In my time, the vicar's warden was called Chudleigh, who helped out, occasionally, by playing the church organ. Sidney Corline, Walter Wyatt and Percy Gibbons were also prominent on the Parochial Church Council and on other active church duties.

There were regular church choir outings to the moors in charabancs (early coaches with hard tyres) to Holne Chase, Dartmeet and Two Bridges, etc. Such were the mechanics of these vehicles that we would often have to disembark on the steep hills and all push to get the coach up to the top! At other times in the year we would get together in the church hall for social occasions, suppers and Christmas parties, etc. with food and drink provided by generous benefactors and hard-working lady parishioners. I remember one such as a Mr Gordon Murray, who lived in Windsor Road nearby, and who was an accountant at Rockeys, in Fleet Street. He would mount the tram at the bottom of his road and stop outside Rockeys, where the conductor would hold the tram there until he had escorted Mr Murray across the road to the shop - a kind service unseen these days!

At this time the Church went through a very unsettled period, and I was constrained to leave Ellacombe Church and eventually be welcomed to join St Lukes. One pursuit which was to occupy a large part of my early life was the Boy Scout movement. At the time I was a child, Ellacombe Church did not have a dedicated Ellacombe Troop, and I joined one under the auspices of St Michael & All Angels Church, then at the bottom of Market Street where Pimlico ends. When a new curate called the Revd Ford joined as assistant to the Revd Higgins at Ellacombe, he took it upon himself to form a church troop to become the 5th Torquay, and I was pursuaded by him to take the job as Scoutmaster, and later, Group Scoutmaster.

The Cub Pack was later formed under 'Rusty' Roberts, the wife of Stan Roberts. Percy Gibbons and Clarry Clark were appointed Assistant Scoutmasters. Percy, who lived nearby (and whose father was a coal merchant in Dunmere Road) was a skilled cornet player, and formed a Scout Band, based in the Church Scout Hut. The band was to become well-known at local functions. At weekends the Troop would attend a 'standing camp' on the side of the River Dart, by kind permission of the Goodson Family, the owners of the land and Sir Hugh a prominent 'scouter'. It was to this camp I would go after work on a Saturday afternoon to enjoy many happy weekends - troop training and with much 'skylarking' amongst the boys.

My second life-long hobby and interest was in the work of the St John's Ambulance. This followed the acquisition of a Scout's First-Aid Badge and the sponsorship of Alfred Boon, who was a member of the Brigade outside his business as a boot and shoe repairer. Altogether I served some 28 years with them, and received a long service medal after 25. The Brigade would attend nearly all local events, being based in the Deep Sea Fishermen's Shelter, at Beacon Quay for the Regatta events and regularly attending the Petitor and Newton Abbot Races.

Although I left Ellacombe School for Torquay Grammar, I was not academically inclined - much preferring to work with my hands at carpentry and metalwork. I do remember the School was very keen on sport, and also recall two lads called Bert Payne and Jowett who, wearing their tasselled cricket caps with pride, were prominent amongst the big sporting crowds at the school playing fields at Cricketfield Road. I felt later that I learnt more after leaving school than at it!

I left early to begin my working life, and remember my father walking the town to find an apprenticeship for me in carpentry and joinery, without success. However, talking to Jack Beasley at Church, who was employed as a plumber by the Torquay Council, I was asked if I would like to work for him. I found employment as an apprentice to a council plumbers' shop, which was situated in the corporation's workshops in the yard at the rear of the Corporation Buildings in Market Street. The Council fire engine was also garaged in this yard - a motorised one which had replaced the horse-drawn variety - and was driven by a man named Blower. I stayed there for some three years of my apprenticeship until, once again, my poor health was my undoing. The heavy work of carrying ladders and fitting gutters and suchlike took its toll on my stomach muscles and internal 'plumbing' until one day I collapsed in the street with a ruptured appendix.

In these days of the National Health Service, and free health care for all, it will be difficult to believe what followed. Whilst I lay in agony, my mother looked everywhere in Town for someone of 'means' to sponsor the cost of an operation, and recommend my admission to the Torquay Hospital for it. Fortunately one was found, and Heal, the cabman from Belmont Road in Ellacombe, transferred me there in Higher Union Street. I was seen, on admission, by a Dr Sir Heathcote-Hetherington, but Dr Lacey did the operation, which was full of complications.

Altogether I spent some ten months in hospital and when I left for convalescence it became clear I could not return to complete my apprenticeship on a job with strong physical demands, so I went into window dressing. I found employment and training with Jacksons, in Union Street, and partly with the Co-operative Society's shoe department, nearby. I think the artistic element in me found satisfaction in this work - stimulated by the various window-dressing competitions held by the Chamber of Trade. Girls in the shop would help my displays by making simulated 'roses' from rolled-up stockings, and the art was to make the displays photogenic to stand the chance of winning.

Unfortunately I was made redundant in a cost-saving exercise. However - the wife of Inspector Coppins, head of the local police in Market Street offered to help, and I found myself training to be a door-to-door insurance salesman at the Refuge Insurance Company's premises next to Cuss' Post Office at Plainmoor. After training, and with plenty of local knowledge of prospective customers, I progressed in my new occupation at £3.50 a week, plus commission at a £1 a policy, until offered an assistant manager's job in the area. After some three years in insurance, the new National Insurance Acts were passed in 1947, and many agents like myself, with equivalent experience, were offered established posts with the new Ministry. I took the necessary examinations and was offered a post first at St Austell, in Cornwall,

and later at Paignton and then finally at Newton Abbot: the latter two posts the result of compassionate transfers, due to the declining health of my wife and to home-sickness.

I retired as an executive officer without ever achieving established status on promotion, although having enjoyed my service with the Ministry and the kindness of managers Arthur Taylor and Gordon Bowden.

I met my future wife at Ellacombe Church Sunday School, and our relationship matured locally and on well-remembered Sunday walks along the seafront after Evensong at Ellacombe Church. Doris lived in Lower Ellacombe Church Road, and her father, Mr Edwards, worked as head of central heating and plumbing at Hardings, the builder's merchants, in Lower Market Street. We 'walked out' together for some five years before getting married at the church on 26 August 1933.

Doris was later a teacher at the Sunday School, and worked at the DBC china shop in Lower Union Street, near what was then Mogridges, the drapers. My mother was pleased to see me settle with a good christian girl, although (as usual) was at first highly critical of her domestic attributes in my mother's own domain. After getting married, we bought a house at 5 Florida Road, where we stayed until transferred to St Austell. Unfortunately we were unable to have children.

My brother - the bright one - had won a scholarship to the Grammar School. He was especially gifted at mathematics, and left school to join a firm of accountants (Boyce) in Paignton, as an office boy. They were so impressed by him that they trained him in accountancy without charging my mother the usual fees for a trainee. He later passed all his examinations and became a chartered accountant with the same company for several years before transferring to a partnership in Bridgewater. There he settled, and later bought out the other partner, and further developed the business to the extent of employing four more accountants - finally retiring in the town. Stanley met, and later married, Evelyn Huxham, who lived at the top of Florida Road, and whose father was a local builder. They also married at Ellacombe Church on 17 July 1937 and had a number of gifted children.

Finally - I remember Percy Bragg , who ran the office side of W. J. Shapley & Son, the furniture removers in Princes Road - one son of whom became a senior engineer with the BBC. There was Jack Kentisbeer and his wife Doris, and Stan Roberts whose sister married a Chave, the garage owners, also in Princes Road. Stan, together with

Mr Callard (the well-known baker and confectioner, with shops in Union and Torwood Streets), and Mr Stedham (of Messrs Webber & Stedham, the builders merchants behind Market Street), a Mr Whatmore (employed in the Torbay Mill) and Mr Dodson were all keen 'Scouters'.

MR and MRS STAN ROBERTS

Stan – I was born at Lustleigh, near Bovey Tracy, in 1909, and my family moved to Torquay just before the Armistice in 1918, when I was nine. My father was a gardener, by trade, working in the area between the two parishes. When work became difficult to find, he looked elsewhere for employment, and found it in Torquay at the house of Mr Swayne, the owner of the Brewery then in Lower Ellacombe Church Road. The brewer lived at Ash Hill Road - a big property with an extensive garden and large glass conservatory across its front. Accommodation was provided in a 'tied' cottage. Later, my father changed his job and moved into another cottage in Warberry Vale, where we lived until his death. Mother was working as a private nurse. I moved out of the family home and into a number of lodging houses in the area, as well as living for a time with my sister. I had no brothers. My sister later married Arthur Chave who, with his brother George, owned the garage in Princes Road.

I have little recollection of my grandfather's history. My father was born in Salisbury, Wiltshire, and the family moved later to Southampton Docks, where grandfather was self-employed as a chemist. My mother belonged to the big Easton family, who were in the building trade at Lustleigh, and well-known there. My grandmother (on my mother's side) was a Bulleid. Both names are recorded in the christian names of subsequent children, plus the name Colleton - rare, with particular spelling in Devon.

On arriving in Torquay I was registered to attend the old Upton School, now rebuilt as the County Court building in Higher Union Street. It was a reasonably happy school. However - an element of children from the under-privileged area of Madrepore were assigned to Upton School at the time, and disrupted the peace and quiet! They were, generally from very poor families, often with boots and no stockings, and much-patched clothing. Obviously there was some

resentment, on both sides, which led to frequent outbursts, confrontations and fisticuffs between pupils of different backgrounds and environments.

Teachers I remember were the Headmaster, a Mr Roberts, 'Charlie' Parr (who later left to teach at Ellacombe School), a Mr Gerry and a Mrs Laskey - whose favourite teaching 'ploy' was a knuckle, on which was lodged a heavy gold ring, to the back of the head! The Headmaster was very strict and heavy with the cane. When this was applied, somewhat over-enthusiatically, troublemakers would often respond with a fusillade of inkwells. On one occasion I recall Mr Roberts was caught on the bridge of his nose with a well-aimed missile!

Later I sat and passed the entrance examination for the Grammar (Secondary) School. Four boys passed at the same time, that year. The initiative to sit for the test was taken by the parents, not the school, as funds for clothing and books, etc. were needed, and some, including my parents, found it a struggle to find the necessary money. I remember a Mr Jowett was the Headmaster of my new school, a Mr Martin (another 'hard' man) taught French and a Mr Ellis (a meticulous historian) taught geography and history.

I left school at 16. All I wanted to do was work in the motor trade - then rapidly expanding and becoming increasingly technically advanced. I was able to obtain an apprenticeship at Chave's garage, and after completing it, moved to work at Couch's garage at Torre (the funeral directors), and then at Callard's off Market Street.

Mr Callard was part of the Callard family that had a dairy there. I stayed with Bernard Callard at his garage, where Union Square now is, until his unfortunate demise. His brother then took over the business, and opened a showroom in Market Street, adjacent to Hardings, the ironmongers. Mr Callard was a conscientious employer, who engaged me on heresay, but rewarded my efforts to give good service by sending me to London for two weeks to train on the very new Crypton tuning equipment.

Eventually I moved again - this time to work as a motor fitter at the Devon General Garage, on the Newton Road. I stayed with them until called up for military service in 1939. By then I had volunteered to join the Supplementary Reserve, which was composed of artisans of all trades, who were paid an annual retention fee, but received no military training whatever. Purely by chance, I did get some military expertise in rifle shooting, given to me by an ex-soldier, and which took

Above: *The 5th (Torquay) Scout Group, 1927. Officials in second row are: Clarence Clark, Percy Dimmock, Revd Ford (Group Scoutmaster) Vicar, Revd Higgins, Treasurer, Mr Beasley and Mr Percy Gibbons, Assistant Scoutmaster.* Below: *The 5th (Torquay) Sea Scouts, 1933, later the 9th (Torbay) Scouts, marching up Hoxton Road to Ellacombe Church Road.* courtesy of the late Stan Roberts

Ellacombe Church Bible Class, 1930. courtesy of the late Stan Roberts

place periodically at the butts on Walls Hill. I was later to become a Warrant Officer in the REME, attached to the 17/21st Lancers (converted to Tanks), and served with the Regiment in North Africa and until the end of the war.

I remember Sam Longthorpe, the garage superintendent, at the Devon General Garage, who was always careful to watch for malingerers 'popping off' for a quick smoke in the toilets! I also remember Jack Langmead, who left the 'pits' to become an outdoor inspector on the buses. I became very much an 'Ellacombe Boy', involved in church affairs, the Young People's Fellowship (YPF), Scouting (particularly), the Men's Bible Class and teaching at Sunday School. Later, I was to become a committee member of the Parochial Church Council and sidesman during the time the Revd Higgings' 'held the living' and the Revd Leslie St Aubrey. This was a somewhat 'stormy' and unsettled period in church affairs following the previous incumbent's (the Revd Stratton) ministry.

I joined the Boy Scout Movement at 16, and became a member of the 5th (Torquay) Baden Powell Scout Group, and at 18, automatically, a rover scout. I was then offered a temporary warrant as an Acting Rover Scout Leader in the 5th. Prior to the formation of the 5th (Torquay) Scout Group, Ellacombe scouts were under the jurisdiction of the Church Lads Brigade, which ceased to function before the 5th (Torquay) was formed. At that time the Torquay Rotary Club, under Mr Callard (the baker and confectioner), Mr Dobson (of Renwick, Wilton & Dobson, the coal merchants), Mr Stedham (of Webber & Stedham, the builders merchants) and others ran the 3rd (Torquay) Scout Group. However - after the Revd

Ford joined Ellacombe Church as a non-stipendiary curate, he encouraged Percy Dimmock to take the job of Scoutmaster and form a new 5th (Torquay) (Baden Powell) Scout Group, of which he later became Group Leader.

There was then a period of enthusiasm for scouting, even to the extent of forming a Scout Band, under the directions and training of Percy Gibbons (a Salvationist), Bill Clarke, Ross Fields and 'Clarry' Clark. We were also very lucky to have the help of an ex-army trained musician named Braun, who was a great asset in extending our musical learning skills. I was recruited to the band as the 'big drummer'!

These were happy scouting times. Many weekends were spent camping at Galmpton and on the banks of the River Dart between Waddeton and Stoke Gabriel. I think we had the use of a small boat, and would row out to swim off sandbanks in mid-stream. After some rather sad accidents, we dropped the Church Army affiliation and were reformed as Baden Powell scouts. As a result of this re-affiliation, and new rules laid down by the Church, we were not allowed to camp without a lady cook/matron being present, and my mother took upon herself that responsibility.

There was a period, after Percy Dimmock took on the 5th, when scouting at Ellacombe lapsed, and only about a dozen members of the troup remained active after Percy gave up. But with the help again of Alec and Bill Clarke and Ross Field, we recharged scouting in the Parish with headquarters in the Parish Hall.

My wife, 'Rusty' took over responsibility for the Cubs, as its Lady Cub Master, so we again had the three sections of Cubs, Scouts and Rover Scouts. Such was our renewed enthusiasm, we self-built (with the help of a local builder) a large scout hut behind the Vestry and Parish Hall to cope with the increased numbers of participants.

The 5th (Torquay) Scout Group was re-numbered the 9th Torbay when the Torbay Boy Scouts Association was created on the formation of the first Torbay County Borough. Its first Mayor was Leslie Goodrich, of A. L. Goodrich, solicitors of St John's Chambers, The Terrace.

In about 1932, we turned over from BP Scouts to Sea Scouts. I met my wife whilst we were both active members of the Church YPF. Their activities were based on the Parish Hall - the centre of all socialising in pre-war days - where we learnt to dance, play badminton and tennis, hiked together in groups on the moors on Bank Holidays and arranged Sunday School outings with others from St Paul's and St Barnabus' mini-churches.

Scout camp overlooking the Dart, 1930. courtesy of the late Stan Roberts

I remember, with humour, occasions when we would dance together in a back room, away from the Revd Higgins (who strongly disapproved of male and female close contact!), with the door locked. He would hammer on the door, and then dash back out of the hall main door, down to the churchyard and back in the rear entrance, only to find we had returned to the main hall and were sitting innocently apart, on chairs awaiting his re-entry! I remember the record we used to dance to: it was called 'Somewhere in Old Wyoming'. We later had our own copy, which got scratched in time.

After we came back to Ellacombe to live, I contacted Radio Devon (David Bassett's programme) to ask if anyone had a copy (he sang the chorus) and George Pridmore produced a copy for us and sent to us for our Golden Wedding.

Rusty and I fell for one another rather suddenly, as I had, for some lengthy period, been 'walking out' with Dorothy Hanson (another member of the YPF) - to the extent of nearly becoming engaged to her. So when Rusty and I occupied the back seat of a coach on an early outing thereafter, we were not very popular with the others!

We were married in Ellacombe Church by the Revd Ford - a lovely man - on the 16 October 1937. I have a suspicion that there was some extra motivation towards the marital state, on the female side, because of the excessive time I spent away at weekends at scouting camps!

Rusty's special memory of the wedding day is of a little Cub Scout appearing from nowhere behind the bride and bridesmaids before entry to the church, with a very grubby face and blowing bubble-gum! His name was Micky something, and I believe lived in Princes Road West.

Rusty (Phyllis Goddard)– I was born in Bickleigh, near Tiverton. We came to Torquay at the end of the Great War, in 1918. My father was a farmer all his life but (strangely) was unable to milk a cow! Father took mother on a preliminary visit to see a house for sale at 91 St Marychurch Road, but such was the poor state of the building, she marched away in disgust - disappearing up the road, vowing she would never enter the place, let alone live in it!. However, he waited until she had calmed down and returned, rather chastened, and eventually she agreed to take up residence there, after purchase.

My parents re-opened a greengrocers' shop in Plainmoor. I lived with, and was brought up by, my godparents, until I rejoined the family. Being a country girl, I had received little or no education until the age of 7 (not unusual in those days), so when I joined Homelands School (before it was re-formed as the Central School) I was considerably behind the rest of the children, academically. However, my schooldays are remembered as happy ones, even after leaving to join Westhill School.

I joined St Paul's (Tin) Church and its Sunday School. My family were rather upset that no vicar had been to welcome us to the area, but a Revd Young met us in a local bakers and bought us

Ellacombe Girls Sunday School outing, 1930. Mrs 'Rusty' Roberts is on the top deck of the tram.
courtesy Mrs S. Roberts

gingerbread, by way of introduction. My first memory of Sunday School, which took place in a little schoolroom behind Victoria Park Road, was of two horrid little brothers called Jack and George Kelly, who welcomed me by putting a snail down my back and squashing it there! I became a Sunday School teacher at an early age, instructing very tiny children. As earlier mentioned - I joined the YPF, and every Sunday St Paul's Sunday School children would join the others at the Mother Church's Sunday services. It was after this, and meeting my future husband, that I helped with the Cubs and became involved with the Scout Movement. My brother also joined the Scout Troop.

I particularly recall a Captain Hutt, who owned a large Lancia, and would take us on trips over the moors. His daughter, Barbara, was first at art classes and then at Slade College, before becoming a bus conductress. Then she met, and married an Army major from Denbury.

After marriage, Stan and I lived for some 48 years at Barton, before returning back to Ellacombe to retire. We have one son - a captain in the Merchant Navy. He was earlier involved in the building, commissioning and crewing the RFR vessel *Atlantic Conveyor* (a container ship) which was badly damaged and sunk in the Falkland's War.

MISS GWEN DOWNEY

My great-grandparents - William and Keziah Downey - came to Torquay from Exeter in 1860. William came from Cadeleigh, near Bickley (in the Tiverton area). My paternal great-grandmother's maiden name was Luxton, and she came from Newton St Cyres, near Exeter. What brought them to Torquay, I have no idea. Their oldest son was William Henry Downey - my grandfather. He was one of twelve children, all of which survived until adulthood. William Henry was born in 1861. It was possible that the children all went to the National School in Pimlico, established in 1826, and where, six years later, it was teaching some 228 children. From the 1870s most were dispersed to other schools in the Town. Later on, my great-grandparents settled in Grafton Terrace, and ran a small cab business. My grandfather was employed as a cab driver, by them, in the business. He died in 1925 at Swiss Cottage, Warren Hill, Torquay.

My paternal grandmother was Louisa Downey - née Willson. She came from a small village called Hittisleigh, in mid Devon (about 8 miles from Crediton). She came to Torquay 'in service', to the Grafton area, where she met my grandfather. They married at St John's Church, Torquay, on 22 July 1888. It is possible that my grandparents' other children attended Ellacombe School. They were - Annie Alice Downey (born 1898); Ernest Frank Downey (b. 1891); Albert Henry Downey (b. 1892); and Louisa May Downey (b. 1903), all in Torquay.

I can recall my father saying that, as a boy, he used to deliver newspapers to the gentry's large houses in the Warberries. For most of his working life he was employed by the Torbay Mill Company (corn and animal-feed merchants), and worked in several of their branches - including their shops in Market Street, Torquay and St Anne's Road in Babbacombe. My father and uncle were born at 3, Exeter Villas, Ellacombe. I do not know if these properties are still in existence, but the name was changed before my time (I was born in 1933). I was told by a very elderly Torquay person that Exeter Villas were in the Cavern Road area.

My late father and his twin (Walter and Charles Downey) are the third and fourth boys from the left in the back row on the school photograph of 1911 (see page 45). They were in their fourteenth year in 1911. Charles was parish clerk, verger and lay reader at St John's Church, Torquay. He was there for almost fifty years, until his death in 1970. The boy second from right, back row, had the surname Spear or Speare, but I cannot remember his christian name. The tall boy - sixth from left - second row, was a Harry Trust. I'm sorry I cannot remember any of the other boys - only a faint recollection that the boy, second from right, middle row, had the surname Bulleid or Bullied. He was killed in the First World War. I believe the 'military' looking chap standing at the far left was the Headmaster - Mr Terry.

When my father and uncle were youngsters, they attended the little 'tin' church at Stentiford's Hill (St Barbabus). I believe the church was attached to Ellacombe Church. My mother, Lilian Downey, née Waller, was born in Newton Abbot in 1897. She moved to Chelston, with her mother and sister, during the 1914–1918 War. It was while she was working in the office of the Torbay Mill Company at Albert Road, that she met my father and married him in 1923. I was

born at 88, Ellacombe Church Road, in the house of my aunt and uncle - Louisa May Downing, née Downey, and Frank Downing. My uncle was a local policeman, and was at Ellacombe until about 1940. They had two daughters - Joan Downing (b. 1924) and Peggy Downing (b. 1930). Another cousin Louie Downey, lived with the family. She was born in 1928, and was the daughter of my father's oldest brother Ernest Frank Downey.

All three of my cousins - Joan, Peggy and Louie Downey - attended Ellacombe School before they left Torquay to live in Barnstaple. My uncle's neighbour, in Ellacombe Church Road, was a policeman - a PC Gooding. A great-uncle of mine - Walter Downey - ran a small tobacconist shop at 36 Princes Road. We know he was there in 1939, but do not know how long he continued in business there after war broke out. Two of his brothers lived in the Ellacombe area - one at 167 Ellacombe Church Road, and the other at Woodville Road. They were Alfred and Charles Downey. I grew up in the Warren Road area of Torquay - living there until 1979.

HENRY (HARRY) HANSON

I was born in Hornsey, London, in 1916 - I remember an aunt there. We moved to Torquay in 1921. My father originally came from East Anglia, and later became a Sergeant-Major in the Argyle and Sutherland Highlanders, whose garrison headquarters were at Stirling Castle. He was badly wounded and gassed in the First World War, and died in a home in Torquay. My mother who was Scottish, and came from Craigniche, bought a house at 14 Kenwyn Road, where we lived until I married.

My father served in the Regular Army for 12 years, part of the time in India where some of his children were born. There was Jessie, Ethel, Douglas, Jean, Freda and I - one brother and one sister died young. Life was very hard for my mother - rearing 6 children on a basic income of 10 shillings widow's pension plus 5 shillings for the first child only. I had a brother-in-law named Lovell (an orphan) whose uncle was employed as a gardener at the Villa Languarde by a Mrs Tweedale - a well-known writer of ghost stories. I started school life at Ellacombe Infants School - risking the cane, at an early age by slipping out of school to run down the front slipway. We had regular book inspections, when a blot on one's page incurred a stroke of the cane, and two blots, two strokes, etc. But the children of those days were brought up the hard way and were used to physical punishment. We had scripture examinations once a year - the best part being the half-day holiday which followed them.

On Empire Days we would have to salute the Flag. Later, as bigger children, we did handicrafts at Abbey Road and Homelands School (I cannot remember the reason for the classes splitting). The girls attended the same premises for house-wifery, needlework, etc. My sisters remembered Miss Phillips, the girls' Head, a Miss Collihole and a teacher called Miss Matthews, who was very hard on discipline. The Schools were quite famous locally for their choirs, under the tuition of Mr (Charlie) Parr. There were many practices before the renowned School Choir Festivals, which took place annually at the Town Hall. These Festivals lasted for some two weeks. Such was the quality of the singing of the Ellacombe School choirs that both boys and girls retained the Constantine Shields permanently for winning over three successive years.

I remember the Emmett family at school, particularly, as the two boys were great sportsmen 'Charlie' Parr coached George Emmett at the Torquay Cricket Ground to the degree that he later became a county cricket player. Arthur was almost as good, and later played for the St Marychurch Cricket Club for many years. A boy named Mills, who lived in Hoxton Road, later became a professional footballer, playing for the Torquay United Football Club. As a youngster I clearly recall we had five hairdressers, five fish and chip shops, and butchers in nearly every street, as well as a number of chemists. Ellacombe was like a very large, almost completely self-contained and integrated family. All residents were part of this 'family' - looking after neighbours and friends in sickness or when some fell on hard times.

I remember Fairs on Plainmoor - particularly 'Co-op Day', when all the firm's horses and carts and vans were decorated in the Abbey Road stables. They would then proceed up Market Street via Ellacombe Church Road to Plainmoor for a big 'field day' for the children who would all be dressed in their 'best bib and tucker'. It was 2d to go in, but sometimes children were let in with-out charge. If one wanted to go out, temporarily, a rubber stamp was impressed on the back of the hand. The high spot was the cycle race - the fastest rider being Bob Oram.

Apart from the Whitsun Fair, the circus from Ellacombe Green would open-up on Plainmoor.

The field where all this took place, originally allot-ments, was given to the Town by a Mrs Marnham - a local JP. I remember the first game played by Torquay United was at the Rugby Ground, versus Leicester City FC. A winger by the name of Billy Bell, of Leicester City, was so taken by the delights of Torquay that, after retiring, he settled in the Town and ran an off-licence in St Marychurch Road.

Torquay United were originally known as Babbacombe Rangers FC. A number of the Brown family, who were connected to St Paul's Church, played for the Rangers. In the early days, there was no established football ground at Plainmoor, as such, and the men would change at home in Victoria Park Road and walk there - returning home afterwards, all muddy and often wet, to wash in the sinks. Later the Browns erected a tea hut near the ground. Mixed bathing on the beaches of the Town was never allowed in the early years - men and women having separate areas allotted to them for privacy. At Oddicombe, for example, there was a men's bathing cove, with its own concrete platform, from which we chil-dren would dive into the sea. The remains of the platform are still visible to this day.

I recall the first arrival of the Royal Blue Coaches, after a regular service from London to Torquay commenced. The coaches were garaged in Market Street - and would have to reverse into the tunnel before reaching the main parking place. The sight of their arrival was such a phenomenon at the time that many folk would stand around and watch the event, quite fascinat-ed. These were the days of the trams, and we children would put a halfpenny or penny, or a nail, on the tramlines just to see what would happen to the objects after the wheels ran over them.

The Sunday School Treat was a big affair - some 200 children from Ellacombe would take part, and four trams would be hired for the event. After collecting the children outside the Church, the trams would run down Market Street to Market Corner (where the overhead cable would be switched) and from there to Torre Station, to embark on a steam train to Bovey Tracey. The children brought their own lunches, but tea was always provided by the Sunday School Teachers and served in the Co-op barn there. Bread would be cut on the bacon slicer (no cut bread then!) and buns ('splits') coated with clotted cream and jam. Everything very 'homely'. The trams would await the return of the children and teachers at Torre Station, where they would be transported back to Ellacombe Church. The destination of the annual 'treats' would, of course, change from year to year. Sometimes we would go to Chagford Rocks or to Lustleigh Cleave - or again to Teignmouth, Paignton or Dartmouth. But the end result would be the same - happy children, bubbling with energy and excitement, but sometimes finding themselves in tears.

As a Sunday School Superintendent, one carried a heavy responsibility. Invariably at any of the venues - Dartmeet or somewhere - a child would fall in the water! I remember, one day, a child was missing and was searched for all day. We returned home desolate, to inform the parents, only to find that the child had been taken home by them earlier!

The Sunday School Anniversary would be held at Christ Church, Ellacombe, but the three Schools would first assemble at Belmont Park, where the Salvation Army (SA) Band would march the children to the Mother Church for the Thanksgiving Service. I seem to remember there were two local Bands, the main SA Band and a 'break-away' one, called the Free Mission Band, based on St Michael's Chapel at the top of Princes Road. If my memory serves me, Percy Gibbons' father was a member of it I also remember hearing of another organisation called the Primrose League, possibly with political connotations, although I knew nothing of it's objectives.

I remember clearly, one Xmas, after a very heavy fall of snow, when, on Boxing Day, the Foreman at Swayne's brewery in Lower Ellacombe Church Road gave the children a number of old barrel staves with which to toboggan down the fields beneath Warberry Copse.

School Sports Day was held first at Plainmoor, and later at Windmill Hill - but the Inter-Schools event was held either at Plainmoor or at the Recreation ground. I was keen on gymnastics, and attended the Gymnastics Institute, which was situated in Albert Road. I remember an Alec Clarke, who was an exceptional athlete in this field. The Revd D. Emery, who lived in Chatsworth Road, ran the Institute. Alan Clarke joined the Army as a paratrooper - transferring later to a Bomb Disposal Unit - but (sadly) died of a heart attack at home shortly after the war.

Another big event of the year was the steeplechase, held on the Petitor Racecourse on Easter Monday and Tuesday. Those who could not afford to enter the ground (and that was the majority!) would assemble on Petitor Hill, overlooking the course, and the crowd there would be entertained by a number of local characters such

as 'Charlie Chaplin'. The SA Band and individual musicians would provide stirring tunes and the wherewithall for dancing on the green. Of course, Walls ice cream was available from tricycles and refreshments served from mobile canteens.

Everybody fit enough would attend the various events of the Royal Torbay Regatta - even the King and Queen, who would review the Fleet. Gentry were plentiful, including such well-known names as Sir Thomas Sopwith and Lipton. They would arrive and stay on board their beautiful steam yachts and go sailing on the huge J Class yachts.

It was a memorable sight by day or by night, to see the Home Fleet (and often many foreign warships) 'dressed overall' with bunting during the day or a hundred searchlights criss-crossing the sky at night. But for the poor, the event of the day was the Fair, positioned around the Inner Harbour and Beacon Quay. There were 'Golden Dragons', 'Diving Dolphins' and 'Chair-o-Planes', and the 'Confetti Fete', until this latter affair got so rumbustious and messy the Council refused to allow it to take place in the future.

The Torbay Regatta always began at Babbacombe before continuing around the Bay. Crossmans, the timber merchants (my future employers) would close down for the event - largely because the timber boats could not be offloaded and serviced from Haldon Pier. Other big events of the year were the large Balls that would take place at the Town Hall. Favourites were the Police Ball, the Hunt Ball, the Firemen's Ball and the St John's Ambulance Ball. At the Firemen's Ball, the opening dance would begin with all the firemen dancing, in full uniform, to the music of 'The Lancers'. Buses would remain in service until the early hours of the morning, to take participants to their homes in various parts of the Town. That was just the way things were - the sort of service rarely seen in this day and age. But, of course, there were few cars!

After leaving school I was apprenticed, as a trainee carpenter, to S.W. Peters, in Kenwyn Road. However - he could not afford to retain me after two years, because of the recession, and I found employment with Messrs Thos. J. Crossman at the firm's premises and timber yard off Union Street, as a wood-working machinist, and later as a general workshop foreman. Crossmans was one of the biggest employers in Torquay, with a fine machine shop and a workforce of some 20 to 30 carpenters and a similar number of machinists. The Company was one of the first to make use of a steam engine in the workshop. My sister was also employed in the office at Crossmans as a general secretary until she retired. The firm was supplied with its timber stocks by sea from sources in Sweden, Finland and Russia. These would arrive by means of some twelve vessels a year and I, as a foreman, was required to supervise their unloading. This was all done by hand then, and took some three days to complete. On one occasion, there was a severe gale, and all the timber being off-loaded was swept into the outer harbour, almost covering the surface of it. It was my job, with other staff, to recover what we could, and got very wet in the process!

Later, delivery and unloading of the timber would take place at the premises of the Teignmouth Quay Company and at the firm's workshops and timber yards which had, by then, transferred to new premises at Newton Abbot. It is a matter of record that Crossmans was the first firm to take an Arbitration Case to the Russian Courts, and win it! Thomas Crossman was also a County Alderman. In the early days, he personally owned two vessels, which were used to transport emigrants to the Americas and return with a cargo of timber. In those days, it was normal for timber stocks to be transported locally by carts drawn by teams of horses. I was always referred to by the Boss as 'the Boy'.

Thomas Crossman was a strict employer, but fair, considering the contemporary times. We were allowed to take public holidays such as Christmas Day and Boxing Day, but without pay, of course! Ironically - we would be given a 5 shilling Christmas Bonus! That was the way of employment in those days. As another example - builders' employees and other outdoor workers would (on two hour's notice) be stood down, without pay, in inclement weather.

On 11 November each year, at 11am. everything in the Town would stop for a two-minutes silence, and many businesses gave 'time off' for attendance at the Cenotaph - but without pay.

Jobs of any sort were hard to find during the recession. Lucky ones were those who were, with some family influence, or with better education, able to find employment in the public services. I remember one colleague at Crossmans called George Baker, who left the firm to work as a cleaner in the General Post Office, and who, later, in the Second World War, joined the Royal Navy, became a warrant officer, and was killed at sea when the aircraft carrier HMS *Courageous* was sunk by enemy action.

After starting work we had to set aside a small sum each week for medical insurance with a local insurance company. I took out a policy with the Liverpool & Victoria Insurance Company at one penny a week. This covered me for normal medical care through a local doctor and in the event of my requiring hospital treatment. These companies imposed very strict conditions. If sick, one had to observe a daily curfew - that is, one must not leave one's home after 7pm in the winter or after 8pm in the summer, unless it was to visit the doctor; and even then the doctor would have to certify in writing that the visit was necessary! And the companies had their own inspectors to police this arrangement.

It was through a colleague at work, called Andy Potter, that I first met my future wife. Andy and I attended a social evening and dance at St Pauls Church Hall, and when he observed that I was interested in a certain young lady, he first egged me on to dance with her, and then bet me I would fail to persuade her to let me escort her home. However, I succeeded in both these enterprises, in the event. She was 'in service' in Warren Road, at the time, and raised no objection to my company. We have been together ever since.

My wife, Evelyn Langdon, was born in Torquay in 1917. Her father, Leonard Langdon, was a butcher from North Devon, who came to Torquay to work for Weddels, the meat importers (from Argentina), whose premises were in Torre. Her mother was called Beatrice Grute, whose family owned a dairy farm at Maidencombe. Her grandfather would deliver dairy products to Torquay by horse and cart, but he died of blood poisoning as a result of a blackthorn embedded in his finger. The family came to live and work a dairy from 1 Hele Road, where we later resided for the start of our married life.

My wife spent most of her working life 'in service' in high-class residential houses at Bayfort Mansions and at Vane Hill. As a result of her training, she set herself a high personal standard. Gentlemen of private means in those days had large hierarchical staff, with strict levels of responsibility from the butler and housekeeper, down to the lowest kitchen maid. Staff were allowed home for the weekend, to visit parents, once a fortnight, and were allowed a half-day off once a week. On Sundays, they were encouraged to go to church after early duties were completed, but had to be back promptly to serve lunch! Nevertheless - although there was a strict order of things, my wife was always proud of her status, and would not accept other employment unless her new employer was 'a lady'.

We began married life together, after the war, first at Hele Road, and then purchasing our present house in Derwent Road. It is hard to believe that the mortgage, in those early days, cost us £9.10.10d a month, and my wages were a mere £2 a week (less when first starting employment).

Horses and carriages were still in common use in the 1920s. C. J. Dimond & Co., the furniture removers off Princes Road, always used all black horses and hearses for their funeral service until some time after motor vehicles became much more popular. The Revd Higgins always arrived to take the service at Ellacombe using his own coach and horse, as did some of the parishioners from the big houses in the Warberries and big houses nearby. Such means of transport was common at the Grand and Torbay Hotels.

Bill Crook (a Scouter) had his own horses, as had various dairies and shops about the town who would use them for delivering their goods and services, including Cuss' Dairy at Plainmoor. I remember that Dodsons at Torre Station had a team of horses, as did Swayne's brewery, with it's own stables behind. I remember there was also stabling behind Alexandra Road.

Two blacksmiths I can recall - one at the top end of Lower Ellacombe Church Road called Mr Lark, and another in Lower Temperance Street called Mr Powell. We boys would love to watch them at work. The latter would often encourage lads to handle the furnace bellows for him. My

close association with St Pauls and Christ Church, Ellacombe began when I was 18 years of age, and my faith in the church and it's teachings has remained (and still remains) strong after 61 years of service to it. I joined the Parochial Church Council (PCC) sub-committee for St Pauls at 21 (the earliest age allowed), and later was appointed a churchwarden for Ellacombe Church. Between times I was a Sunday School Teacher (later Sunday School Superintendant when Miss Winifred Avery died suddenly) and also took the Bible Class. We were married in St Marychurch Church but came back to St. Pauls, which was the centre of a very close-knit community, and in it's own special way provided fine pastoral support from it's own curates and Church Army captains. Among them was the Revd Fanshaw and the Revd Benson, who for many years lived at St Andrews, nearby.

As part of my work for the little church, I painted the whole of it's exterior surface, including the taking down and gilding of the cross and returning it to its former position. During the last war I recall one lady was killed by a machine-gun bullet (which remained embedded in the porch woodwork until the church was demolished).

A visiting curate and his son were injured in the same attack. It was on this occasion also that German aircraft set ablaze the gasometer at Barton, and people living nearby had to be evacuated until the danger was past.

St Paul's Church Choir, taken in the vicarage grounds c. 1922. courtesy Harry Hanson

St Paul's Church Choir c. 1928. In the front row, second left is Mr Bailey, the blind organist, and fourth left is the Revd Stanley Stratton. In the back row second left is Mr Bradford, fourth left is Andy Petter, seventh from left is Mr Dart, and Mr Howard stands on the far right. courtesy Harry Hanson

The treasurer of St Pauls, during my time, was called Jack Taylor, who also worked at Crossmans with me. Whilst, of course, the Mother Church ran the main PCC, each 'tin' church (St Barnabus at Stentiford's Hill and St Pauls at Plainmoor) had it's own sub-PCC, raised it's own funds through church sales, offerings, donations, etc. and was self-supporting and ran it's own affairs.

It was a very sad time for me when, despite my efforts in fighting for a re-building project, the decision was taken to demolish it. So I turned my church activities over to Ellacombe.

Interior of St. Paul's 'tin' Church. Harry Hanson

During my period at Ellacombe, the following incumbents were in office - the Revd Stratton, the Revds Higgins, Leslie St Aubrey, Burton, Peter Cranch, Paul Irwin (a lovely man), Roger Beck and (currently) the Revd Roy Taylor. The churchwardens (CWs) hold full responsibility for the funding and upkeep of the church fabric, communial plate, hymn books, etc., in consultation with the vicar and CPS, and are elected each year.

I recall a Mrs Fremlett, late of Ellacombe Church Road, among many other kind benefactors, leaving a substantial sum to the church. During the incumbency of the Revd Jack Burton, the organ was removed from the back of the chancel and re-sited on the balcony, thereby enabling a Chapel of Healing to be erected in it's place. A gentleman gave an altar of remembrance for those who died in the Great War, although memorials to the fallen in both World Wars appear to have disappeared. Two windows were also donated, but flags, which were once flown at the Cenotaph on Remembrance Day, have been taken down.

The Church organists at Ellacombe I remember were - first a Sunday School Teacher called Weaver and after him, Sidney Bryant.

During the early days there was always a Christmas supper for the choirmen and a tea for the choirboys. At these events there was singing around the old stoves in the church hall before the advent of central heating. My sister would produce and direct plays at the same venue. I can recall, in the Revd Stratton's time, the church hall being packed for two or three days at a time - the plays were so popular. On a number of occasions the Mayor and Mayoress would attend in full evening dress, in support of the event. Such were the stringent rules of the church then, that the Revd Stratton found himself in trouble for allowing a whist drive to take place - especially without a licence!

Two final memorable (if sad) occasions remain in my mind. The first was when a lad called Bobby Walfton, whose father - strangely - was a safety officer on Torre Abbey sands, fell over the cliffs and was killed. As he had been a choirboy at St Barnabus Church, the Scout Band turned out in full dress and headed the procession at his funeral, all the way from Stentiford's Hill to the service at Ellacombe Church. Also I remember a huge fire, in the 1920s, when the Methodist Chapel in Union Street was completely burnt to the ground.

MISS LILIAN BROWN

I was born in 1908 in Forest Road, Torquay, where my father and mother lived for twelve months, and until we moved to Victoria Park Road in Plainmoor. My grandfather had owned a big house in what is now Torwood Gardens - that is, before the houses, shops and garages were erected in the vicinity. I can clearly remember the house. We would meet my aunt and uncle (who lived at Paignton) on the Strand, and together visit grandad and grandmother there. Such regular family visits were routine in those days.

The front part of the house was set out as a dairy. In the rear part of the property was the 'scalding room', where the clotted cream, butter, etc. were made. Beyond the back door was a paddock where free-range chickens and ducks were accommodated. It was a family dairy - as my uncle would deliver the dairy produce, by pony and trap, to premises in the main street of the Town.

I suspect that my great-grandparents were farmers in Marldon, and supplied the raw materials for the dairy, as both my grandparents were born in that village and are buried there, together with a baby called Lilian Brown. Strangely - I remember much less of my own parents early life. My father

was, I know, a carpenter by trade and was born in the dairy house in Torwood Gardens. He lived in Cockington before he married, sang in the Cockington Church choir and played rugby for Torquay 'Tics' and was a great supporter of the Club all his life. Like so many, he served in the First World War, and remained in bad health thereafter, as a result.

My mother originally came from Chagford, before her family moved to Torquay and settled in the poorer area of St Edmond's Road, Plainmoor. There was much overcrowding - indeed, an aunt living in the front part of a house there had an Italian family of organ-grinders domiciled in the rear. I can remember poor children, ill clad, sitting on the doorsteps and pavements, with bare feet, washing them in the gutters. A year after my birth we moved to Victoria Park Road, in one of three houses my grandfather had built there. At the time there was a lot of vacant building land available in the area bordering Boston Fields (Plainmoor). My father was given one house, an uncle another and an aunt the third.

There were six of us children - Tom, Ernie and Harold (boys) and Eileen, Edith and myself (the girls). All were brought up in the Road until they married, and even then, have spent most of their lives in the Plainmoor area. I have lived for nearly 87 years in the same property.

I first went to school at Victoria Park Infants, and from there to the old Upton School in Higher Union Street, where the County Court now stands. Two of my brothers were the last Protestants to be admitted to the St Marychurch Catholic School, before a ban was imposed. I do not remember to which schools the other three went - possibly Ellacombe.

At the Infants School the Headmistress was called Miss Woodleigh, and the only other teacher was a Miss Phillips (not to be confused with the Miss Phillips - later Head of Ellacombe Girls' School, I believe). Both teachers lived nearby. Later, I returned to the Infants' School for a period of a few years after leaving Upton, to help Miss Phillips with the babies.

I remember little of my schooldays at Upton - only of a single, large schoolroom, with a big stove in the centre to provide heating, and around which we would all huddle for warmth whilst we ate our packed lunches. I do recall the caretaker had his accommodation below the classroom. My mother, whilst a temporary patient in the old Torquay Hospital, would wave to me in the playground from her ward window. I started full-time work with a friend at a house in Walnut Road,

Chelston, owned by a family called Barnes, who had a small business accommodating visitors to the resort. From there I went to work at Alfred Bruce's shoe shop in Fleet Street for some years until the early part of the Second World War.

At that time, all females not in reserved occupations had to be employed either in the Services or on specific war work. I was given the choice of either joining the Fire Service at Barton, or taking employment at the new Torbay Hospital. I opted for the latter, and after a short spell of time cleaning floors in the wards, became a regular house worker in the nurses' home nearby, and there remained for some 23 years until I retired.

I always enjoyed my work, although it was hard - particularly as we had to work split shifts. This meant two journeys each way, walking from Plainmoor to Lowes Bridge and back, often with my colleagues Winnie Taylor and Florrie Emmett - a long and tiring day. I remember the names of the Matrons in my time as the Misses Swift, Foal and Stamp. I also recall there was a bungalow near the gates of the Hospital occupied by an electrician.

Every Christmas a party was arranged for the domestic staff, following a lunch in the hospital canteen, in the main building, where we were served by the staff sisters.

I have been closely connected with St Paul's Mission Church all my life. As a young child of the times, we were introduced to the church environment and religious training at a very early age, and the only social life we knew and enjoyed was provided by the Church. Like the others I joined the Sunday School, and later took over the teaching of the infants when I grew older myself.

The boys were able to enjoy the benefits of a games room in the Church Hall (the 'Welcome'), but the girls were looked after by the Girls Friendly Society (GFS) - talks on religion interspersed with walks and picnics, for example, on Babbacombe Beach and Broadsands (walking each way!). A Miss 'Gertie' Kentisbeare (who lived in Windsor Road) ran the Sunday School. Her sister looked after the Infants. The two Miss Comptons, who lived at 'The Chase', in St Marychurch Road, also helped with the Sunday Schools.

The local street meeting place was the corner of Victoria Park Road and St Edmund's Road, with shops on all corners - Billy Bell had the off-licence, and there was a grocers called Norrish, a 'mixed' shop called Rendells, Canns the bakers and another fruit and vegetable shop called Gooders. St. Marychurch Road was known to the locals as the 'Front Street'.

The males would wander off to the games room at the Welcome for recreation, after the usual gossiping. Local boys knew my father as 'Joss', the caretaker.

Sunday School outings were usually on trams to Paignton, starting from the old Tram Depot at Westhill. We girls would all fight for seats on the top deck to see all there was to see en route. Lunch was taken, but the Sunday School Teachers would provide the tea. Once a year a Sunday School Festival would be held at Ellacombe Church, and we would all march, in our sunday best clothes, behind the Salvation Army Band, from St Pauls, via Belmont Park, to the Mother Church. We children loved these parades - they were the 'high spots' of our young lives.

The Whitsun Festival was another. We would march to Ellacombe Church, via Ellacombe Green, always in white frocks and with bunches of flowers, to a special Service of Thanksgiving, as we did at Harvest Festival time. During the year we would learn to dance, under strict supervision, in the Welcome, and play organised games such as musical chairs. I remember the Fairs at Plainmoor, held in the big open space used by all the local children as a vast playground. In the centre was the 'hallowed' football ground, on which we dare not tread.

Most of the area then was flat - bordered on one side by a few fruit trees and bushes known as Homelands Drive. An annual bonfire night was also held on Plainmoor Fields - supervised by the parents - and the Co-op Children's Field Day was also held there.

There was always a Christmas party at the Welcome - the big event of the year   There was no entrance fee, as everybody contributed towards the food, prizes and entertainment.

I recall the most influential lady at St Pauls was undoubtedly Miss Florence Skirrow JP, who lived in Marnham Road. She took the Mothers Bible Class in the Welcome on Sunday afternoons - a class so popular that many of the local mothers attended. She was the secretary and treasurer of the Welcome for many years, and attracted a large number of influential people to the bazaars in aid of Church and Church Hall Funds.

The St.Pauls 'Tin' Church was always financially self-supporting to its end. Later I joined the St Paul's Church choir, and remained a member for many happy years. In my time, and before the Church closed in 1966, the officiating clergy were the Revd Stratton, the Revd Young (curate) and the Revd Higgins (very strict). We also had some fine officiating Church Army captains by the

St Paul's Church Choir outside the 'Tin' church c. 1940. courtesy Lilian Brown

names of Fanshaw, Massey and Godfrey. It was a very sad day for all of us when, despite the desperate efforts of the Friends of St Pauls the Church was closed in 1966, and the building that had given so much to the local people through the years, was razed to the ground for development. We were all very upset.

GILBERT and WINNIE FURNEAUX

Gilbert – My earliest recollection, as a young child, was of being domiciled in Carlton Road, where I was born on 25 January 1913. My father was a surgical bootmaker, employed by a Mr Boon, whose premises were situated below the shops opposite Ellacombe School. It was his duty to attend customers' homes to measure up and specify bespoke-made boots for those whose limbs required them and to make them up. Later he left this employer and started work at the Co-operative Society on a piece-work basis.

My mother was called Clarke, before her marriage, and her parents had a bakery at the bottom of Madrepore Road. Both my father and grandfather were born in Torquay. The latter

lived in St Edmund's Road, in Plainmoor, and was a stonemason by trade. His ancestor was a prisoner of the Napoleonic Wars (hence the French surname), and was marched from Plymouth to incarceration in Princetown Prison - then used to accommodate both French prisoners and those from the American War of Independence. Whether he escaped or was later released is not known, but he found his way to Buckfastleigh, where he met and married a local housemaid and settled there.

It was during the First World War that we moved house to 60 Ellacombe Church Road, alongside George Davey. I have fleeting memories of this war. As a very young child I would walk down with my mother to the Military Hospital huts, erected in an open area on the banks of the River Flete behind the Town Hall (erected in 1913) and give out a few Woodbine cigarettes to some of the wounded Canadian soldiers (bought for 2d for a packet of five). I vividly recall walking up Market Street, after seeing my father off back to war after leave at Torquay Station, my mother warning me that if I broke into tears she would quickly 'box my ears' for my trouble!

I also remember seeing what we called in those days a 'blimp' hoisted in the air above Warberry Copse. My father was recruited and served as a saddler and barber in the Royal Horse Artillery.

He survived the war with only a small shrapnel wound in his back, and died in 1950-55 at over 70 years of age. After the war we moved to Megla Villas, whose back entrance was in Pennsylvania Road.

My elder brother joined the Royal Navy as a boy seaman - much against the wishes of my mother, who refused to sign until he threatened to enlist as an orphan. He spent his first years of naval training aboard the old wooden ship HMS *Impregnable* - later rising through the lower deck (torpedo) ratings to the commissioned rank of Lieutenant Commander. During the Second World War he was taken prisoner in Java after his ship, HMS *Jupiter*, was sunk by the Japanese. He remains alive in Plymouth at nearly ninety years of age.

My other brother learned his trade as a plasterer, but sadly died of a heart attack at work at the age of 65. I have no surviving sisters.

Winnie – My father (my maiden name was Southcott) came originally from Stockton-on-Tees, although I have no idea why he came down to Torquay. He married my mother here and they lived at Mount Pleasant Road. I had one sister, 14 years older than me, who worked at Dinhams, the photographers, in Union Street. She was later a keen member of the Torquay Operatic & Dramatic Society. My brother, 9 years older, worked at the Star Tea Company, grocers, also in Union Street, delivering groceries to private houses by bicycle. Later he left to learn his trade as a plasterer, like his brother-in-law.

My father was employed as a stage manager at the Royal Theatre in Abbey Road until 1919, when we left to go to Surrey on a venture to provide laundry facilities for the nearby barracks at Camberley. We never settled, and returned to Torquay two years later. Having no job, my father was lucky to meet the manager of the 'Royal', Arthur Pearce, who offered him his job back at the theatre. For a while we lived at an aunt's house, until moving to Hoxton Road. I recall, as a child, many of the neighbours, in rooms without proper cooking facilities, would all trip over to Furze, the bakers, to have their Sunday meals cooked in the baker's oven. My mother was lucky enough to have a range in which to cook hers. Many a twopenny meal of chips, peas and 'scribbles' were purchased at Martin's fish and chip shop in Cavern Road.

Memories of my early days spent at school at Ellacombe are vague, as we grew up so quickly. I remember Miss Phillips, the Headmistress, Miss Collihole and Miss Saunders; twopenny 'hard-bakes' at Hookways; Burgoynes the chemist and Coombe's laundry opposite the School. I sang in the School choir and took part in the Music and Drama Festivals at the Town Hall, where we won the Choir Shield. I also remember we would dance around the maypole in the playground - girls only! Boys would do sword dances in groups of eight in their playground - but 'never the twain would mix'! We would walk to Rock Road for cookery lessons, whilst the boys would do the same for woodwork and metalwork. Gilbert would go to Plainmoor for sports before Windmill Hill sports ground was in use by the School.

Sometimes we would be kept at home to help out, but dreaded a surprise visit from Mr Rooke or Mr Jaggs, the school attendance officers (the latter a poor man with an iron hook in place of his lost hand).

I particularly remember, as a child, at Regatta time, when my mother would take me to Addisons Cafe for a cream bun, and we would sit for hours on Princess Pier watching all the big yachts and enthralled by all the colourful activity in and about the harbour. Gilbert's memories of school at Ellacombe were more of swimming and Eisteddfod festivals than academic studies. Mr Terry was still in charge until Mr Collett took over as Headmaster. The latter was a strict disciplinarian, and kept a heavy cane always to hand underneath his desk, which he often applied when he was sitting down. I remember on one occasion when a rather naughty lad from Alexandra Road was being given three strokes when he dodged from under the cane and the Headmaster gave himself a nasty swipe on his own leg! I was only caned once, and did not transgress again (or was not caught doing so!).

Gilbert – Winnie and I first met at 13, when we would walk home from school together. As was remarked by Winnie, we grew up quickly. Before the age of 14 I worked after school, and in the evenings, at Singer's sewing machine shop where Mr Bowden from the Mission Hall in Market Street worked as a machine repairer. My part-time job was to deliver repaired machines locally in a wheelbarrow-cum-trolley. I carried on with this work after leaving school until aged 15, when I became an errand boy for a bakers in Tor Hill Road. My principal job there was to deliver 150 bread rolls each day to Torquay Station in time to catch the Torbay Express leaving at midday. However - I had by then decided to try and better my prospects by learning a trade. I really wanted to become a plasterer, but being left-handed was an impediment in working with a right-handed mate. So I took advantage of a chance to learn my trade as a signwriter and decorator under Harry Pearce, whose premises were in Lower Thurlow Road. Harry was also a lecturer at the Torquay School of Arts & Crafts in Braddons Hill Road West, near the General Post Office. Every Tuesday and Thursday I would attend evening classes under my boss-cum-teacher, which meant some disadvantages in the summer months waiting for the school to open. I was (diplomatically) loath to do what my fellow students did in dodging classes to chase after the girls in their summer frocks who were passing by to go for a stroll along the seafront. What a frustrating youth! I did get a good technical grounding, however, and became a specialist in wood-grain simulation, which stood me in good stead later when I went to work for the South West Electricity Board.

A painter's job then was much more complex in that the paint materials had to be mixed, coloured and filtered by hand from lead in casks cut out by trowel and mixed with linseed oil, turps and driers. Then the skill was to mix the colours to the exact shade required, and woe betide the craftsman who mixed up a fraction more or less than required or got the shade wrong! Some of my better work was done on wood graining on a front door of Electric House after damage to it following a burglary, and on partitioning in the 'boss's' office there. I felt the matching was so good as to defy any obvious differences from the original.

After a working life of similar work I retired after 27 years with the Board. Harry Pearce, my earlier boss, and Winnie's father were pals. Mr Pearce's sister-in-law kept the Alpine Inn on Stentifords Hill and Winnie's father would deliver theatre handbills to the premises. However - as I became known to be Harry Pearce's apprentice, and later worked more than adequately on the theatre safety screen, his attitude towards my friendship with his daughter then changed, and I was allowed to paint his house!

Our romance really began when we were at school together at age 13, and we have been together ever since. My earliest recollection was of the somewhat unmasculine job of holding skipping ropes for the girls in Cavern Road. One of the excuses for managing some early courting was to take out Winnie's niece in her pram, and in this way we were able to walk miles together legitimately - until at times being caught in places like Bishop's Walk by relatives. Later we would

enjoy visits to the Empire Cinema at 9d a seat in the stalls on a Saturday night with a halfpenny block of Cadbury's chocolate for a shilling. For years I kept a scrap book of all the films and artists we saw on the screen there.

Winnie – Whilst Gilbert was on first-aid duty at Plainmoor or elsewhere, there were dancing classes to attend, run by a Mrs Andrews under the chemist shop in Hoxton Road on a Saturday afternoon, and where a dance was held for older couples on the same evenings. I remember going to the Royal Theatre at Christmas times, courtesy of my father, seeing Cliff Weir and another performer named Fredericks as pantomime dames, 'ad libbing' without scripts, and Pearl White in variety. I particularly remember seeing Gracie Fields perform 'on the boards' there when she was a relatively unknown variety artist and, I believe, married to an Arthur Pitt.

We used to do much 'baby sitting' with Nancy - and miles and miles were walked in the process. Gilbert had 'magic fingers'. When he was in charge the baby never cried. On one occasion we were sat nursing the child on an iron seat at the top of Stitchhill Road when an outraged elderly husband and wife got the mistaken impression that we were teenaged parents, and a look of utter disgust came into their eyes!

Gilbert – Winnie went to the Sunday School of the Presbyterian Church at the back of Torwood Gardens. I, because my father was an alto in the church choir at St Marks, perforce, joined the same choir as a boy there. Choir practice was held on Tuesday and Thursday nights at the Torwood School. Living in Ellacombe made life energetic, if not sometimes difficult. For example - on a Sunday we would walk through the Warberries and Erith Road for morning service and back home for dinner. After dinner a similar walk was required to Meadfoot Lane for Sunday School, after which we boys would go down to the Fish Quay to collect spratts. A handkerchief full (if we did not get our hands stamped on by the fishermen in the process) could be captured from the tubs-overfill on the ground, and we would arrive home for tea proud as punch with our efforts to supplement the family food supply. Then all the way back to St. Marks for Evensong!

When 15-16 I joined Miss Camble's bible class, which was held at her house in Erith Road called 'Stapleton'. After two years of this, and in between, I joined the St. John's Ambulance Brigade, with whom I served for many years until the War in 1939, and was awarded the Brigade's long service medal. The St John's Ambulance Brigade, of course, provided first-aiders for the sports ground events, regattas and on other public occasions, and I was enthusiastic enough to enter many first aid competitions. In between these activities I helped to run a Sea Scouts troop in the Braddons. Our Scoutmaster was an ex-naval lieutenant, and our HQ was in the Sailors' Rest at the Harbour. At weekends I would often take 7 or 8 cadets and set up a tented camp at Hopes Nose. Our Scoutmaster was able to 'pull some strings' and allow us to go on board Royal Navy ships when the Home Fleet visited Torbay. My proudest moment was to be sent up to the coastguard hut on Daddyhole Plain on one occasion to semaphore a message of thanks, on behalf of the troop, to the C. in C. aboard his flagship.

Winnie started work as an apprentice dress-maker at Rockeys, in Fleet Street, and remained in their employ until we were married in 1935 at the age of 22 each. Her father was ill, and died before the wedding, and her mother was also unwell, so it was a very quiet wedding. Afterwards we lived for twelve months with my mother at 45, Hoxton Road, until moving to our present home in Princes Road East. We shared these premises with Gilbert's father and mother until our three children arrived. With one boy and twin girls the house soon became overcrowded, and later my parents were able to move to a pensioners' bungalow at Watcombe. When the War came in 1939, George Davies and I set up a course of first-aid instruction in the Grey Cars garage in Torwood Street with civilian students as old as 75 - a very difficult age to teach body mechanism!

After the lads came back from Dunkirk I felt I was wasted doing this work, so went off to Exeter to enlist (I thought) in the RAMC. In typical 'Fred Karno' fashion, the RSM there tried, despite my expertise, to enlist me in the infantry. I adamantly refused, and ended up as a gunner in the Royal Artillery - a light AA unit stationed at Bristol. However - the Unit's medical officer was impressed with my first-aid qualifications so I was soon co-opted to lecture, once again, and ultimately given promotion to add the necessary authority to my lectures to the troops. My Army career took me, in due course, by troopship from Scotland, via Capetown and Mombassa (U-Boats everywhere) to Bombay and Ceylon, and straight into the jungle.

However - I was to be sent back to England as a long-serving soldier, and I remember being in the Indian Ocean when the Japanese surrendered. I

recall mostly bad food, weevils and flies, flies, and more flies!

MRS STELLA MARGETTS (NÉE COOMBE)

My paternal grandfather came from Launceston, in Cornwall, was a grocer by trade and came to Torquay before the First Woirld War to set up a grocery business in Princes Road, Ellacombe. My father set up home there in 1928 and began the fish and chip cafe (and later, ice-cream) business, which continued until just before the second world war began. On leaving Princes Road, my paternal grandfather went to live in Victoria Road, in the end house opposite Ellacombe Green. All my aunts were born in the Princes Road house. My father began his working life in the grocery trade and was employed as such by the Co-operative Society in Union Street as a young man.

My maternal grandfather came to Torquay from London to manage the Prudential Insurance offices, which were then based at 117 Union Street. It was there that I was born in 1914. My mother also came from London, and my parents married in the Zion Church, in Torquay. Later, my maternal grandparents bought a boarding house called 'Brighton Lodge' (now 'Lindham Lodge'), in Abbey Road, and it was here that I lived as a young child. I recollect that I had a number of relatives in London, whom I visited, but for some reason I never went to Cornwall to see any of my Cornish family. My father left the Co-op to become an insurance agent for the Prudential, covering the Dartmouth area. He set up home, for a period, in Stoke Fleming, where my sister was born in 1915. After the war was declared in 1914 my father was called up to serve in the Army, where he remained until wounded shortly before the Armistice was declared in 1918. After discharge he returned to live with my mother's father in Union Street for a time, until moving to Princes Road.

My brother was born in Union Street during that period. My mother suffered a nasty fall during pregnancy and the child was premature, and very frail and tiny. But he survived on heat from an anthracite stove, brandy and Nestle's milk - the only thing the poor child's stomach would take. As a young girl I was sent to a private school run by a Miss Strickland in premises on the St Marychurch Road. Later, the school moved to a new site, now known as the Abbey School. From there I transferred to another on the Newton Road, where I had the traumatic experience of being locked in a cupboard for naughtiness at aged 7. This so upset me that I had a nervous breakdown, and was at home in the care of my grandparents for nearly a year. During that time I recall being happy, walking the lanes and on the beach with my grandfather and his dog. After this my sister and I were sent to Homelands School, at Plainmoor, to study. I remember we had to walk from Abbey Road to Plainmoor every day to school and back - also during extended lunch hours. A kindly taxi driver, based at Castle Circus, would sometimes pick us up in his horse and carriage whilst delivering or collecting fares to and from St Marychurch. To expect such a safe and sure kindness would be most inadvisable in this day and age.

I was a bright child at school, usually ending terms in the top one or two places in class. I am in no doubt that I could have passed a scholarship examination at the time, but there were other considerations, in those days, preventing acceptance of a place at the Grammar School. A Mr Allwood was the headmaster until the Central School was formed and Homelands was renamed Westlands. It was the practice, in those days, for the same teachers to take the same children through the ensuing years of instruction until leaving school. I remember particularly mine - Mr Slee and Mr Blake. A Miss Dutton taught us cooking and housewifery. She had an unoccupied school flat in which we girls learned our skills. The flat was kept spotless and highly polished by the childrens' elbowgrease. A Mrs Laskey taught us sewing and embroidery, etc.

I recall the football ground next door was surrounded by a high fence, but we could play on the open ground behind. My brother first went to the old Upton School in Upper Union Street, but when we moved to Princes Road he transferred first to Ellacombe School and then (because of temporary reading difficulties) to Babbacombe School, where he could receive more individual attention under a Miss Leach. For a time after leaving Abbey Road we lived at 144 Windsor Road.

My sister and I were keen dancers, as children, and received dancing instruction (mine in ballet, and my sister in acrobatics) at Miss Meek's dancing establishment in Union Street. The dancing school was situated above three shops near (what was then) Albert Road. Miss Gooding (of the Castle School of Dancing) was then a student dance teacher at the School, and taught us both. We both took part frequently in dancing entertainment at both Conservative and Liberal functions, and my mother would make our dance dresses (of crêpe paper) in red, white and blue for the Tories and orange for the Liberals! I recall we also took part in larger dancing festivals at the old Pavilion, and rehearsed for these at Upton School. I remember little of note of my early childhood - except that for much of the time I was engaged in furthering the early stages of my swimming career.

I attended Sunday School at the Zion Church. Sunday School outings were invariably at either Galmpton Village, where we would have tea in the school room or the village hall, or we would travel to Chudleigh Rocks. My maternal grandfather played the organ at the Zion Church, and when that closed, he continued as organist and choirmaster at Belgrave Church. If he practised the organ during the week or held a choir practice, then my sister and I would be co-opted to pump the organ - and when we tired, would try to continue by sitting on the large, wooden arm!

Most of the summer we would spend our school holidays on the beach, or in watching our brother roller-skate on Princess Pier. I remember, on one occasion, going to Stoke Fleming to visit friends of my parents and also Blackpool Beach. We rarely went far from home. In the earlier years, in Abbey Road, my parents employed a nursemaid to look after us. I loved the Torbay Regatta - especially the water and swimming events - and the fireworks, although I would hide under my mother's skirts when the rockets exploded!

It was at Westhill School where a Herbie Clow excited our interest in swimming. He encouraged the children to go to Oddicombe beach to learn the art. My mother, however, was an early member of the Torquay Leander Swimming Club (TLSC) before the war, and gave us every encouragement also. My sister and I would spend much time at Torre Abbey Sands, where a boatman, called Bob, would tow us out to the raft, hanging on the back of his boat. Then we would be dropped off to swim back - distance largely dependent on the state of the tide! Later we took part in a schools' race in Paignton Harbour with a Myra Kent (now Mrs Rayner), my sister and another girl. The latter fell sick, so I was invited to fill her place in the team and we won the event. Such excitement! From then we both never looked back. My sister took up diving rather than pure swimming, and stayed with the Oddicombe

Swimming Club (OSC), whilst I joined and remained with the TLSC. We both took part, annually, in the Torbay Regatta swimming events, which were then held in the Outer Harbour. My sister would enter the diving events held from the Pier diving board - over thirty feet above the water, and I below in the water ones.

I was the only eventer to be allowed on the Langmead Committee Barge during the races because of a tendancy to sickness. I left school at 14 to work in my father's shop. I remember, particularly, the bonfire nights at Ellacombe Green and in Brewery Park - mainly because I was always made to work extra time in the cafe feeding the returning revellers with lashings of fish and chips. My sister did, too, for a short period, before going to work in a wool shop in Fleet Street near the General Post Office (where the Wimpy Bar is now situated) until she married. Apart from running a fish and chip cafe, my father ventured into ice cream manufacture.

The idea arose through Mr Cavalier, who ran the quayside chip stall, and who had no premises from which to commence making the ice-cream. So my father started production in a rear room in Princes Road himself, and operated under his own name. I recall using gallons of milk to make the custard base. Later, he purchased a motorbike and sidecar to deliver ice-cream to local retailers (including Corbyn Beach) and certain Dartmoor village shops. He had an elementary freezer in the car - a tub packed with chemical ice. As the business expanded he bought a van to replace the motorbike and sidecar. At Christmas he would make a special 'Tutti-Fruiti' type of ice-cream, with nuts, cherries and clotted cream, especially for the Palace Hotel. Every day, also, he would journey to Brixham to buy his supply of fish for the cafe - mostly skate and cod. The shop premises were later extended by a flat for my grandfather. This was a biggish extension, necessary to accommodate a grand-piano in addition to the usual offices.

I remember down the back of the property was a spiritualist church which to us young girls was very scary, and frightened us with the thought of ghostly things! Eventually the shop and premises were sold in 1935 - just prior to the outbreak of the Second World War, and we were living in Avenue Road when my mother died in 1940.

I first met my future husband through my swimming activities. He was then living in Newton Abbot , and was employed as a railway clerk at Heathfield Station when I first met him. He was born in Exeter. He had represented his school at swimming and his schoolmaster encouraged him to train at Torquay, where there were proper facilities. It was at his school he became Schools' Champion for Devon in 1926. When not at work, he would take the train to Torquay, walk along the seafront and train at the Marine Spa Baths before coming back to our shop for supper. Bill and I were married at the Abbey Road Congregational Church in Torquay in 1935. Afterwards we set up home in Kingskerswell. I remember often pushing the pram containing our first child Ann through the lanes to visit my parents, and would return home on the train. We moved into our present house in Walnut Road, Torquay, in 1939, first as rented accommodation. Much later my husband and I bought the premises as sitting tenants when the owner died, and have lived there for nearly 60 years. My husband sadly passed away in 1995.

We have three children, Ann, who later married an electrician in Chelston; David, who is married and a doctor in Canada and Robert, also married, and a teacher at the Torquay Grammar School. All have children who are doing well. I first met Don Roberts through my swimming activities and career as a swimming official. My husband and I, Ilse Locke, Peter Harris, B.Sc., and Don were closely and actively involved, with Councillor Damerell, in the development and building of the Plainmoor Swimming Pool under the title of 'Swim Torquay Limited'. Seven Directors were appointed for this project - two from the TLSC, two from the OSC and three from outside. Fund raising was a massive exercise. Tom Brown was persuaded to offer a car as a prize in a raffle, and tickets were sold from empty clothes shop premises on the Strand and an initial £5000 was raised. Eventually, with aid of more fund-raising projects, a Government Arts Grant, and the physical efforts and support of the students and lecturers from the building and engineering section of the Torquay Technical College, the current swimming pool was finally erected and completed in 1975 and officially opened by the Sports Minister, Denis Howell, in January, 1976. Don was a long-standing member of the Management Committee.

My father, during the last war, worked as a barrack warden for the Royal Air Force Initial Training Unit, which was based in Torquay, principally at the Grand Hotel. I was brought in to help in 1941, when my husband joined the Army, and made masses of blackout curtains for the Hotel. My father went to Bath with the RAF after hostilities ended and remained there until he retired.

DON ROBERTS

I was born two minutes past midnight on 5 August 1930 at 23 Berea Road, Ellacombe the first born son of Thomas Jesse Roberts and Millicent Kate, formerly Lyle.

My mother and father were married at All Saints, Babbacombe on 25 June 1927 as my mother's parents lived at Aston Villa, 150 Babbacombe Road. Mother's father, Albert Broad Lyle, was born 8 April 1878 in 1 Grosvenor Terrace, Warren Road, Torquay, and had grown up to become a builder. He had in fact built the terraced houses at the top of Berea Road where I was born, and the semi-detached house where he lived in Babbacombe Road, together with the terrace of limestone-built houses opposite what is now the Babbacombe Pottery.

My father was a blacksmith working for T.L. Harding & Sons. At the time of my birth, and from the time I could walk, mother and I used to proceed to the bottom of Market Street to meet him every day from work. The large double-wooden gates had a small door for personnel to go in and out and hid the yard, which seemed to be strewn with lengths of iron, old wheels and large girders. I did go inside the blacksmiths' shop once, and apart from the fire which glowed brightly, it was to me like some horrible black cave with tools large and small everywhere. Father had learnt his trade from his father William Roberts, who had come to Torquay from Lewtrenchard in the early summer of 1901 to work as a blacksmith for Harding himself. The following photograph of all the Harding's workers in 1902 gives a good idea of the size of the enterprise in Market Street. William Roberts had been born on 3 April 1865 at Bratton Clovelly and baptised in the village church the very next day. The Roberts family can be traced back from Bratton Clovelly, through Bridestowe to circa 1718, and beyond to Crediton, circa 1687 and earlier in North Devon.

My mother's mother was Thirza Counter, born at Sampford Courtenay on 22 June 1875, the daughter of Thomas Counter, the village blacksmith. She had come to Torquay ahead of her sisters, one of which had followed the rector of Sampford Courteney when he, the Revd Thomas Wright Little, became vicar of St Marychurch in 1906. My mother's paternal grandfather was James Broad Lyle, who was born at Launcells in

Cornwall on 29 September 1839. The Counters can be traced back to the mid-1500s at South Tawton. It may be interesting to note that my father's mother (Leah's) father was a mason who worked on the buildings of the Blenheim Palace estate, and Leah helped as a maid with the children of the Revd Sabine Baring Gould, whose brother became the first vicar of Christ Church, Ellacombe in 1868. When my father was apprenticed to his own father at Hardings in 1915, one of their tasks was to walk to Oldway Mansions from Ellacombe to make splints for wounded soldiers who came to the hospital set up there.

Grandfather was a staunch conservative, as he believed it was the rich people who provided work for the lower classes and he was grateful for that. When T.L. Harding died, my grandfather helped to bear his coffin at the funeral, but lost half a day's pay for the privilege! The family lived at 11 Ellacombe Church Road: the premises could be entered from the lane at the rear. Grandfather had a mini-blacksmith's shop in an outhouse and was able to do small blacksmithing jobs there. So for nigh on thirty years William Roberts traversed his back lane, Mount Pleasant, and the double-sided steps down to Alexander Road, and then through Ellacombe Green to Market Street to work at Hardings and return at 5pm.

As a child I was always, when visiting, fascinated by the pink-and-white valerian which grew profusely out of all the limestone walls protecting the rear of the property. My early days in Berea Road were carefree. The road had not been made up - it was rough and bumpy, with large limestone boulders protruding here and there. The milkman would come with his horse and cart from the Co-op, and in addition, Mr Perry Squires would arrive carrying his large milk churns from which he would ladle half or a pint of milk directly into our own jug.

Motor traffic was unknown. I was not short of friends to play with - the Underhill boys at No. 2; the Fowler boys at No. 8; Clifford and Jim Higgins at No. 20, on the opposite side to me; Francis and Mervyn Smith were at No. 9 and Leslie Newband and his sister Kathleen at No. 17. We were all lucky to have the use of a little triangular field at the top of the road in which to play, and access to the back lane of our house could be made from this field. It seemed that, in those days, the summers were always lovely and sunny and one day we crowned Kathleen Newband our Queen of the May, only to be told soon after that she and her family were emigrating to New Zealand. It was almost impossible for me to comprehend, at

Employees of T.L. Harding & Co. outside the company premises in Market Street c. 1902. Don Roberts

age 5 to 6, a journey to the other side of the world by sea which would take 5 to 6 weeks. For many, many years we never heard from them again until, through other means, we heard that poor Kathleen had died quite recently in New Zealand.

I also had quick access to the Lower Ellacombe Road swing park - down our long back garden, down the lane between Jimmy Smart's house and the Richardson's and you were there. The fir trees at the top of the park were well established like those in Warberry Copse that dominated the head of 'Ella' combe, but the poplar trees planted before I was born were making good progress skyward. The disused Swayne's Brewery was always a mysterious place for me - talk of rats certainly deterred me from going in there!

I was sent to Babbacombe School in the January of 1935, as there was no more five-year-old places available for me at Ellacombe School at that time. I have few memories of that experience, save the fact that the toilets didn't smell very nice! I joined Ellacombe School in the September of 1935, and the first year class was taken by Miss Kirkham. My first report in July 1936 gives my teacher as Miss Walton, but I have no recollection of her at all. There were 36 in the class and I was placed 17th - my conduct was good but I was deemed to be very careless and very untidy. The

Headteacher was Blanche G. Phillips. Miss Collihole taught in the classroom next to mine and she, I thought, was a wonderful lady - very 'high up' in the St John's Ambulance Brigade. In the September of 1937 I moved into Form 1 and Miss F.M. Blackler took charge of my education. Now there were 56 in the class and Miss Blackler knew how to keep order. She must have read my report about being lazy so for the first week of the term I was called out to the front to have the ruler put across the back of my legs to wake me up! I responded very well and was placed 8th in the class in the end of term report, which made much more pleasant reading than the previous one, although I was still a bit careless in arithmetic - gaining only 16 out of 20 in the test. The report at the end of the year placed me 8th again, and this in spite of 56 absences due to a series of very painful abcesses in my ears.

I then went into Miss Hilda Packe's class. I was pleased to be its form monitor and I can recall many of the activities that went on in that class: the correct writing of letters that would lead to 'joined-up' writing; the use of the Stave for understanding and reading music - I played drum (the blue notes), others the triangle (red notes), others the clappers (black notes). Miss Packe was keen on country dancing and we had special practices for that, especially when the inter-schools festival was about to be staged at the Town Hall. Looking back, I realise what wonderful training those dances were. 'Flowers of Edinburgh' and 'Circasian Circle' were among my favourites, but others were very much more complicated. The music was good for training the memory and timing. Physical training took place in the playground and the oval coconut mats were always laid out for ground exercises. This was a tremendous year for learning and experience. I was introduced to needlework and did drawn-thread work and made raffia mats. Geography, history and nature study were introduced and my report said I was keenly interested in these lessons. Once again carelessness in arithmetic lowered my position in class down to 16th out of 48. Miss Packe described me as a keen leader!

There were some nice sunny days in 1939 but the situation in Europe was far from happy. On one such day Mervyn Cummings, Arthur Stead, Jim Fowler and myself sat in a circle in a grassy part of the Quinta discussing the possibility of War in Europe. Mr Chamberlain seemed to be working for peace but we all thought that the worse might happen. I was not yet nine but here were four young boys contemplating and feeling the worse for the future. I also remember that the conversation changed to the fact that if we lived, the year 2000 would see us all 70 years old! Arthur Stead and Jim Fowler will not make it - they both died in the 1980s.

Miss Crocker was an excellent teacher of Form 3 and I had two school reports on my work in December 1939 and July 1940. The class was consistent with 50 members. By this time I was working well and gained 6th. and 9th. positions in class respectively. It was during this year that I made my one and only misdemeanour - I was caught passing a note to Joan Guntrip in class: I will not disclose what it contained. For this I found myself in Mr Collett's room, as he had become Headmaster following the opening of Audley Park School and Miss Phillip's appointment as its Headmistress there. Mr Collett made me promise I would never do anything wrong again and let me go back to class. That short visit set me up for life! I have often thought how I would have learnt such a lesson if I had not passed the note!

Things were really happening for me at this time. I had become a church chorister at All Saints, Babbacombe, under Mr Ernest Winship. This meant three practices a week and three services on Sundays. I loved singing and learning

new settings for the canticles and psalms. There were 16 boys in the choir and I sang on the decanai side and my friend Ray Slocombe and Richard Kingdom on cantoris. My father had sung as a boy in Upton choir under Mr Trotman, who was a very strict disciplinarian.

Having been taught to swim at the Marine Spa baths by my father during police sessions run by P.C. Gooding, I joined the Oddicombe Swimming Club in 1939 and was coached by Herbie Clow. In the summer of 1939 I did the Babbacombe Pier to Oddicombe Beach swim, the last time this event was held until after the war.

It was about this time that Berea Road was 'made up'. It was fascinating to see the men at work laying the concrete road and the masons setting the curb stones and laying the paving stones. Each time I returned from school I assessed the progress of the work. Also the park at Ellacombe was laid out with the lovely shelter set at the centre of the geometrically designed paths. New swings were introduced and the playground became a mecca for all the children in the area. The bell-shaped roundabout was a great favourite, but rather than make it go round we used to hang from adjacent bars to see who could hang on the longest - a real test of skill!

In July 1940 Ellacombe School swimming team narrowly failed to win the inter-primary schools swimming gala at the Marine Spa. I had won the breast-stroke race for ten-year-olds and we had a number of seconds, but we lost out on the relays. In September I moved into the top class with Mr Charles S. Parr as teacher. Mr Parr worked us all very hard. Dictation every Monday morning and arithmetic every day. Spelling and composition was rigorously doled out and mental arithmetic practised. Geometrical drawing and model making also had a place in the lessons, with nature study and reading offering some relief. We read *Beowolf*, which was enough to stir anyones imagination, learned about the Bedouin Arabs and the life in Britain at the time of the Domesday Book. We grew peas and beans in jam jars, the seeds being trapped by linings of damp blotting paper, carefully monitoring the method and speed of growth.

Mr Parr took the swimming team to the Marine Spa after school on Mondays, and at the end of the year the team of John Barter, Mervyn Cummings, Arthur Stead and myself won the Primary Schools Championship for the first time in its history - a great moment for us all. Also at the end of the year, as a result of the 11+ examination taken at the Grammar School earlier in the term many of our class learned that they had secured a place at the Grammar School to further our education. My report of 31 July 1941 saw me placed 3rd. out of 44 - beaten by two very clever girls named Norma Causley and Helen Smith. After that, I set off from Ellacombe School to begin a new educational career.

Ellacombe was a marvellous place to grow up in. I knew all the back lanes like the back of my hand, and there were the many series of steps that linked the parallel roads. The bank at Denys Road provided an exciting playground, and on occasion I must have run up and down its paths there some hundred times during the course of a morning. The alleyway between Lock's Hill and Selley's always fascinated me and the bits of alabaster used to fall out of the left and were used for numbering our hopscotch squares or drawing the grid. Mr Beck, of Lower Ellacombe Church Road, I remember as always walking so uprightly as if he had a steel rod in his back. I also remember a Mr Chesterfield and a Mr Denzyl Nenner being the gardeners for Warberry Copse, Mr Jimmy Smart a retired coachman at Ardvar House, and George Lark had his blacksmith's shop at the rear of Ellacombe Church Road.

During the war I remember a Bofors gun placed at the end of Warberry Copse, near to Normount Cottages. At the top of Berea Road we had an armoured vehicle manned by members of the RAF Regiment. A machine gun was always ready for action, and the crew was changed three times a day. We boys were privileged to go inside and talk to the soldiers.

On 8 January 1943 I had been to Lincombe Woods to play in the morning and had arrived home about 1.05pm. I was having lunch with the family when at 1.15pm we suddenly realised another 'tip-and-run' raid was imminent, as we heard firing. My brother and I slid under the kitchen table and my father followed. Mother made for the Morrison Shelter in the front room. The bang was enormous and accompanied by an intense blue flash. The ceilings came down and the glass windows shattered. We emerged from under the table and shook the plaster and glass out of our ears and hair to find mother uncon-

scious on the floor. She had been struck by the front door, as the blast had blown it in with great force. Mother soon recovered and was labelled as a 'walking wounded' and treated by the local wardens. The scene outside was unbelievable - glass and slates everywhere, but there was no evidence of any crater made by the bomb. Later we solved the puzzle, as we found the shallow groove the bomb had made as it bounced on Lydwell Road, shot skywards, cutting the top off a fir tree and losing its fin, before hurtling on over the top of Berea Road and exploding in mid-air.

After the end of the war Mrs Treeby and Mrs Heard were well to the fore in organising an exciting street party at the top of Berea Road.

Top Class - Ellacombe School July 1941 as I recall included: Peter Collier; Norma Causley; Derek Barker; Joan Guntrip; Barry Nichols; Christine Bassett; Arthur Stead; Helen Smith; Keith Beck; Jim Fowler; Christine Mayne; Flora Stoneman; Don Tozer; Cynthia Heath; Mervyn Cummings; Bill Cann; John Barter; Mary Lamble; Ethel Tapley; Arthur Cole; Alicia Onions; John Alford; Peggy Drake; Jean Coyd; Derek Atkins; Elston Peters; Pam Heywood (Hayward); Derek Fowler; Dennis Penny; Sheila Walker; Betty Brown; Bob Thomas; Raymond Chilvers and Ted Bragg.

Other familiar names I remember are: Mr Babbage; Mr Wilson; George Lark the blacksmith; Jack Lark, who was George Lark's brother and also a blacksmith at Hardings, and who will be remembered for his lovely garden at the corner of Ellacombe Church Road and Carlton Road; Mrs Layers of 41 Victoria Road; Barry Stoyle; Blanche Phillips; Sammy Maddern; John Lloyds the builder; Wedden of 27 Victoria Road; Hookways the bakers; Richard Kirsopp of Hoxton Road; Fred Friend; Mr Beck; Mr Sid Blackler; Chave's garage; new garage behind Savages off-licence; old Mr Treby; Miss Tregale; Mrs Eva Carslake; Peter Jenkins; Mr Holloway the baker of Woodville Road; Miss Cottey of 9 Market Street; Clement Berry the dairyman; Tom Hingston of 25 Congella Road; William George Pack; Tony Holloway, and many others. I have many, many fond memories of Ellacombe.

Chapter 11 - Conclusion

The early 1930s were innocent times - before the pill, teenage sex, glue-sniffing, drugs, discos and the all-invading, image-making television. But we were mostly happy and without guile. We did not have much in the way of material wealth, but found our happiness in the simple things in life.

Happiness was sixpence spent at the local 'flea pit' watching Deanna Durbin, or Mickey Rooney and Judy Garland; the Young People's Fellowship at the church hall; a choir-boys' supper and choosing our pick from the Harvest Festival fruit; spending our coppers at the harbourside Fair, and watching the land and water fireworks of the Torbay Regatta from my Uncles' committee barges.

Innocence was following the Salvation Army Band to the Quay in our Sunday-best suits after evensong, and promenading along the sea front with our pals making cheeky remarks to the girls we fancied; the joy and excitement of the first stolen kiss; the pride and commitment of 'walking out' in earnest.

Reality was unemployment without Social Security, hot soup at a 'kitchen' in Rock Road during the 1930s slump, owning one suit, and with cardboard in our shoes. Security was a penny a week on the 'National Deposit' and a doctor on the 'Panel'. In those days promiscuity and irresponsibility were punished by ostracism.

Then we did not have motorways and carbon-monoxide, out-of-town supermarkets and multi-storey carparks, colour TVs, leisure centres, radiation and chemical pollution. Instead we had stable family relationships and corner shops; wild life abounded in the fields and hedges; we could walk at night without fear of mugging; we could lose a purse on a bus and be sure it would be returned. We could walk home from school unmolested, without passing a McDonalds or a Col. Saunders on the way, and find 'mum' waiting with a home-made tea by a glowing fire.

Womens' Lib was a mild stirring of female spirit and Neighbourhood Watch schemes were not desperately needed by an overworked police force: when the local 'bobby' was a gentle giant, but feared and respected by every child. Puberty was a slow and gentle awakening without constant instruction and publicity. Friendships were made and lost in groups. Parents were often stern and feared, so assignations were sometimes made in the oddest ways. I remember 'courting' the headmaster's (can you believe?) daughter in secret by whistling 'Monday Night at Seven' outside her parents' bungalow, when she would find an excuse to pop out and post a letter, or run to the nearest shop on a spurious errand! And when mother did find out - I was threatened with a terrifying 'umbrella in my spokes' if I was caught! Love's awakening was gradual and engagements long. Virginity was highly prized, and not an award lightly offered for an evening's entertainment.

Stress arose from fear of hunger or want, not concern over poor performance on the executive ladder, or from listening to the TV news or from inability to 'keep up with the neighbours'. We prepared, over a long period of courtship, both financially and physically, for a lifetime partnership and bringing up a family, and did not run for divorce at the first signs of incompatability. We did not expect a fully-fitted house and all the modern gadgets before we embarked on marriage, and grew more closely together working to achieve these things over the years to come. And when we did, we valued what we had worked for greatly.

Grammar schools were mainly fee-paying, and winning a 'scholarship' was a prize indeed, and a guarantee of a bright and rewarding future. Parents sought employment for their sons and daughters with security uppermost in mind. The Civil Service and local government posts were priorities, as were the banks and insurance offices. Entrance to the better posts and levels was highly selective, and a high pass-mark in an examination was no guarantee of a post. Even humble beginnings were often a grant of someone's 'influence' - a family friend or relation already in the same employ, or a post offered by someone of note in return for a past favour.

Promotion came after many years of toil and effort and small annual increments depending on performance, and often was granted only to fill 'dead man's shoes'. Politeness and respect for one's superiors was a vital pre-requisite, as was tidyness and neatness. Hours were long and holidays few. Overtime payment was unheard-of and one worked on until the job was satisfactorily completed - often simply from personal pride. And there was a great respect, not necessarily reflected in pay, for the craftsman in every field. Motor mechanics were not foiled from lack of factory-made replacement parts - they re-made a faulty part, by hand, on a lathe or work bench. The days of mass production by computerised machinery were still to come. Furniture, like clothing, was often bespoke-made and one differentiated between a dressmaker and tailoress.

Eggs were free-range - there were no battery hens, poor things. Butter was butter and not a by-product of vegetable oil. Meat had taste, and was not impregnated with hormones and colourings. There was no Milk Marketing Board and cream was often produced in the home, on individual farms or in small dairies. Bread was mouth-watering and untouched by chemicals and preservatives, and the weekly home cake-making and autumn 'preserving' a 'must' for housewives.

Christmas was the religious 'high-spot' of the year - not a commercial marketing exercise under the guise of the Birth of Christ. Father Christmas was a believed enchantment of the very young. Stockings were hung with the expectation of a miracle - seldom realised. They were often filled only with a rare orange or apple and some home-made toy lovingly fashioned by the parent - not some highly expensive electronic toy, a five-minute wonder easily discarded. Nevertheless - the Christmas Dinner was the great meal of the year - paid for over many months of hard-worked saving through the 'Xmas Club. Great family gatherings were 'the order of the day'. Christmas carols were sung around the family piano, paper hats were worn, Stone's Ginger Wine, and a precious bottle of sherry were produced, and what excitement when one found a three-penny piece in the Christmas pudding!

We were often poor, but proud. We paid our way without plastic cards, and we looked after our own without 'the Social'.

Then came the Second World War, and after it Socialism and Comprehensive Education, the 'National Health Service', 'Social Security' and the modern scourge of the environment - the internal combustion engine. Life never stands still, however, and evolution will continue despite inbuilt misgivings that progress is not necessarily always for the better. We may be much wealthier today - in the widest possible terms - but happier and more contented in spirit in this day and age? I very much doubt it.

Now you and I are older lad, but we have
  a bond to treasure -
We can look into each others eyes with pride
  too great to measure

Nancy Mayhew

Subscribers

Mr T R Abrahams, Torquay
Shaun And Denise Acton, Torquay
John Andrews, Torquay
Mr F Annear, Torquay
Mr Bernard Backwell, Torquay
Mr Roy Backwell, Torquay
Mr J S Bannister, Torquay
Mrs I Barker, Brixham
Gladys E Barnicoat, Ellacombe
Mrs Phyllis M Barritt (Carter 1928),
    Brixham
Mrs M Batley, Torquay
Josephine Bell (née Eales),
    Culmstock
Mr D Bellworthy, Torquay
John Bennett, Torquay
Mrs P Berryman, Torquay
Eric Bickford, Torquay
David Blackler, Torquay
David B Blackler, Ellacombe
Charles Blake FRIBA, Torquay
Mrs M A Boffey, Ellacombe
Mrs N Bond, Abbotskerswell
Ms M J Bovey, Torquay
Dianne Boxall
E J Bragg, Twickenham, Middlesex
H J Bragg, Sandwich, Kent
Alan G Braund, Torquay
Mrs Winnie Braund (née Down),
    Newton Abbot
Mrs A M Briand, Fife, Scotland
Mrs Barbara Brimicombe, Torquay
Mrs Margaret Brinicombe, Torquay
K J Brown, Torquay
Mrs B E Browning, Babbacombe
Leonard Burden, Torquay
Mr And Mrs Glyn Burton, Torquay
Mrs G M Butler, Kingsteignton
Miss Sylvia Byrne, Torquay
S Byrne
Mr P A Byrne, Torquay
J L Caldicott, Torquay
Mr And Mrs A Carruthers
Mrs Rosemary Carter (nee Wyatt)
Miss M Chaffe, Babbacombe
B A Chalker, Paignton
Ms Karen S Chapman, Ellacombe
Mrs M Chappell
Mr R C Chidgey, Torquay
Mike Chittenden BA, Torquay
W H Church, Ellacombe
Miss D T Coe, Torquay
Mr Derrick M Collier, Ellacombe
Mr Peter J Collier

Cook Family, Torquay
Geoffrey Leslie Cooper RJDip.
Director Of Abacus Gem's Ltd
Miss M Corline, Torquay
Barry Cornall, Paignton
Derek Cox, Torquay
Mr D M Crawford, Torquay
A K Crews, Torquay
David F Crispin
D Critchett, Uxbridge, Middlesex
Mrs I M Davey, Paignton
Mrs C Davies, Ellacombe
Miss L Davis, Ellacombe
Mrs F E Dennis, Torquay
Mr R G Dimmock, Kingskerswell
Mr George Barry Doan,
    Babbacombe
Mr W R And Mrs E Doidge,
    Torquay
Miss G M Downey, Exmouth
J J P Drake, Torquay
Geoffrey Dredge, Upton
Mrs B Duggan, Torquay
John Dunn, Torquay
Eric And Rowan Easterbrook,
    Ellacombe
Mrs V Edgecombe, Brixham
Mrs Edwards
Ellacombe Primary School, Devon
Lt Col W J Elliott, Torquay
Mr David Janes Ellis, Newton
    Abbot
Mrs L Ellis, Torquay
Mrs Gladys I Evans, Torquay
N I K Eynstone-Hinkins, Torquay
Captain Michael S J Farley,
    Paignton
Mr R Farman, Torquay
Mr V E Fellowes, Epsom, Surrey
Mrs Lesley Finch, Ellacombe
Mr P H Fish, Torquay
Mrs P A Fleming, Torquay
Adrian Foster, Torquay
Mrs Denise Francis
Mrs Roberta Franklin, Torquay
A Freer, Ellacombe
Mr Colin F Frost, Torquay
Gordon Furneaux, Ellacombe
Mr G Furneaux, Torquay
David Fursdon, Torquay
Mr K Fursdon, Ellacombe
Mr G I Gale, Torquay
Gordon Gee, Barton, Torquay
J Gibbes, Torquay

Mr J A Gibbings, Torquay
Mr K W L Gibbons, Peterborough
Mr And Mrs B Gill, Ellacombe
Mr C J Gillard
Mrs B Glanfield, Torquay
Marilyn Godfrey, Ellacombe
Mr C And Mrs J Goodwin, Torquay
Mrs M E Grandin, Brixham
Gladys Green, Torquay
Mr Russell Green, Torquay
D F Greenhill-Tanner, Torquay
Mrs P H Grubb, Witheridge
Heather Hall (née Mc Millan)
Mr G E Hannaford, Torquay
Miss V I Harris, Ellacombe
Mrs B R Harris, Torquay
Mrs S A Harris, Newton Abbot
Mr David Brian Harris, Ellacombe
Austin Hawkins, Torquay
Stephen Haywood, Torquay
Mrs Yvonne Heath (née Leaman)
O T Higgins, Torquay
Clifford Higgins, Ellacombe
A R Hill, Torquay
Mrs W Hillgrove, Torquay
M Hitching, Torquay
Audrey Hodges (née Eales),
    Ellacombe
Mr T B Holtom, Torquay
Brenda Hookway, Torquay
Cynthia Hooper, Paignton
Miss M L Hore, Torquay
Mrs D E Horwill, East Grinstead
Mr J Howard, Torquay
Helen Howells, Ellacombe
Joyce Humble (née Eales),
    Exmouth
John C Jackson, Ellacombe
Ricky Jago
T C James, Torquay
Beryl Johns, Ellacombe
Jacqueline Johnson, Torquay
David P D Johnson, Torquay
G A Johnson, Torquay
Jennifer D Kellow, Ellacombe
Peter Edwin King, Torquay
Mrs Nancy Kirby-Selves, Newton
    Abbot
Mr Steven A Knapman, Torquay
Mrs Mary Kneil, Ellacombe
Mrs Laline Knight, Paignton
Mrs J Knott, Paignton
Mrs V A Lamb-Brown, Brixham
Mrs Margarite Lane, Ellacombe

THE ELLACOMBE BOOK

Thos. W Lane, Plainmoor

Mrs I. Langmead, East Hendred, Oxon.

Mr Ian Langmead, Brecon, Powys

Mr H A Langmead, Worthing, West Sussex

Patrick Langmead, Shaldon, Teignmouth

Miss Briony Langmead, Brecon, Powys

Miss Nicola Langmead, Brecon, Powys

K R Lasseter, Torquay

Gordon Latham, Ellacombe

Mrs Diane Leach, Sheffield

Mr T J Leaman, Torquay

Robert (Bobby) Lear, Newton Abbot

Mrs Betty Lee, Torquay

Margaret and David Leishman, Sampford Peverell

John W Lewis, Ellacombe

Mrs Angela C Lowney (née Farley), Coventry

Mr H J Martin, Paignton

Paul Martin, Torquay

Mrs Gladys Martin, Torquay

Mrs R Matthews, Paignton

Mr John Maynard

Shona McMillan, Ellacombe

Tom McMillan, Warminster, Wilts

Jacky McCallum, Torquay

Dr D A McCarthy, Torquay

M P McElheron, Kingskerswell

Gordon, Medway, Ellacombe.

Mrs Mellish

Mrs D N Midgley, Torquay

Terry Milden, Ellacombe

Eric A Milton, Ellacombe

Mrs J I Mollart, Calne, Wiltshire (formerly of Ellacombe)

Mrs M Molloy, Torquay

Mrs A P Morris, Torquay

Mr Tony Moss, Paignton

Mrs P Mudge, Ellacombe

Mrs M E Nicholls

Mrs J Nickells, Torquay

Gerry Nield, Denbury,

David Olding, Torquay

Gordon Oliver, Torquay

Patricia Osborn, Brixham

Alan Palmer, Torquay

Mrs Beryl Palmer, Torquay

Mrs Patricia Parker, Ellacombe

Mr G E Pearce, Torquay

Mary Peel, Ellacombe School

Mr C Pendered, Torquay

Mrs M Penny, Ellacombe

Mr John Pering, Torquay

David Charles Pering, Torquay

Andrew Richard Pering, Torquay

Benjamin Pering, Torquay

Richard Pering, Torquay

Mrs Irene Perry (née Sarahs), Ellacombe

David Phillips JP, Abbotskerswell

Mr John Antony Pook, Teignmouth

Mrs C L Pook, Torre, Torquay

Mr M Pool, Torquay

Mrs P M Pool, Torquay

Mrs M Pope, Torquay

K J Pope, Torquay

Alan J Pope, Ellacombe

Mrs V I Potter, Torquay

Mr K A Powell, Barnstaple

Mrs E Pugh, Kingsteignton

Mr F A Radford, Paignton

Mrs J Rallison, Torquay

G J Rawle, Kingskerswell

Phillip G Redwood, Babbacombe

Denis Reid, Torquay

Mrs D Richards, Stokeinteignhead

S C Rider, Torquay

H A Rider, Torquay

Gregory Julian Roberts, Ellacombe/Liskeard

Alex James Roberts MSc, Ellacombe/Dawlish

Donald John, Roberts MSc. ACP, Ellacombe

Mrs P. Rodgers (née Lowe), Harrogate, Yorks

Brian Rooke, Ellacombe

Margaret Rooke

Mrs M A Ruelens (née Back), Torquay

Mrs G L Searle (née Siveyer) Crownhill, Plymouth

K J Selley, Torquay

Mr R E Setter, Torquay

Mr S V Setters (former Ellacombe family)

Deryck Seymour, Torquay

Mrs Martine Caroline Shapley

John C Sidebotham, Ellacombe

Raymond Skinner, Ellesmere Port, Cheshire

Mrs E L Skinner, Polegate, East Sussex

P W Southall, Babbacombe

Dr John G Speake, St Marychurch

Mrs L D M St John-Clifford, Torquay

Mr G W Stephens, Paignton

Mrs Linda Stinson, Chelston

Miss L E Stockman, Ellacombe

L Stockman, Ellacombe

Joyce Stonelake, Westhill, Torquay

Mr And Mrs D Summers, Ellacombe

Mrs Freda Symonds, Torquay

Bernard Tapley, Highweek

John Tapley, Neyland

Garry Tapping, Torquay

Mrs G Tarr, Torquay

Mrs F Taylor, Torquay

Mr John Taylor, Torquay

Miss E M M Taylor, Babbacombe

Lillian Thomas, Ellacombe

Noel Thomas, Paignton

Mrs R Thompson, Paignton

Torquay Central Library

Miss Githa Townsend, Torquay

Alan Tozer, Torquay

Joan Tozer, Ellacombe

Mr J B Vowden, Torquay

Mr A H Vowden, Torquay

Philip And Mary Wade, Torquay

Miss Eileen M Waldron, Wareham, Dorset

Peter Waldron, Wareham, Dorset

Mr R Wannell, Babbacombe

Mr D Ward, Torquay

Mr I J Way, Ellacombe

Miss S Webber, Ellacombe

Mrs J Welch, Ellacombe

Julia E West (née Woodfin), Ellacombe

Mrs Edna L White, Torquay

John Royson Williams, Warrington

L W G Williams, Torquay

Dorothy J Williams (née Maynard), Bristol

Ken Windeatt, Ellacombe

Mrs C Windsor, Babbacombe

Mrs T Winstone, Skewen, West Glamorgan

Ian Woodford, Torquay

Leonard Wyatt, Torquay